Verbal Dueling in Heroic Narrative

Verbal Dueling in
Heroic Narrative

THE HOMERIC AND OLD
ENGLISH TRADITIONS

Ward Parks

PRINCETON UNIVERSITY PRESS

PRINCETON, NEW JERSEY

Copyright © 1990 by Princeton University Press
Published by Princeton University Press,
41 William Street, Princeton, New Jersey 08540
In the United Kingdom: Princeton University Press, Oxford

Library of Congress Cataloging-in-Publication Data

Parks, Ward, 1952–
Verbal dueling in heroic narrative : the Homeric and Old English traditions /
Ward Parks.
    p.   cm.
Includes bibliographical references.
ISBN 0–691–06780–5
1. Epic poetry, English (Old)—History and criticism.
2. Literature, Comparative—English (Old) and Greek. 3. Literature,
Comparative—Greek and English (Old) 4. Epic poetry, Greek—History and
criticism. 5. Dueling in literature. 6. Heroes in literature. 7. Speech in literature.
8. Homer—Technique. 9. Dialogue.
I. Title.
PR205.P37   1990
829′.1—dc20   89–10609

Publication of this book has been aided by a grant from the
Paul Mellon Fund of Princeton University Press

This book has been composed in Linotron Baskerville

Princeton University Press books are printed on acid-free paper, and meet the
guidelines for permanence and durability of the Committee on Production
Guidelines for Book Longevity of the Council on Library Resources

Printed in the United States of America by Princeton University Press,
Princeton, New Jersey
10 9 8 7 6 5 4 3 2 1

Contents

Preface

THE REAL SUBJECT of this book is war-in-dialogue and dialogue-in-war. War itself as armed conflict has long been parading in all its multicolored regalia through the annals of history. In some ages it is celebrated, in others execrated. Either way, its face is well known to us. But how does it speak? In what terms does it declare itself? I do not refer here to war merely as the corporate venture of nations, but as the manifestation of one aspect of our humanity. To this there can be few better witnesses than the heroes of ancient epic. War to them was a way of living; and the poets who told of them opened the mind of the warrior to view as only great artists can. In the verbal duels of these heroes in battle, the discourse of war finds perhaps its superlative expression.

I came to this topic initially because I was struck by the extent to which the literature that I was studying featured it. Yet on further reflection, these dialogues seemed to me to be linked with problems of undeniable importance. No era could know better than ours the terrible toll that war exacts. Tens of millions have died on the battlefields of this century alone; and full-scale global conflict now would spell holocaust indeed. Against such a backdrop, the contemporary peace movements bespeak a worldwide and heartfelt desire on humanity's part to cast off its violent heritage. Yet recent experience has also shown that war arises from within us and is not merely imposed from the outside. Hitler was empowered not just by his own ambitions but by mass support; his dreams of conquest were shared by much of the German nation. Unfortunately this recognition that the causes of war fester within the average person tends to dampen the enthusiasm of those who want to end it. Unable to follow Prospero in acknowledging their own creatures of darkness, sincere peace-marchers keep shooting themselves in the foot by blaming all war on the power mongering of politicians and governments. Yet because this is only a half-truth, because we the people are the true authors of our own violences, many of the best men and women wind up denying reality to affirm their conscience, adopting intransigent policies and noble postures that could not possibly be held to for any length of time by the mass of human beings as they are. The effect of this is ultimately to forfeit control in these matters to others whose ideals do not similarly handicap them. Thus the precious resource of an intelligent idealism gets wasted—and the hope for peace continues to languish.

Yet peace does not have to remain a pipe dream forever. But before we can close and seal up the tomes of bloodshed, we need to understand them better. Warriors are not simply bloodthirsty, sadistic, and crazed for killing. To the contrary, the greatest martial heroes are usually quite principled in their own way and, if we can avoid undue cynicism, heroic epos can teach us much. Warfare almost always entails collaboration not only between confederates but between enemies. One of the conclusions of this book is that heroic adversaries are subtly bound into interdependency, that their verbal and martial hostilities are, in covert ways, joint ventures. Have we not all read or heard or even lived through the story of the longtime rivals who come to realize that they have grown into a mutual respect, indeed, that in a curious way they have become friends? The contestants of epic speak war from the inside and so might spotlight for us both its perils and felicities. If peace movements can take as their starting point that idealism inscribed in the heart of warfare, they can catalyze a transformation that will succeed where the mere vilification of violence never will. The warrior mentality will always be with us. Yet by waging war against those habits of mind that precipitate in external destructiveness, the better aspirations of our time might finally come to fruition.

It is toward this larger purpose that my probings into the verbal duel in this book are dedicated. The book itself is the culmination of a long effort that has taken shape in bits and pieces and in various places. Some of it found its first approximation in chapters 4 through 6 of my doctoral dissertation, written at the University of Missouri at Columbia in 1982 to 1983. Parts of that material subsequently appeared in article form. Chapter 2 enormously enlarges on an idea set forth in "Flyting and Fighting: Pathways in the Realization of the Epic Contest," published in *Neophilologus* in 1986. The third section of chapter 3, on "speech functions," is based on "The Flyting Speech in Traditional Heroic Narrative," published in the next volume of that journal; the discussion of the *Alliterative Morte Arthure* in the second section of chapter 4, though developed along somewhat different lines, shares material with "The Flyting Contract and Adversarial Patterning in the *Alliterative Morte Arthure*," forthcoming in an anthology entitled *New Views on Old Masterpieces: Essays on British Literature of the Middle Ages and Renaissance* (University of Delaware Press, 1990). Finally, chapter 5 is a modified version of "Flyting, Sounding, Debate: Three Verbal Contest Genres," published in a 1986 issue of *Poetics Today*. While I would not wish to deny its relationship with this earlier research, I must emphasize that the present study is far more than mere recapitulation. Aside from the maturation that my thinking has undergone in the past several years and my introduction to an array of new topics during the unfolding of this inquiry, the exigencies of the extended, book-length argument have demanded a rigorous interconnecting of ideas that is wholly lacking in these shorter, more exploratory treatments. I nonetheless wish to thank the original publishers for their kind permission to reprint or paraphrase from these earlier works. I would also like to express appreciation to Oxford University Press for permission to reprint from *Homeri opera*, vol. 2, 3d ed. (Clarendon Press, 1920), pp. 175–78 and 181, and to the University of Chicago Press for permission to reprint from Richmond Lattimore's translation, *The Iliad of Homer* (1951), pp. 409–11 and 413, on pages 118–26 of my text.

Those who have undertaken projects of this sort will no doubt feel as acutely as I do how much they owe to the generosity of others. I would particularly like to thank Professor John Foley of the University of Missouri and Father Walter Ong of Saint Louis University, both of whom served as readers for my dissertation and have helped me since then in more ways than I can enumerate. Other colleagues, particularly at Louisiana State University, have contributed in various ways; nor can I fail to mention the students of my graduate seminars who have vastly enriched my experience of the primary texts. But most of all I want to thank my wife Karin, who has borne with me with love and patience while the struggles of ancient times found new battlegrounds in my imaginative replays. Well I know that any work of mine can exist only through the accommodations of other people. Nor would I wish it to be otherwise; for in these debts lie the affirmations that join us into community.

Baton Rouge, Louisiana
January 31, 1989

Verbal Dueling in Heroic Narrative

Introduction

As TWO hostile armies first square off against each other, or later, during a lull in the storm of battle, or at a public assemblage, or in the beer hall, or at a tournament or athletic contest, a hero is engaging in provocative display. A second hero takes umbrage at the public attention the first one enjoys and draws him into in a verbal contest. Flyting ensues: The adversaries name and abuse one another, compare ancestries or accomplishments, debate their relative heroic merits, prognosticate on some projected competition or exploit. After a physical contest in the shape of direct combat, athletic competition, or some other feat, a winner is eventually determined; and his victory receives a ceremonialized acknowledgment, by the boasts and curses of winner and loser respectively, or through reconciliation and an exchange of gifts.

This scenario has been repeated unendingly in many of the world's great narrative traditions. One is reminded, to cite just a few examples, of the showdown between Achilles and Hektor in book 22 of the *Iliad*, or the disguised Odysseus's skirmishes with Euryalos, Polyphemos, Antinoös, and other adversaries; that ominous encounter in the *Mahābhārata* when Arjuna and Karṇa first meet in a tournament of the martial arts and begin their long enmity, or the trading of insults and curses between the Pāṇḍavas and Kauravas at the great dicing match; the verbal sparring of Beowulf and Unferth in the Old English epic poem, or that of Byrhtnoth and the Viking messenger in *The Battle of Maldon*; the *Lokasenna*, *Hárbarðsljóð*, and other flytings in the *Poetic Edda*; of the exchange of verbal barbs between Skarphedin and Flosi at the Althing in the *Njáls saga*; Siegfried's belligerent displays upon his first arrival at the court of Gunther in the *Nibelungenlied*, or in the quarrel of the queens Kriemhild and Brunhild in the same work; the single combat of Charlemagne and Baligant in *The Song of Roland* or of Lucius and Gawain (acting as proxy for Arthur) in the *Alliterative Morte Arthure*; the boast-and-battle sequences pitting members of the Heike and Genji clans in the fourteenth-century Japanese *Heike monogatari*; and numerous other episodes from epic and romance. Yet while heroic narrative is particularly rich with examples, the phenomenon itself is not confined to these genres. Brawling shoot-outs in the town saloon made for standard fare in the great age of cinema and television Westerns, just as today professional wrestlers rant into the camera about the barbarisms planned for next week's victims. And would it surprise us to find similar displays in the school-yard or in ghetto gang wars, such as were depicted in the well-known musical *West Side Story*? Like it or not, such verbal belligerence, often wedded to violent action, has lived long in the roughhouse of yarn and history.

Yet dialogic warfare cannot be exiled off into "heroic" settings, ancient or modern; to the contrary, it springs up in every kind of context, leaping across historical, geographical, sociological, and linguistic boundaries. A perspicuous literary survey of the verbal duel or poetic contest, for example, might uncover a deep complicity between many of our most highly prized creations of verbal artistry and agonistic mind-sets. Epic aside, much of the cream of Greek literature—the plays of Aeschylus, Sophocles, Euripides, and Aristophanes, or the Pindaric odes—was composed for the Greater Dionysian poetic competitions or to celebrate winning athletes in the Olympic festivals. In the Middle Ages rivalries between troubadors and Meistersingers thrived in courts and poet guilds; the late medieval Scottish flytings, we may be sure, did not fail to entertain. Even today bards battle through ten-round matches before an audience and three judges in the World Heavyweight Poetry Championship at Taos, New Mexico, held each year on the summer solstice. And could we very well deny that competition for jobs or fellowships often inspire literary creation? Yet the verbal contest has served not only for many a poet's Muse but for his matter also. Violent Aeschylean or Sophoclean stichomythia vies with the barbed banter of Shakespeare; even the gentle eclogue sponsored singing matches. Roman and neoclassical satire did not eschew the quip and the repartee, traded between characters in a dramatic fiction or flung at living historical persons. Medieval disputation reigned in poems of *débat*, *The Owl and the Nightingale*, the Middle High German *Wartburgkrieg*; Chaucer's *The Canterbury Tales* is precisely a literary "representation" of a reportedly oral tale-telling contest on a grand scale. Unlike their epic heroic counterparts, these literary adversaries do not typically kill each other. Nonetheless, might not the same motivations have been in force?

But even literature and the narrative arts collectively stake out too small a turf for verbal duelists; others among our most venerable cultural forms and institutions have long played host to their wars. Systematic philosophical inquiry, for example, took shape through the Platonic dialogues that were much in the manner of contests, Socrates' protestations to the contrary notwithstanding. Medieval university theologians forged their proofs out of the crucible of *disputatio*; the very forms of their written discourse, such as the *sic et non* of Peter Abelard or the argumentation through objection and rebuttal in Aquinas's *Summa Theologica*, seem to represent the reduction of combative dialogue into modes suited to continuous, univocal exposition. And still in the academy today, the very insistence on *proof*, on *demonstration*, presupposes a critically disposed readership that will find faults whenever there are faults to be found and that will accede to persuasion only when every other possibility has been ruled out. In an important sense, through much of the history of Western intellectual inquiry, my audience is my enemy. Much the same holds for our system of law, which defines justice through an adversarial process.[1] What is a trial, after all, but a verbal contest with its labyrinthine rules and procedures honored in their own right, even when truth itself gets cast out of court? One cannot "win" a robbery or a murder; but that winning is what he is paid for no lawyer can afford to forget. In short, verbal dueling is built into our way of life, so profoundly, so inextricably, so variously, that few of us can even begin to fathom the extent of our involvement.

Yet despite its pervasiveness and institutionalization in Western civilization, study of the verbal duel remains in its infancy, particularly by comparison with canonical literary genres such as epic or drama or novel, or even the philosophical dialogue.[2] A brilliant pioneering effort in this respect is Walter Ong's *Fighting for Life* (1981); although its subject is the contest itself and not the verbal contest more narrowly, it opens windows on the latter topic. Most of the earlier sections of his book devote themselves to establishing the psychobiological bases of contest behavior, which by Ong's argument plays a dominant role in the establishment of male sexual identity. The second half (118–209) traces broad patterns in the development of the academy, in diverse spheres of contemporary culture, and in the movement of consciousness toward increased interiority. Although the agonistic drive emerges as an invariant element in the psyche, it is historically conditioned in its manner of expression and does not always attain to equal ascendancy in the major arenas of cultural interchange. Indeed, as Ong argues in detail, the literacizing of Western civilization over the last three millennia and in an accelerated fashion in recent centuries seems to have encouraged the interiorization of conflict and the displacement of overtly polemical displays in education, politics, religion, and other domains of contemporary life.

My purpose is not to survey the verbal duel in all its manifestations.

Rather, I plan to concentrate—especially in the first three foundational chapters—on a particular genre of verbal disputation that I will call "heroic flyting." In brief, heroic flyting is agonistically styled verbal disputation with martial overtones. Because this form of verbal dueling crops up in genetically and geographically remote civilizations, it cannot be treated merely as the product of a particular cultural history or tradition, though of course such factors contribute their share. My selection of a limited corpus of material from Homeric Greece and Anglo-Saxon England is intended to facilitate an in-depth inquiry while establishing the cross-cultural generality of the phenomenon. In chapters 4 and 5, I will enlarge into other historical periods and discursive traditions, but here too my primary aim will be to give further definition to my genre by viewing it in these other contexts. Thus the project of this book is, in a sense, a limited one. Yet in the larger world of disputation, verbal and otherwise, heroic flyting has two special virtues. First, it can stake strong claims to chronological primacy in the sense that it appears in some of the earliest Greek and English texts, thus antedating and probably influencing other disputative forms in these societies, and perhaps in other cultures as well. Second, it displays the agonistic mind-set underlying all verbal contests in a particularly bald, even naive, form; indeed, I cannot think of another body of material that does this so well. Because modern prestige culture is generally embarrassed by vulgar macho displays, agonistic motives at work in its own life are seldom admitted. Homeric and Anglo-Saxon heroes had no use for such concealments. Their pronouncements, therefore, have a special power to reveal a domain of the psyche that civilized modernity—often for the best of intentions—has tried to wish away.

The word *flyting* might mislead some who associate it with the flamboyant and wildly abusive volleys of invective of Scottish *makars* such as William Dunbar.[3] In fact, for reasons to be set forth in chapter 5, such "ludic flytings" must be generically distinguished from the "heroic flyting" of epic with its martial entailments and serious truth claims. Yet the term has long been used among Germanicists also; in an important article Clover (1980) has recommended it as a general expression for verbal contesting of the north Germanic type, in preference to native Icelandic terms such as *senna* or *mannjafnaðr*. Although the word flyting as such does not occur in Old English poetic usage, there are numerous attestations to the verb *flitan*, meaning "to strive, contend, dispute, rebel" (Bosworth and Toller 1898).[4] I feel that the word will serve us best if we take it as a general designation for *verbal contesting with an ad hominem orientation*, as distinct from dispute whose subject matter is nonpersonal. This definition enables us to study flyting as a cross-cultural genre, though, of course, further refinements become necessary when one turns to any particular body of material. Within this larger category of flytings, then, heroic flyting stands as a subclass, whose precise characteristics we shall be specifying in due course.

My analysis of heroic flyting draws in the main part from Homeric and Anglo-Saxon narrative poetry. The *Iliad* will furnish the greatest number of examples, since its battle books are virtual showcases for heroic display. The *Odyssey*, by contrast, tries to suppress its flyting movements; there are several superb instances anyway, and the poem's very ambivalence toward verbal *agōnia* will yield some noteworthy insights.[5] Other early Greek narrative, as in passages of Hesiod's *Theogony*, or in the prose summaries of the Trojan Cycle, or in the histories, would not serve my purposes well, since they do not dramatize contests in the epic manner.[6] In Old English literature, our attention will center on three major episodes and two minor ones. The principal flytings are Beowulf's, first with the Danish coastguard (*Beo.* 239–319) and then with Unferth (449–610), and Byrhtnoth's with the Viking messenger (*The Battle of Maldon* 25–95);[7] though they are abbreviated and obscure, *The Fight at Finnsburg* and *Waldere* will be drawn upon from time to time. Other Anglo-Saxon disputes, such as that between Elene and the Jew, between the fiend and Andreas or Juliana, or between Solomon and Saturn, though of interest in themselves, do not constitute flytings of the heroic type.[8] More Germanic instances could be adduced if we broadened our purview to take in the *Nibelungenlied*, the *Poetic Edda*, Saxo Grammaticus, and a sampling of Icelandic sagas. This would lead me outside those fields I know best, however; also, this larger corpus of material would greatly complicate the analysis by forcing me to treat a variety of questions (generic, historical, political, ideological) tangential to my inquiry. No treatment of verbal disputation in the family sagas, for example, can ignore the institutionalization of feuding whose intricacies Byock (1982) has sketched out; yet patterns rooted in the legal history of medieval Iceland do not generalize easily. The Greek and Old English heroic material, by contrast, seldom resists in-depth comparison; and the Old English examples, though small in number, do fortuitously provide a wide spectrum of heroic flyting types. I have, nonetheless, tried to keep other literatures in mind, and I believe that the principles I develop are widely applicable. To illustrate this, the fourth chapter breaks out of the Greek-to-Old-English axis and applies these formulations to literary works of ancient India, medieval France, and England of the Middle English period.

Obviously a comparative enterprise such as this one demands repeated transgressions across disciplinary boundaries. Although I have tried to cast a wide net, I cannot pretend to have read all the criticism that might bear on my subject; moreover, the exigencies of my argument have seldom allowed for detailed commentary even on those secondary works most crucial to my thinking. In fact, few interpretations of Homer or *Beowulf* focus on verbal dueling *as such*, and fewer still see it as a cross-cultural phenomenon. Yet the construction of a coherent outlook on the heroic flyting genre is a challenging task in itself; and its rigors will not permit those kinds of digressions necessary to relate my observations on that genre to the conventional topics of the literary criticism dealing with these particular epics. Therefore I do not wish to mislead my reader into expecting anything on the order of new "readings." To the contrary, I have ignored literary complexities whenever possible and used my texts unabashedly as sources of examples. If an apology is required for such practice, I submit that verbal dueling is an important topic in its own right and that present-day scholarship must admit sufficient critical pluralism as to allow for its study. Nonetheless, I do feel that my observations on heroic flyting will pertain to literary interpretation, as the conventions of any genre will to the study of a literary work that employs or plays with them. For neither Homer nor the *Beowulf* poet (nor anyone else) created flyting out of whole cloth. To appreciate their achievements, we need to understand it as one of the materials with which they worked.

The major ground for my Greek-to-Old-English comparison, then, resides in the integrity of heroic flyting itself. The very genetic, geographical, and chronological distances between these civilizations give support to this explanation. Yet there are other similarities that make this selection of material felicitous. Both societies were Indo-European, although the Indo-Europeans cannot claim the credit of inventing a genre that also flourishes among red deer and herring gulls, as we shall see. More significant, my material derives from what has been called the "heroic age." This does not refer, of course, to a historical era in which the conditions described in heroic epos actually prevailed, but to phases in the literary expression of diverse cultures in which a heroic *ethos*, in various forms but with recognizable consistencies, played a major and often dominant part.[9] My particular slant on the "heroic," which will be set forth in more detail in chapter 1, draws on sociobiology and, in a loose sense, psychology. It centers, as I see it, in an agonistically defined concept of the self, in the establishment of which the ritual contest figures largely. Such agonistic inclinations are common not only to humans but to many spheres of animal life. To attempt to study specific expressions of contest behavior without recognizing these broader affiliations would be as myopic as to analyze the sexual patterns of a specific group as though they were the particular inventions of that group, unrelated to sexuality in general. This is not to say that agonistic conceptions prevail to an equal degree across the entire heroic landscape, since obviously this narrative is variously eclectic in its concerns, depending on the work and tradition. Archaic heroism entails more than just contesting. Yet contesting is a necessary if not a sufficient condition. Thus, contests from diverse cultural settings can be interilluminating for the very reason that they help to create the "heroic" aura that these literatures are generally felt to share.

A second consistency in my focal material is that almost all of it (until the last two chapters) is epic in its narrative style. I am thinking of epic not as a Western literary tradition running from Homer through Virgil to modern authors such as Milton (though a history of flyting in this context would be well worthy studying), but as a worldwide narrative mode encompassing, for instance, the *Mahābhārata* and *Rāmāyana*, the *Cid*, *The Song of Roland*, the *Heike monogatari*, *The Wedding of Smailagić Meho*, the *Popol Vuh*, and the like. What is essential from my standpoint is that flytings and the contests to which they belong be fully dramatized scenically, preferably within the sweep of a broader narrative. It is true that the label of epic fits *Beowulf* better than the other Old English poems. Although *Waldere* may derive from something of the sort, *Finnsburg* does not; in any case both survive in mere fragments and will be alluded to only occasionally. *Maldon*, however, while lacking the dimensions associated with epic, nonetheless develops its battle episode with an epic and scenic expansiveness, and for this reason it can sustain comparison with the flyting and fighting episodes of *Beowulf* and the *Iliad* quite well.[10]

The third basis for the comparison consists in that the Homeric epos, *Beowulf*, and, to a lesser extent, *Maldon* all have roots in oral tradition. I will not claim that any of these works is itself the direct product—that is, the transcription—of an oral performance; neither do I rule out this possibility. Yet it would not be unreasonable to suppose that all of them are to various degrees residually oral, drawing on oral-traditional resources and habits of mind.[11] One of these is the disposition of oral poets to employ formulas of various sorts. This subject is fraught with controversies in which I do not wish to get embroiled; in any event, formulary tendencies are not the only characteristic of oral expression. But since oral composition must rely on memory heavily, stereotypic patterns suited to mnemonic recall serve well the economy of oral thought; oral formulaic research has sorted out various types—lexical formulas, themes, type scenes (*typischen Sce-*

nen), story patterns, and other concepts (like motif and motifeme) borrowed from folkloristics.[12] *Type scene* probably characterizes heroic flyting better than *theme* or *motif*; Carol Clover has argued persuasively that flyting transpires within the scenic framework, which in her view constitutes the base level for saga narrative movement.[13] Yet while scenic constraints are often involved in the realization of flyting, to incorporate the concept of the unitary scene into its very definition is in several respects misleading, at least for its epic manifestations. Oftentimes, for example, chained flytings succeed one another in the course of a mass battle sequence. Is each of these necessarily a separate scene? Also, as chapters 1 and 2 argue at length, heroic flytings are tied to martial encounters that frequently do not materialize for many hundreds or even thousands of lines—well beyond scenic boundaries. As I see it, heroic flyting is best characterized as a traditional dialogic mode or dialogic genre with particular scenic and narrative entailments. At present, dialogic types are not admitted into most inventories of the traditional oral "wordhoard." Yet the traditional dimension of heroic narrative lends itself to many kinds of analysis not yet accommodated within the existing oral-formulaic typologies. Plainly this branch of study will in coming years be compelled greatly to enlarge its conceptual vocabulary.

In what follows, then, these three grounds of comparability will be taken as sufficient for the direct juxtaposition of Greek and Anglo-Saxon materials without further apology. At the same time, it would be churlish to deny that verbal contesting owes greatly to its historical settings. Nagy (1979) has discussed many of the traditional matrices in which the archaic Greek concept of the hero is embedded; plainly this must affect the Greek concept of the "heroic." Nor is the form of the Iliadic contest unrelated to Homeric battle practices, the precise character of which has long been disputed.[14] At the same time, the Homeric poems had or took on a pan-Hellenic significance in association with the great athletic festivals, whose roots extend well back into the early eighth century.[15] There is nothing in Old English literature remotely comparable with the great funerary games for Patroklos in book 23 of the *Iliad* or even, on a lesser scale, the competition and festivities on the island of the Phaiakians in the *Odyssey*. The sense of sport and athletics does, in fact, directly enter into flytings of what I will later call the guest-host variety and accounts for specific differences between the ways in which the Greek and Old English guest-host contest patterns realize themselves.[16]

Perhaps there is a certain similarity between the incipient pan-Hellenism of Homer and that perspective out of which the major Old English epic arises, casting back upon an era of tribal migrations yet itself belonging to an age of increasing centralization and even emerging nationalism. The extent to which one might wish to press this claim would depend on whether one dates the poem from the eighth or tenth centuries—the earlier date prior to and the latter following the unification of England under Alfred and his successors. Yet Old English flyting may well be related to traditions of disputation or *streitgedichte* that flourished on the continent.[17] Some of these forms, such as the French or Provençal *tenso* or Latin debate poetry, reached their apex later in the Middle Ages; Norse saga similarly postdates *Beowulf* and so could not as such have been an influence. Yet in some sense all these debate modalities might have resonated within a common world of discourse. Pizarro (1976) provided a comprehensive review of early Germanic tradition of the *senna*, which includes the exchange between Alboin and the followers of Turisind in Paul the Deacon's *Historia Langobardorum* 1.24, the *Hárbarðsljóð*, *Lokasenna*, episodes from Saxo Grammaticus and the *Völsunga saga*, and other instances, particularly in Norse saga literature. The topic has sponsored other important studies by Lönnroth (1979), J. Harris (1979), Bax and Padmos (1983), and Clover (1980), who argues specifically for Germanic "flyting" as the best interpretive context for the Beowulf-Unferth exchange. Another relevant topic is the duel, which, particularly in Iceland, is fraught with legal implications.[18] A major study in this subject by Byock (1982) derives Icelandic family saga feuding—elaborated through the three "feudemes" of conflict, advocacy, and resolution—from a rather unique historical and legal background. Since these societies were intermittently in contact with each other throughout the Old English period, and often enough in warlike settings that would have sponsored this very type of dialogue, it should hardly surprise us if their flyting traditions were interactive. None of this, of course, can be illumined by the flytings in Homer.

Before concluding, I should comment briefly on a very different problem, that is, the sexual bias inherent in my subject matter. The literary corpus that I have selected precludes more than a short note on this issue, for all the instances that I am treating pit males as adversaries. Yet this is not altogether unrepresentative, for by far the greater number (though by no means all) of the examples of highly formalized verbal dueling that I have encountered in ancient literature are between men. In chapter 1, moreover, I will argue for the association of heroic contesting with intermale combat in the animal world. This link with gender, in my view, needs to be squarely recognized. Epic heroes are far from "liberated" where sexual stereotyping is concerned; to the contrary, the proving of one's "manhood" is central to the whole heroic project.[19] Whether we like it or not, the reality of sex roles in the literature of ages past should be recognized for what it was and not distorted into something we think better.

A study of verbal contests in which women take an active part would demand very different methods from those I have found suitable for heroic flyting.[20] Even if one concentrates on the more formal, ceremonialized exchanges, as opposed to simple quarrels, interfemale or female-male contests seem hardly to be of a single type. For example, the altercation between the queens Brunhild and Kriemhild in the *Nibelungenlied* centers not on the merits of the disputants themselves but on those of their husbands; likewise, the obligation for martial resolution devolves upon the men. From a structural standpoint, then, this contest seems like a typical intermale flyting whose speeches, though targeted at the husbands, have been taken over by the wives. Radically distinct from this are the erotic-amatory "flytings" between men and women who pose as adversaries but are really courting or seducing each other, sometimes unbeknownst to themselves.[21] Outstanding examples include the ongoing verbal skirmishes between Beatrice and Benedick in Shakespeare's *Much Ado about Nothing* or the stylized courtly debates in book 1 of Andreas Capellanus's *De Amore*. Although this dialogic form is both ceremonialized and long-lived in Western literature, surely one must differentiate flytings aimed at romantic and sexual consummation from those conceiving victory in terms of the physical extermination of the foe.[22] Still another form of "verbal combat" between women and men is the goading on to vengeance that women such as Hallgerd in the *Njáls saga* direct at their husbands or other relatives. Yet these exchanges are not contests between adversaries who contend with each other on equal terms; rather, they center on charges (such as cowardice or ugliness) to which one sex or the other is specially vulnerable.[23] Then again, the altercations between Cecilie and the tyrant Almache in Chaucer's *Second Nun's Tale* or between Elene and the Jew in the Old English *Elene* take on the character of a theological debate, a distinct verbal contest genre. Perhaps most fascinating of all is *The Wife of Bath's Prologue*; although it presents us with abundant quarreling reduced into monologue, it cannot, even so qualified, be called verbal dueling in the same, ceremonialized sense. For finding herself confronted with a hegemonic tradition of antifeminist discourse, the Wife delights precisely in flouting the rules of good medieval argumentation, with its proper use of authorities, avoidance of ad hominem accusations, adherence to principles of logic, and so forth. My point is that these highly heterogeneous forms—and an enlargement of the sampling would only increase the heterogeneity—demand an inquiry based on different principles than I have employed here. No study that took mere "contesting" as its root term could get far into this material.

Yet even within the narrower confines of strictly intermale heroic flyting, women and the image of femininity are pivotal, though covertly so, because to flyters throughout the world the establishment of sexual identity is a paramount preoccupation. This concern expresses itself in many forms, as in the flyter's imputation of feminity to his adversary or his rejection of it in himself. This pancultural theme is particularly evident in the verbal duels of male adolescents as have been studied by Labov (1972), Gossen (1974), and Dundes, Leach, and Özkök (1972). Plainly such rejections and exclusions of femininity mark it out as an unconscious force. Nor should we fail to note the extent to which women or the desire for them motivates heroic exploits. Even though the *Iliad* often depicts its women as pawns of war, nonetheless the entire Trojan expedition resulted from the abduction of Helen, and the quarrel over Chryseis and Bryseis sets the entire epic plot into motion. The Greek and most other heroic traditions seem to me to express male sensibilities for the most part. Thus men dominate the foreground of action, and women become visible in only a few scenes, important though these often are. And yet this very disproportion between the number of lines devoted to them and their central role in the structure of several epic stories signals the centrality of the feminine in the male-dominated heroic imagination. Once again, since it can be approached more through what is excluded than through what is actually expressed, this issue of femininity in the unconscious or semiconscious aspect of heroic narrative expression cannot receive adequate treatment here. Yet to the degree that it provides a coherent account of what heroic flyters do express, this study may provide one useful foundation for such an inquiry.

The argument that follows divides into two major sections. The first three chapters, which develop the Greek-to-Old-English comparison, attempt to provide a comprehensive definition of heroic flyting through detailed analysis on several levels, moving from the broader to the narrower. The first chapter, "Flyting and the Contest Paradigm," situates verbal disputation within its larger behavioral (or sociobiological) context, reviews several of the major characteristics and significations of heroic contesting, and discusses the constituting elements and structures within the contest as a larger whole. The heroic encounter is here viewed in static terms. Chapter 2, "Flyting-to-Fighting Pathways," schematizes the lines of movement that adversaries trace through the contest exchange. Flytings are still viewed within the larger contest setting; yet attention here centers on the dynamics of process, particularly as these are influenced by the social environment in which the encounter takes place. I turn to analysis of the conventions of the verbal contest itself in chapter 3, "The Flyting Exchange," which first describes the dynamics of quarreling and contesting as simultaneous, complementary flyting processes, turns then to an inventory of the rhetorical moves by which individual speeches are generated, reviews the sequence of mirrorings by which flyters respond to one another, and concludes with the detailed review of a specific contest, between Aineias and Achilles in *Il*.20.158–352. With this chapter the analysis of heroic flyting per se is completed.

The remainder of the book will examine heroic flyting in other, broader settings. Chapter 4, "The Contest Paradigm in the Structure of Epic and Romance Narrative," tries to document how large-scale realizations of the flyting-fighting pattern help inform the narrative movement of several major works of heroic epic or romance outside the orbit of the ancient Greek and Anglo-Saxon worlds. A review of key episodes in the *Mahābhārata*, the *Alliterative Morte Arthure*, *The Song of Roland*, and *Sir Gawain and the Green Knight* shows basic flyting patterns at work, though modified and transformed by ideologies not fully in accord with the heroic ethos. Nonetheless, the contest paradigm proves to be fairly maleable; and far from limiting the creators of these extended narratives, it serves as one of the bases for artistic vision. Finally, in "Genre and the Verbal Duel" (chapter 5), I try to situate heroic flyting in the larger world of adversative dialogic forms. My method here is to identify parameters of generic differentiation on the basis of which one can distinguish between heroic flyting, ludic flyting, and academic debate, these three representing a broader spectrum of diverse verbal contesting types. Eschewing a formal in favor of a pragmatic approach, I find diverging (binary) tendencies in four areas: subject matter, referential mode, locus of resolution, and social context. While these variables are derived empirically from a limited sampling, they may serve taxonomic purposes in studies of other verbal contest material.

Although at present mainstream scholarship relegates verbal dueling to the margins as a scurrilous footnote to the history of narrative and dialogic forms, I am convinced that in coming years this will change, as the agonistic underpinnings of modern civilization emerge into plainer view. For in these duels of the heroic era, agonistic display was overt, uncamouflaged, nakedly parading in its own natural colors. Today this is less the case, at least in "literature" and other preserves of prestige culture, and this change registers a genuine and laudable disenchantment with the violent heritage of the past. Yet in reality flyting is far from dead. It thrives openly in the games of adolescents, and covertly in the polite rebuffs of scholars on the conference circuit; more perturbing, it animates much of the discourse of high politics, diplomacy ("we went eyeball to eyeball with the Russians, and they blinked"), and other spheres whose impact on the fates of millions of human lives is incalculable. For those interested in the conditions of war and peace in the modern era—and in a nuclear age what problem could press itself upon us with greater urgency?—the "naive" frankness of epic heroes unmasks certain human realities that we would do better to acknowledge. It is here, in the depths of our own self-honesty, that these ancient masters of abuse can speak to us.

Flyting and the Contest Paradigm

Behavioral Ecological Backgrounds

Why do flyting, and other types of formalized contesting, exert such an appeal on the human psyche? Why does the author of the *Iliad*, like many of his bardic brethren, devote hundred- and even thousand-line stretches to the grisly detailing of battle slaughter, the redundancy and gratuitous violence of such scenes notwithstanding? The answer must lie in the psychobiological sources of agonistic behavior. Ceremonial contesting manifests variously not only among human beings but widely throughout the animal kingdoms. In assessing the significance of flyting between epic heroes, then, we need to reckon with our own biological and evolutionary past.[1]

The agonistically styled intermale rutting contests among red deer in Scotland, as described in a well-known study by Clutton-Brock, Guinness, and Albon (1982: esp. 105–42), illustrate the affiliations between human and animal behavior. These fights for control of harems broke out in the rutting season, from September through October, between harem holders and intruding stags. While most single stags preferred to skulk at a distance, prospective challengers advanced to approximately two to three hundred meters of the harem holder. At this juncture the adversaries engaged in a curious roaring match in which each tried to outdo his rival in the intensity and frequency of his roars. After several minutes of this, the intruder ordinarily withdrew. If he advanced further to within one hundred meters,

> the contest was more likely to escalate first to a further exchange of roars and then, in the majority of cases, to a parallel walk, with the two contestants moving tensely up and down, typically at right angles to the direction from which the approacher came. At any moment during a parallel walk, either stag might invite contact by turning to face his opponent and lowering his antlers. Opponents almost always accepted his invitation, turned quickly, and locked antlers. Both animals would then push vigorously. . . . In the course of longer fights, contestants frequently separated for a few seconds at a time, rejoining after one of the pair invited contact again by lowering his antlers. Fights lasted until one of the pair was pushed rapidly

backward, broke contact, and ran off. Winning stags seldom pursued losers for more than 10 to 20 m, though if a stag slipped in the course of a
fight his rival would immediately attempt to horn him in the flank, rump,
or neck. (Clutton-Brock, Guinness, and Albon 1982: 129–30)

Although contestants did not fight to the death, injuries could be se-
vere and sometimes ultimately lethal (132–35).

Much in this scenario is specific to red deer. The precise form of
combat, for example, owes much to cervine anatomy; nor does all
intermale competition center on mating prerogatives as these fights
do. Nonetheless, the ritualization and stereotypy evident in these red
deer displays recur throughout the animal world. As Barash puts it
(1982: 355), such agonistic encounters are often

> so stylized as to be more aptly described as tournaments rather than fights,
> programmed by rules and perhaps containing a touch of pageantry as well.
> Although written by evolution rather than by a human hand, the strictures
> appear to be no less real, and adherence is remarkably complete. Animals
> whose behavior is characterized by such rules are no more likely to break
> them than a human prizefighter is to pull out a revolver and shoot his
> opponent.

Thus dueling tomcats, according to Leyhausen (1979: 170–88), progress through a series of stereotypic attack and defense postures, many
of them in slow motion (and superbly illustrated in Leyhausen's pho-
tographs and drawings), as lead-up to a caterwauling frenzy of bites
and blows; the contest ends when, after such a "round," one of them
gives up, which he signifies by remaining in the defensive posture.
Even rats, a species singularly unsusceptible to primitivist human ro-
manticizing, manage their fights between intruder males and colony
alphas in a stereotypic fashion. According to Blanchard and Blanchard (1984: 8–9), the alpha first piloerects, then bites at the intruder, and chases him when he runs off. The intruder halts and
rears up on his hind legs, using his forelimbs to "box" off his attacker,
while the alpha moves laterally, making occasional biting lunges. In
the next stage the stranger rolls on his back while the alpha tries to
turn him over. Remarkably enough, the target of the alpha's attack,
according to Blanchard and Blanchard, is the intruder's back, a region far less vulnerable to deadly or incapacitating injury than other
bodily parts that the intruder makes no effort to defend. As these
and other examples show, the ritual stylization of combat particularly
between conspecific adversaries is no mere fiction. When we see such
phenomena in human affairs, then, we may legitimately suspect that
the ultimate causes go beyond conscious human artifice.

That stylization figures prominently into the interhuman contests of heroic literature much of this book will be trying to show. Yet one need not leaf back through the annals of the past; rules and ceremonies contour much human aggression even today. Consider, for example, the boxing match. Two adversaries, who in pregame promotional interviews profess to hate each other, try to inflict bodily injury, but only in certain ways. Neither uses weapons, such as guns or knives; neither kicks or hits below the waist; and both desist at the bell ending each round, so that pats or slaps on the back administered immediately afterward are interpreted as friendly gestures, not attacks. Now nothing in human genetics has determined that boxing should be conducted in precisely this way. Boxing as such is a creation of human consciousness. Yet the disposition to enjoy stylized combat *of this kind* probably does owe to biology. Why else should it appeal to so many viewers? Of course, the world of athletics provides many such illustrations of the acting out of aggression as play; yet the same is often true of warfare.[2] A superb example appears in the "live and let live system of accommodation between the opposing forces" in World War I.[3] According to a German soldier, evening bombardments came with a predictable regularity (Axelrod 1984: 86): "At seven it came—so regularly that you could set your watch by it. . . . It always had the same objective, its range was accurate, it never varied laterally or went beyond or fell short of its mark. . . . There were even some inquisitive fellows who crawled out . . . a little before seven, in order to see it burst." The Germans likewise directed their artillery fire according to a predictable pattern, so that a certain Colonel Jones of the opposing army "was able to take what seemed to uninitiated Staff Officers big risks, knowing that the shelling would stop before he reached the place being shelled" (J. D. Hill, quoted in Axelrod 1984: 86). Such systems of reciprocal restraint did not succeed in avoiding all bloodshed, of course, any more than they do in heroic epic. Yet through the reciprocal restraint underlying this rituality, the scope of aggression can be—and for the most part is—contained within certain boundaries.

But let us return to the red deer of the island of Rhum in Scotland. Perhaps the most striking aspect of their rutting encounters are the roaring matches. And these were indeed a very real part of the contest process: each stag seemed to be trying to outroar the other. Thus some intruder stags gave up and withdrew after the roaring; and in those cases where fights did ensue, the rates of roaring correlated with fighting success (Clutton-Brock, Guinness, and Albon 1982: 136–38). Other species similarly use precombat threat display as an occasion for mutual assessment by contestants. Territorially combative herring gulls, according to the Nobel prizewinning Niko Tinbergen, prefaced physical contact with a kind of "mutual bluffing" in which the birds tore at bundles of moss or grass (1961: 56). Sometimes the assessment centers on anatomical characteristics, as among American bighorn sheep, who compare the size of their horns (Maynard Smith 1979: 482).· Yet red deer are not alone in vocalizing their threats.[4] Indeed, there may be a generalizable semiology involved; according to Morton (1977: 855), "birds and mammals use harsh, relatively low-frequency sounds when hostile and higher-frequency, more pure tonelike sounds when frightened, appeasing, or approaching in a friendly manner." All these threat displays, and particularly the vocalizations, seem to provide clear behavioral analogues to heroic flyting. For like their animal ancestors, flyting heroes are trying to represent themselves as better fighters than their opponents; like animal threats, human boasting may either escalate into physical combat or terminate the conflict (when one contestant flees the battlefield or modulates from aggression into appeasement). From a sociobiological perspective, then, flyting is continuous with interactive patterns that not only antedate ancient Greece and Anglo-Saxon England but, indeed, precede the human race altogether. Thus, heroic flyting may stake a claim to being one of the most long-lived of all dialogic genres.

What are the causes of such ceremonialized aggression? The question is a complex one, first, because the category is by no means clear-cut, and second, because causation can be conceived from so many different perspectives. The problem of categorization of aggressive behavior has led to various taxonomies. Wilson, for example, identifies eight major forms: territorial, dominance, sexual, parental disciplinary, weaning, moralistic, predatory, and antipredatory (1975: 242–43). Taking environmental stimuli and motivation as well as physiological and motor functions into consideration, Moyer (1976) derives six categories: predatory, intermale, fear-induced, maternal, irritable, and sex-related.[5] On the other hand, the integrity of "aggression" as a behavioral class can be challenged on various grounds, such as the physiological, for no single center for an instinctual and unitary aggressive drive can be identified within the brain.[6] Yet one needs some rubric under which to compare violent creaturely interactions; and "aggression," riddled with ambiguities though it may be, will have to serve. Perhaps the class of "agonistic" duels that I plan to study could be more precisely defined as "high-display intraspecific aggressive encounters," with aggression conceived as behavior intended to produce physical injury. This definition fits heroic flyting contests, the dueling matches of red deer and tomcats, and other such interactions that ethologists have generally agreed are related.

The matter of causation can be approached in various ways, not all of which conduce equally well to literary interpretation. Causation can be conceived in physiological terms, as when one studies the relation between aggression and androgens. Unfortunately, such approaches are not productive for the literary exegete studying fictional characters who are unavailable, for example, for blood sampling. More promising are behavioral causes found in social situations (to be studied extensively in later chapters); Goodall, for example, schematizes a number of these in her discussion of aggression among chimpanzees (1986: 320–21). Then again, causes can be identified as "resources"—such as food, territory, or mating privileges—that individuals fight to control.[7] Heroes too compete for such things. The quarrel between Agamemnon and Achilles, like the one between Menelaos and Paris that gave rise to the entire Trojan war, hinges on the possession of a woman; war between the Achaians and Trojans plainly takes on a territorial dimension as well; the *Scél Mucci Mic Dathó* (N. Chadwick 1927) features a brawl arising explicitly out of the division of food at a feast; and the struggles between Grendel and the Danes or between Odysseus and Polyphemos are constructed on a predatory model. In all these respects, then, the sources of heroic and animal conflicts are much alike.

Yet all these "proximate" causes are, from a sociobiological standpoint, subordinate to "adaptiveness" as the ultimate cause. Those phenotypic characteristics that promote the survival and reproduction of the organism, or, more exactly, that perpetuate the genes that it carries, are adaptive and for this reason ensure the reappearance of these genes in subsequent generations. In a sense, adaptiveness is as much an effect as a cause, in that it is the product of biological, developmental, and environmental factors. But since it selects the patterns that repeat themselves subsequently, it can be said to govern the other more immediate or proximate causes.[8] To return to our subject, aggression is plainly adaptive in many circumstances, as in those involving control of resources necessary for survival or propagation. A successful red deer harem holder will have greater impact on the genetic pool than will that stag intruder who gets outroared and outgored year after year.

But if aggression is adaptive, why do aggressors ceremonialize it? Why do they not always pursue the most ruthless and violent course? The reason is that aggression has its drawbacks as well as its payoffs. For while aggressors potentially benefit in terms of both survival and reproduction, they incur risks of injury that would vitiate their prospects in these areas. Thus, aggression becomes a kind of strategic interplay in which potential contestants weigh prospective benefits and losses. Maynard Smith and others have conceived of contesting as a kind of evolutionary game in which a population progresses toward a state in which those policies that consistently produce the greatest payoffs are regularly adopted.[9] Such an "evolutionarily stable strategy" (e.s.s) would plainly include this ceremonialization of conflict in many, though not all, situations. It would not benefit a cat stalking a mouse, since in predatorial situations surprise is the key to success; however, it would on the average benefit tomcats fighting each other, since one's long-term chances of survival are improved if such intraspecific contests are so orchestrated as to permit escape or submission. Then again, agonistic combatants are susceptible to deceivers and tricksters. Thus, a newly molted mantis shrimp, soft-shelled and vulnerable to attack, tries to drive off hard-shelled intruders by increasing the frequency of its claw display, although it invariably runs off if actually attacked (Trivers 1985: 409–10). One is reminded of many a coward-braggart in heroic epos whose gab outbites his spear jab. But continuous overbluffing would, in due course, confer the advantage to those who always challenge the bluff; indeed, in the natural world, deception sometimes provokes "moralistic" aggression that restores "honest" interactive reciprocity. Thus both rule observation and rule breaking contribute to the gaming balance of evolution. Achilles and Odysseus both have their place.

So much, then, for general sociobiological rationales for heroic contests. But since we will soon be examining many particular heroic incidents in assorted contexts, can we define some of the characteristics of these fights more precisely? In particular, what are some of the variables relevant to the amount of display and ritualization in conflict?[10]

Perhaps the most crucial distinction sorts out conflicts of the interspecific and intraspecific varieties. Although there are many exceptions, usually interspecific conflicts are less restrained than intraspecific conflicts can be, partly because predators habitually seek victims from other species. There is no reason why a lioness stalking a deer should ritualize her approach: Her aim—finding food—pragmatically demands no more than that she kill her prey. Although humans and other creatures often connive in like fashion for the death of their fellows, it is nonetheless among conspecific adversaries that the most elaborate rituals usually develop. In fact, this distinction several times makes itself felt in epic material, for the most ruthless and least ritualized conflicts are between humans and nonhumans. The violence that Odysseus metes out to Dolon or Achilles to his sundry victims cannot match the horror of Grendel's or Polyphemos's grisly feasts or the massacre of Odysseus's men by the Laistrygonians (*Od.*10.80–132).[11] For, as I will try to show in later sections, the inter-human fights occur in negotiative and formally contestational settings that give the violence a meaning intelligible to those who engage in it. Flyting brings fighting into the human ken. But you cannot flyt with Grendel. And the unsociable Cyclops, while he can at least be engaged in conversation, refuses to play by the rules.

Another factor influencing the likelihood of combat is kinship. From the evolutionary standpoint, since close relatives bear many of one's own genes, their survival and propagation secures, to some degree, the continuance of one's own genetic line.[12] And thus altruistic behavior flourishes more between close relatives than among nonconsanguineous members of a common species. Female ground squirrels, for example, are more likely to give the alarm call, which benefits the group while increasing the hazard of predatorial attack for the caller, when among close kin; similarly, among *Macaca fuscatas*, a breed of Japanese monkey, relatives such as parents, offspring, or siblings are more likely to be the recipients of altruism in such forms as grooming or defenses against attack (Trivers 1985: 110–21). There are, of course, countervailing forces: When relatives live in close proximity, they are more likely to be rivals for food, parental attention, and so forth. Similar rivalries often divide human kinfolk as well; nonetheless, the kinship principle is strongly in force in most heroic traditions. In the early Germanic world, kinsmen were obliged to uphold and protect each other in war and to avenge a blood relative's killing; and the literature is replete with illustrations of how seriously such duties were taken. Homeric heroes honor kinship ties, as Agamemnon does in the solicitude he repeatedly shows toward his brother Menelaos, or as do the many pairs of brothers who fight together; here again, close relatives of slain warriors feel a special call to vengeance.[13] Thus, kinship in heroic narrative spins important networks of mutual support. And while the killing of kin can happen, it ranks among the greatest of crimes.[14]

Yet even more pervasive than kinship in its evolutionary impact is the principle of *reciprocity*.[15] Reciprocal altruism is indeed of inestimable adaptive value. Such relationships can span the distance between species, as it does between tropical cleaner fish and their hosts, or between dolphins and whales; it also manifests in intraspecific social relations, as in the food sharing of vampire bats (Trivers 1985: 47–49, 382–86, 363–66). Yet within a species, it especially pertains to members of a single group, because these individuals interact most frequently. Not surprisingly, violence percolates closer to the surface in intergroup settings: as Wilson has observed, "the xenophobic principle has been documented in virtually every group of animals displaying higher forms of social organization."[16] In heroic literature, the principle of reciprocity conditions contesting in various ways. Men bound by intimate reciprocal ties—such as lord and thane, or fellow members of a *comitatus*—are less likely to compete in ways that are life-threatening.[17] Thus ingroup contesting is liable to follow on physically less violent tracks. Deadly combat flourishes most in intergroup settings, although here too, since contests as rule-governed interactions are built on the recognition of reciprocity, the flyting negotiative process offers loopholes by which fighting can be avoided. Even mortal enemies, if they are engaged in long-term warfare, come to recognize the need for certain reciprocal observances. Thus, the Trojans and Achaians in book 3 of the *Iliad* try (though unsuccessfully) to make a single duel between Menelaos and Paris substitute for continued hostilities between the armies. Reciprocity is, in fact, most absent from those violent meetings that are thoroughly nonagonistic. Grendel, a noncontesting predator anyway, further rejects the possibility of reciprocal relations when he disdains paying wergild for the Danes he has eaten (*Beo.*149–58); Polyphemos mocks guest-host reciprocity when he promises Odysseus a guest-gift (ξεί-νιον, *Od.*9.356) that turns out to be only the assurance that he will eat Odysseus last, after all his men. Reciprocal exchange patterns, including the contestual, have a wide scope of influence; but their power too has limits.

The last variable bearing on the manner in which contests realize themselves is sex and sexual identity. By and large, males of most species are more aggressive than females are, and the association between aggression and androgens suggests that this difference may have a biological component; more to the point, it is particularly among males that *agonistic* combat thrives. Ong (1981) develops at length on this issue, arguing that the male attraction toward agonistically styled conflict derives from the greater evolutionary expendability of individual males: "A colony of one surviving male and twenty females can in most species reproduce itself with a proficiency that cannot be matched by a colony of one surviving female and twenty males" (1981: 53). It is consequently more advantageous for the species and the genetic pool if males perform the more dangerous tasks; and the males achieving dominance in ritual combat would be those most fit for these functions. Thus, a man's self-concept is far more likely to be invested in his proficiency in such arenas than a woman's is; indeed, as Ong argues, the male ego is beset with a sense of insecurity and a need to prove itself as the female ego is not. It is difficult to make these observations in the current climate of opinion, which is ill-disposed to recognize any kind of sexual difference. Yet men today are often criticized on exactly these accounts—that their bravado and macho belligerence mask underlying weaknesses. To castigate men for behavioral proclivities that may owe in part to biology and evolution would surely be a lamentable form of sexism. And to pretend that there are no differences between female and male participation in agonistic patterns would entail vast falsification of the ethological and human historical records. Yet recognizing such realities does not mean playing the apologist for them.[18] Indeed, my purpose here is neither to condemn nor to condone but rather to *understand* heroic contesting in a nonjudgmental way.

Agonistically styled conflicts are usually intermale. According to Lorenz, in some species the males are much inhibited against inflicting serious injury on females (1966: 117–21). According to Goodall, however, most adult male chimpanzee attacks are directed against females (1986: 341–50, esp. 344). Yet, female chimpanzees seldom attack back, and the major, drawn-out adult struggles with mutual high display are rarely bisexual.[19] Similarly, while red deer harem holders will herd and chivy harem hinds, they roar and lock antlers with other stags. In the heroic world, despite notable and (from the macho perspective) traumatic exceptions such as Virgil's Camilla or the *Nibelungenlied*'s Brunhild, warrior contestants are, in most cases, all men. What makes this gender link so unavoidable is that it holds such importance for the warriors themselves. Heroes repeatedly, and throughout the world, interpret successes in battle as proof specifically of their manhood; and the imputation of "womanliness" to adversaries is a standard cross-cultural insult in heroic literature.[20] This representation of womanhood is entirely from a male-dominated viewpoint, of course. The heroic mode with its macho ethic cannot easily represent femininity with any degree of interiority. Homer best succeeds at this, significantly enough, in the *Odyssey*, by far the less agonistic of the Homeric epics.

While the behavioral ecological perspective brings out all these lines of affinity between human and infrahuman aggression, it does so through reference to determinants that do not necessarily figure into the subjective consciousness of aggressors and their victims in the same way that they do into the theories of sociobiologists. In fact, sociobiology is little concerned with consciousness, intention, and other subjective mental states, except to the extent that they can be shown to derive from or contribute to adaptiveness. This austere outlook cannot be maintained in literary analysis, however. For literature is nothing if not an expression of the subjectivity of human beings and humankind. Epic poets, like other human narrators, tell stories that are above all of interest to other people. Thus, aggression—especially agonistic aggression—is depicted not as an objective reporter might do but as it articulates the concerns and imperatives of the traditional community for whom these tales are intended.

Obviously we could not expect heroic epics to conceptualize evolutionary function as sociobiologists do. In fact, although much heroic narrative material is quite frank in depicting warrior interests in those material advantages that are the "payoffs" of Maynard Smith's game strategists, it is usually even more concerned with underlying concepts of heroic selfhood. This is not to deny the line of evolutionary continuity that joins ritual combat among animals with that of epic heroes—quite to the contrary. Yet human beings are insistently interiorizing, insistently self-reflexive. That which presents itself to the human consciousness in material terms is thematized, reconstructed in a language intelligible and conducive to the needs of the human ego. Thus, heroic epic, when it turns this reflexiveness on the agonistic exchange, generates abstract significations that are as important as the fights themselves. Heroic contests may originate in struggles for dominance, territorial control, wealth, or sexual mates. Yet in the context of the contest paradigm, these gains are construed, as Huizinga says, as the *prizes* of victory, effects of the successful establishment of oneself, the concomitants of honor (1955: 50–52). Material advantages are the outer faces of a happy "me"—a me, from the heroic standpoint, established and upheld agonistically. For the contest is perhaps the central image in the heroic system of social codes by which one's right to these things is defined. Within the socialized, traditional idiom of heroic narrative, it is not enough for the warrior simply to secure the object of his desire. Such tales, though having their own grounding and enjoying their own appeal, do not satisfactorily emblematize the agonistic process by which meanings and claims can be vindicated in a public way. The agonistically styled hero demands that of which the prizes of victory are but the tokens. By his own self-conception, his real quest is for martial glory.

GLORY, IDENTITY, AND CONTEST

The interiorizing turn of human consciousness invests agonistic activity among epic heroes with a new significance. Of course, the sociobiological causes of aggression remain in force. Odysseus's quarrel with the suitors centers on what in the nonhuman domain we would call territorial and mating rights; the Achilles-Agamemnon flyting exhibits characteristics of a dominance struggle with sexual prerogatives as the winner's gains; the Beowulf-Unferth exchange gives an elaborate and carefully controlled expression to intergroup rivalries. Yet to the heroes involved, according to the ideologies by which they themselves conceive these conflicts, the issue is one of honor. The *Iliad* does not generally depict Achilles as suffering for the loss of Briseis personally. His grievance centers on the insult that he has endured. In *Beowulf* (2435–71), Hrethel dies of sorrow—not so much because his biological son Herebeald has been killed, but because the Germanic code forbade his exacting vengeance on a killer who was, in fact, another son, Hæthcyn. Thus, although the notion of honor is plainly responsive to evolutionary determinants, it acquires a motivational force in the minds of heroes that may even induce them to act against their own "better interests." What is at stake, from the warrior's viewpoint, is his own self-concept. Honor and glory stand at the foundation of heroic identity and thus of the heroic ethos.[21]

The heroic vindication of self through the winning of honor is at once an individualistic and public enterprise. Expressed martially, the glory motive drives the hero toward the establishment of a very *personal* superiority. Ong associates agonistic behavior with the male ego's need to differentiate, establish its separative identity in the face of what is perceived to be a female environment.[22] Since individuation is a dieretic process, agonistic settings serve it well. By winning, the hero affirms himself, while by losing, he forfeits claim to self-possession and self-mastery, as the word "surrender" implies. When Achilles vaunts over a fallen enemy, he is proclaiming this triumph of heroic selfhood in the face of opposition. Achilles' gain is Hektor's loss;[23] yet to the loser also some measure of honor accrues, for as Priam says (*Il.*22.71–73):

νέῳ δέ τε πάντ' ἐπέοικεν
ἀρηϊκταμένῳ, δεδαϊγμένῳ ὀξέϊ χαλκῷ,
κεῖσθαι· πάντα δὲ καλὰ θανόντι περ, ὅττι φανήῃ·

It is altogether fitting for a young man
to lie slain by war, torn by sharp bronze;
although he is dead all is beautiful, whatever might show forth.

That heroic honor depends on personal worthiness is well illustrated in the subject matter of heroic flyting exchanges; for the contestants regularly set forth their attacks and self-justifications on an ad hominem basis. Flyting heroes in the *Iliad*, *Beowulf*, and other early epics do not usually address themselves in the main part to ideological, theological, or political issues. Of course, such questions do arise, both in other parts of these epics, and sometimes within the flytings themselves. Yet, as discussed in chapter 4, the heroic flyting process draws on nonheroic ideological considerations less for their own sake than for the light they shed on the relative personal merits of the two adversaries. This insistently personal orientation in heroic flyting distinguishes it from other debate forms, such as academic *disputatio*, for although the vindication of one's intellectual powers may in reality motivate many of these later nonheroic exchanges, the explicit matter of debate is, by convention, nonpersonal. To attack one's adversary overtly is to confuse the person with the issue and thus to accede to the ad hominem fallacy. Bragging and abusing, to the academic, merely betray bad taste.

Yet while honor plays a crucial role in the valorization of the heroic individual, it simultaneously binds that individual to his community.[24] Selfhood is not self-determining in the earliest strata of oral epics; the hero must first establish himself in the eyes of others. As Havelock has pointed out, this externalized, communalized, contingent concept of self only became supplanted in ancient Greece in the age of Plato.[25] And so a generation later Aristotle could reject honor's candidacy to the title of the "supreme good" on the grounds that "it appears to depend on those who confer it more than on him upon whom it is conferred. . . . [M]en's motive in pursuing honour [τιμὴν] seems to be to assure themselves of their own merit."[26] In Homer, by contrast, this rigorous distinction between inner merit and outer recognition or honor does not function in the same way. Of course, individual heroes like Achilles might feel that they have not received their due. In this sense, then, an inner self-assessment might stand at variance with external judgment. Yet no one in Homer could accept the radical cleavage between the individual self-conception, founded on a rational and often counterintuitive delving into first principles, and the public subsumption of the individual into itself—a cleavage epitomized in the person of Socrates and made possible by the critique of orality that the Platonic dialogues represent. Although enraged at the dishonor he feels he has received at Agamemnon's hands, Achilles never rejects the ideal of honor itself—quite to the contrary.[27] Odysseus operates in a far greater degree of freedom with respect to conventional behavioral norms; yet he too, after the fall of Troy, can find no peace until he has reestablished himself in the highly traditional role to which he feels himself entitled and, in the process, acts vigorously toward the public vindication of his honor.[28] In Old English poetry, the haunting specter of the exile attests to the necessity for a community setting for the heroic life.[29] For both societies, the attempt to affirm heroic identity through winning honor remains meaningless without community endorsement.

For these reasons I will assume that the modern English words *honor, glory, fame*, and the like stand, if not in a relationship of synonymy, at least in one of metonymy, in that all allude to a single complex or continuum whose common roots are as I have been describing. In fact, the Greek and Old English vocabularies often do attest to perceived interdependencies between inner worth and external recognition of that worth.[30] For example, an important Homeric term for honor, *timē*, can carry the senses of "worship," "esteem," "price," and even "compensation for damages." Thus "honor" exists in the context of someone according it to someone else, often in a material and economic form. The cognate verbal form *timao*, translated by Chantraine (1977: 1120) as "honorer" or "manifester son estime par des cadeaux" ("to show one's esteem through gifts") illustrates this same association. Pointing to the oral world of "sayings" passed along chains of speakers and hearers is *kleos*, denoting "rumor," "report," "fame," "glory," cognate with *kluein*, "to hear."[31] Situating itself on the expressive rather than the receptive end of the oral exchange, *eukhos*, meaning "glory" or a "vaunt" or "boast," can also signify "the object of prayer," a sense made plainer by the verbal form *eukhomai*, meaning "to pray." The boast, then, is a formal commitment, whose fulfillment can be accomplished through dispensation of the gods but which would nonetheless bring the hero glory. More fully reified in its connotations, *kudos*, "glory, renown," is often described as being conferred by the gods or won by heroes, almost as though it were an athletic prize (*aethlon*). Some of these same associations can be indirectly linked to *aretē*, a key Homeric term meaning "excellence" in the sense of "manliness" or "valor." It is cognate with the superlative *aristos*, "the best," and the derived nominal form *aristeia*, used in the *Iliad* to denote the supreme deeds of a great hero in battle. And so, although *aretē* does not, like several of the other terms, imply the public conferral of this excellency, it can be gained or established in a competitive (and thus public) sphere.

The same tendency to associate terms for honor and glory and related abstractions with interactional settings can be found in the Anglo-Saxon as well. An example is the key term *dom*, encompassing a range of meanings from "judgment" and "sentence" through "power, glory, praise." It is related to the verbal form *gedon*, "to do, perform," through the association that what is done or performed is a judgment; it is further cognate with the Greek noun *themis*, "*that which is laid down* or *established, law*" (Liddell and Scott 1925–1940: 789). Here again, glory accrues from without, through the judgment of others. *Lof*, "praise, renown," cognate with *leof* ("dear"), *lufian* ("to love"), *liefan* ("to allow, permit," as "as sign of favor to a dear one" [Barney

1985: 23]), and *geliefan* ("to believe"), connotes—in the context of Old English heroic values—a community of peers and kinfolk, among whom praise is circulated. *Mære* ("excellent, illustrious, distinguished, famous") and *mærðu* ("fame, glory") connote an oral world where renown passes from tongue to tongue (Barney 1985: 31); the relationship with *ma* ("more") and its cognates implies that this greatness and fame result from one having proved oneself superior to others. Bosworth and Toller's citations (1898: 988) for *tir* ("glory, honour"), while related to the Norwegian *tir* and the Greek *delos* (Holthausen 1963: 349) through the idea of light, often suggest a substance that can be won through deeds or distributed by a lord. *Ar*, "honour, glory, rank," closely related to the verbal form *arian*, can also mean "kindness, favour," or "property, possessions, an estate" (Bosworth and Toller 1898: 47); this nexus of meanings again suggests the context of symbolic exchange suffusing material relations within the *comitatus*.[32] Even *ellen*, which does not directly suggest fame but rather the qualities of strength and courage, can be used (as in *Beo*.3) to denote those deeds through which these qualities are manifested and become known. The weak masculine noun *hlisa* is similar to its Greek cognate (through the Indo-European root *kleu-*) *kleos* in deriving meanings of "fame" and "glory" from "sound, rumor, reputation." This list is, of course, incomplete. I must emphasize, moreover, that my argument is not an etymological one, for these words are quite disparate in their origins and fuller range of connotations. My point is simply that in Homeric and Anglo-Saxon heroic usage, a natural relation between the establishment of heroic excellence and its recognition is implicitly understood. Public and private terms of valuation meet.

The nature of heroic honor as a mechanism for the social valorization of the individual is reinforced by the insistent dichotomizing movement that defines it through praise and blame. Honor stands in opposition to shame, which is its other half and a condition of its being. Old English poetry provides superb examples of such polarizing, as in *Maldon* 185–264, where the cowardice of the sons of Odda is contrasted with the bravery of Byrhtnoth's faithful retainers, or in the final section of *Beowulf*, where Wiglaf's loyalty in the fight against the dragon shames the other retainers who hid in the forest. Opland (1980), taking the hint from Xhosa and Zulu analogue traditions, derives Old English epic narrative from eulogy. Nagy (1979: 211–75) discusses in some detail the opposition of praise and blame as "a fundamental principle in the archaic Greek community" as well as in the constitution of the Homeric hero.[33] Whatever might be said for the evolution of genre in either culture (and I myself am disinclined to grant priority to either narrative or lyric), the heroic ethos in the epic material we will be surveying is upheld through the mechanism of praise and blame. Through it, society exerts its control over what might otherwise become a purely individualistic display.

Of course, concepts of honor are socialized in senses other than those upon which I have been dilating here. In any culture, heroic activity registers the imprint of the dominant ideologies, religious beliefs, social structures, and so forth; all of these have a role in conditioning agonistic expression. Early Anglo-Saxon literary tradition, for example, consistently celebrates the *comitatus* and the bonds of loyalty among its members—which frequently included kinsmen. Thus, charges of treachery take on a particularly heinous coloring.[34] Nothing quite comparable with the *comitatus* and all that it entails can be found in the Homeric epos. On the other hand, in the *Odyssey* and, even more, the *Iliad*, the epic cosmological purview is vastly enlarged to take in the world of the pantheon. The Olympians are perpetually embroiling themselves in the course of human combat, and this fact complicates heroic agency and the proper allotting of martial glory. Indian epic situates the martial and the heroic within the much larger ethical-philosophical context of the *dharma*, which concerns itself not merely with the code of the warrior but with the interrelationship of all aspects of Indian life in all castes. Indeed, the great king Yudhiṣṭhira in the *Mahābhārata*, though himself of the kshatriya (warrior) caste, conceives of honor in a fashion that dissociates him from the more bloodthirsty aspects of the heroic ethos reviewed in this book, although the same cannot always be said for Yudhiṣṭhira's brothers. In the medieval Japanese *Heike monogatari*, heroic action is interpreted in the context of Buddhist Pure Land salvationism mingled with themes of karma and *mono no aware* ("the pity of things"); a haunting awareness of the ephemerality of human glory and its attainments everywhere colors the work's treatment of the great deeds of the Gempei War. In short, themes of heroic honor in any particular epic tradition interpenetrate with institutions and ideologies that, whether in their individual strands or larger configurations, are culture-specific; and comparative study by itself cannot illuminate these dimensions of the subject. The brand of martial glory that I am singling out, however, does constitute a common element in all of them. Indeed, this particular aspect of honor comprises what I consider to be the essential heroic strain in these and other works in the heroic mode.

The formalized contest provides the most natural medium for the winning of glory and the public establishment of heroic honor.[35] Huizinga provides an excellent discussion of the intimate relationship between play, contest, and honor as the prize of winning,[36] noting that whereas competition is by nature "for" something (the notion of a stake or prize is integral to the very root idea of "contest"), the winning is of a symbolic order. This is not to deny that material advantages accrue from winning. Indeed, sociobiology points to these advantages as the evolutionary cause of such behavior. Yet as a behavioral paradigm in its own right, the heroic contest highlights the sheer fact of winning itself, and the gains of winning figure as tokens of this. The ritualization of heroic contests, particularly when realized narratively as single combat, serves to screen out the "static" of irrelevant detail so that these thematic concerns can be dramatized as effectively as possible. The ceremonialized contest thus provides the "purest" format for exploring those concepts of selfhood and identity with which heroic epic is centrally concerned.

I do not mean to imply that all martial activity in heroic epic is formalized and ceremonialized, since even the most cursory recollection of epic incident will bring to mind many famous "cheaters." Odysseus is an outstanding example, and the fact that his Trojan horse engineered that military overthrow that all the contest display in the *Iliad* could not bring about surely relativizes agonistic achievement in this epic tradition. In the *Mahābhārata* Krishna plays a similar role: During the battle of Kurukṣetra a series of impasses from which the high-minded policies of King Yudhiṣṭhira could never have delivered his army are broken only through Krishna's stratagems, which temporarily suspend the rules of fair play. These examples relate to the "global" level of plot; yet "rule breaking" is always a hazard to which the more conventional contestants in the thick of battle must keep alert, as the Heike warrior Takahashi in the *Heike monogatari* learns to his grief when he is treacherously murdered by the young Genji warrior Yukishige whose life he had just spared.[37] Indeed, according to many readings, the *Maldon* poet is critical of his main character, Byrhtnoth, for the *ofermode* (89) that induced him to forfeit an important strategic advantage so that both armies might fight on equal terms (on dry land). Quite obviously, then, poets of the heroic recognize styles of combat other than the agonistic. In fact, deception and mimicry in many situations are well known to the animal world (Trivers 1985: 395–420). The tension between the "openness" of ceremonialized combat and deception in the service of private interest pervades the world of aggression, both animal and human.

Yet we would be mistaken to conclude from these examples that formalized contesting is a mere romanticized idealization. Ethological research makes it clear that such behavior does indeed occur in the "real world" (unshaped by conscious human artifice) of animal combat. Tinbergen's description of the territorial struggles of herring gulls or Clutton-Brock, Guinness, and Albon's superb exposition on the ceremonialized matches of red deer during the rutting season are only a few examples from a wide literature on this topic.[38] Indeed, Harris sparrows, among whom darker plumage signifies higher dominance rank, actively punish those unintentionally deceptive low-ranking birds whom experimenters dye dark (Trivers 1985: 411–15). Thus "moralistic" responses to cheating and deception are not unique to humankind. Returning to the literary representation of human aggression, a mere cynicism toward heroic attitudes cannot account for the way in which the agonistic paradigm, with its rules and standards of fair play, keeps insinuating itself into the action, even in the behavior of heroes (like Byrhtnoth) whose self-interest would be better served by ignoring it. Moreover, heroes themselves on occasion express the view that a martial victory secured out of conformity with a set of heroic standards does not wholly redound to the victor's credit. Beowulf, for example, refuses to bring weapons or armor into his conflict with Grendel, since his adversary lacks these advantages (*Beo*.671–87). Conversely Diomedes, after having been shot in the foot by Alexandros, retorts that his opponent has little to boast of in a victory secured in this way (*Il*.11.384–95). I do not mean to imply that great heroes are purists who categorically refuse advantages of every sort. The Achaians have archers of their own; nor does any of their force find cause to complain of the trick by which Odysseus secures the overthrow of Troy. My point is simply that heroes do recognize an unstated set of norms corresponding to what we are calling the ritualized contest, and seem to feel that a conformity to these norms imparts honor to a victory secured in this way, whatever might be said for or against other means to success.

These, then, are the contours of my subject area: the theme of honor, disengaged as fully as possible from culture-specific ideological environments, as it figures itself through the agonistic paradigm, extrapolated (in turn) from heterogeneous battle narrative. While any expression of these themes cannot help being informed by its specific cultural history, the contest has biological and psychological roots that ignore historical and geographic boundaries. Therefore, my analysis cannot promise to illumine what is unique to *Beowulf*, the *Iliad*, or any other particular literary work, except insofar as this in turn sheds light on cross-cultural patterns. Yet these in the end are more important, for they bring out that dimension of heroic contesting that derives not merely from some historical occasion but from our own nature.

THE STRUCTURE OF THE HEROIC CONTEST

What is the shape of this contest paradigm that keeps insinuating it-self into the narrative? I am deferring discussion of *verbal* contesting until the next chapter; and because the interrelation between the ver-bal and martial dueling—flyting and fighting—generates much of the narrative dynamics of contesting, I will likewise reserve comment on those aspects of the contest that unfold in time. It may be useful at this juncture to recall the distinction between the *events* and *existents* that jointly compose a story. The events distribute themselves through a story's temporal dimension whereas the existents inhabit its spatial dimension.[39] Excluding events for the present, then, let us typologize the existents—characters and settings—that heroic con-tests regularly employ.

In the way of preliminary definition, I propose to take the individ-ual, one-on-one encounter as the paradigmatic expression of the rit-ualizing agonistic impulse. By thus privileging single combat, I do not intend to imply that all warfare in epic is reducible to this pattern, since such plainly is not the case. In the *Iliad*, for example, both single and mass combat claim the narrative foreground at different times, although single combat seems to be especially featured.[40] On occa-sion, matched single encounters dissolve into melee. Sometimes we see a warrior coming to the rescue of a beleaguered colleague, or several teaming up on a single enemy. On other occasions, strings of individual attacks are narrated seriatim, or in "chains of retribution": B kills A, C kills B, D kills C, and so forth.[41] Even when heroes do match off individually, as often as not the encounter is narrated in too abbreviated a fashion to be characterizable as a duel. In the *Iliad* again, the symmetry of the single duel is repeatedly disrupted by the intervention of gods or goddesses. This failure of the matched en-counter to achieve inviolable closure and autonomy in heroic epos should hardly surprise us, since the complexity of actual battle is bound to register in its narrative representation. Ethological studies likewise illustrate considerable variation in aggressive patterns. Among baboons and chimpanzees, for example, the outcome of dominance struggles depends as much on a male's success of forming coalitions as on his sheer strength displayed in one-on-one match-ups.[42]

Nonetheless, if we conceive of it not as an indivisible "atom" but as an underlying concept that can individuate and distinguish itself to varying degrees, greater or lesser, in accordance with the war context and narrative design, the single combat can be used to bring out many of the most crucial coherencies in heroic martial exchange.

Again, it is worth recollecting that single combat figures significantly into intraspecific animal aggression, as in the rutting encounters of red deer (Clutton-Brock, Guinness, and Albon 1982: 104–42) or between a rat colony's alpha rat and a male intruder (Blanchard and Blanchard 1984: 8–13). The disposition toward single combat, in other words, is not merely the product of human ideological systems but exists in nature.

Yet among literary forms epic exhibits marked predilection for such single encounters, and the fact that the most developed duels commonly feature the greatest heroes at moments of greatest strategic importance in the narrative must be taken as an indicator of their centrality to the heroic project.[43] Several outstanding examples in our material include the great matchoffs between Menelaos and Paris (*Il.*3), Hektor and Aias (7.219–307), Achilles and Aineias (20.161–352), Achilles and Hektor (22.248–377), Odysseus and Euryalos (*Od.*8.158–415), or, in *Beowulf*, between the Geatish hero and Unferth (449–610). In all these cases, the two principals compete with a minimum of outside human intervention.[44] The narratorial disposition to isolate the agonistic dyad is repeatedly displayed in the *Iliad*—a comparatively realistic poem—in Homer's practice of seeming to suspend action so that heroes can exchange lengthy speeches in the middle of heated battles. Expanding our purview, we find the same orientation toward single encounters in the insistence of Heike and Genji warriors in the *Heike monogatari* on seeking out a "worthy opponent"; thus too the ancient Gauls, according to a passage from Diodorus of Sicily (5.28–39), shouted challenges at the enemy ranks with the aim of enticing out a single foe; thus the quarrel between men of Ulster and of Connaught in *Scél Mucci Mic Dathó* takes the form of a series of verbal exchanges in which Cet mac Matach verbally humiliates the men of Ulster *one at a time* rather than *en masse*, and while these flytings take place the others keep their silence;[45] thus Garulf, before attempting to force entry into the hall held by the Danes, first asks the name of the adversary holding the door against him, even though the circumstances—a treacherous nighttime attack—hardly conduce to open formalized contesting.[46] Further, heroes themselves often seem to acknowledge a special propriety and significance attaching to victories achieved in the one-on-one manner. An excellent example is the dying Patroklos's complaint to Hektor (*Il.*16.844–54) that his Trojan adversary is unfairly claiming credit for a victory that it took two men and a god to bring about.[47] In short, it is plainly the single encounter that represents the apex of ceremonialization in heroic battle narration; and the *movement* toward this, while not always carrying to its logical culmination, is in many places evident in incipient forms. My aim in what follows will be to define the characteristics of this paradigm that wields this thematic importance, concentrating on its "purer" instances but recognizing its immanence in much of the rest.

When it occurs, the single combat presupposes a comparability of contestants. Indeed, the most developed contests usually pit heroes of roughly comparable eminence, measurable in terms of proven heroic accomplishment, rank in the political hierarchy, or lineage. Thus, the climactic encounter in the *Iliad* opposes Achilles and Hektor, the champions of their respective armies. Similarly, Charlemagne—despite his great age—brings battle with the heathen in *The Song of Roland* to its culminating point in his head-to-head encounter with his archenemy, the Emir Baligant, while in the *Alliterative Morte Arthure*, the two definitive contests pit Arthur against, in the first instance, Lucius, the Roman emperor, and in the final sequence, Mordred, the usurper and pretender to the British throne. The Beowulf-Unferth exchange has its own special characteristics, in that Beowulf flyts with the Dane but fights with Grendel (discussed in chapter 2). Yet even here a kind of rough initial equivalence binds the two men. For although Beowulf has the makings of a great warrior and leads his own *comitatus*, his heroic credentials have yet to be established, and he is still a thane, not a *dryhten*. Unferth, for his part, though ineffective against Grendel, remains Hrothgar's *thyle*, evidently a post of distinction.[48] This positive correlation between contest development and the comparability of contestant ranking seems to hold at various levels of the heroic hierarchy. Almost an entire book of the *Iliad*, for example, is devoted to the formal duel between Paris and Menelaos, neither of whom emerges as a great one-on-one fighter in this epic (though Paris does excel as an archer). Yet while equivalently undistinguished as heroes, each stands in close blood proximity to his own respective king (Agamemnon or Priam), and the two of them are the main rivals for Helen's affections in the quarrel that brought about the Trojan war. This complex of rivalries and equivalencies lends special interest to this encounter, a battle of claims to manhood whose outcome, according to a subsequently violated agreement, will end the war.[49]

While contests between equals or near-equals furnish the prime material, epic poets do take interest nonetheless in encounters in which one warrior finds himself grossly outmanned, as, for example, Lykäon does in his meeting with Achilles in *Il*.21.34–135. And so significant stretches of battle narrative can be devoted to the *aristeia* in which a preeminent warrior overpowers adversaries, one after another. Such conflicts are, for the most part, quickly told; the contest pattern tends to be elaborated to the extent that real parity exists. Indeed, as we shall see, flyting allows for capitulation by the weaker force, just as the exchange of threat displays does in many intermale animal contests, and thus physical combat can be avoided altogether.[50] Yet even in those cases where, despite the unequal distribution of martial talents, combat proves unavoidable, the narrative insistence on comparability, without which a true contest is impossible, motivates insinuations—usually projected through the boasts of the inferior warriors—that the disparities might be overcome, that one advantage might be counterbalanced by another. It is in this light that we should interpret Aineias's speech during his flyting match with Achilles when he compares their genealogies (Il.20.199–258). While Achilles may be the better fighter, Aineias means to imply, he himself might win the contest anyway by virtue of his lineage. Asteropaios likewise rehearses his ancestry before Achilles (Il.21.152–60); and although the Trojan indulges in no explicit comparisons, the fact that Achilles feels compelled after the fight to assert the superiority of his own blood line (184–99) suggests that he has construed Asteropaios's speech as a challenge. In Il.20.430–37 Hektor, while openly acknowledging that Achilles is a greater warrior than himself, introduces the superordinating principle of divine judgment, asserting that he himself, despite disadvantages, might prove victor, since the outcome rests on the knees of the gods. In Maldon 42–61, Byrhtnoth adopts a more direct strategy when he simply refuses to acknowledge the Vikings' claim to superiority at all. Comparison presupposes comparability; contesting presupposes an uncertainty as to who will win. This principle of assumed initial parity is rooted in the structure of the contest itself and exerts an appreciable influence on the way it is conducted.

While the combatants seize the active role in contests, witnesses as passive participants play an indispensable function also. As Ong points out, the idea of witnessing is rooted etymologically in the very English word "contest," which

> comes from the Old French conteste, which in turn derives from the Latin contestari. Testis means a witness and derives from the Proto-Indo-European root trei (three) compounded with stā (stand), to yield the form (unattested in extant literature but pointed to by phonological patternings) *tri-st-i, meaning a third person standing by, as in a dispute between two others. Thus a testis or witness, a "third stander," implies an agonistic situation between two persons which the testis or third person reports from outside.[51]

These implications are no mere accident of the modern English vocabulary and its peculiar history but derive from the nature of the contest. The witnessing function is, in fact, regularly presumed by epic heroes in their quest for *kleos* (fame or glory). Such fame can be achieved only through the agency of observers. In this connection heroic epic contrasts curiously with medieval romance, in which combat often takes place in the remote wilderness. In some works—the romances of Chrétien de Troyes, for example—this movement from public to private contest can be associated with the greater interiorization and subjectivization of narrative brought about by the love theme. Even if Lancelot's achievements and identity elude worldly report, Guinevere knows of them, down to the smallest detail. Thus in *Le Chevalier de la Charrette* the seemingly omniscient queen, ignoring an extraordinary series of knightly achievements, sees fit to condemn Lancelot for the most miniscule of slips in chivalric behavior, and one that, so far as can be ascertained, she had no means of learning about. Through most of the romance, Lancelot adventures anonymously: it is Guinevere herself who first identifies him and, figuratively speaking, gives him a name. Thus Guinevere has displaced the warrior's peer group as the center from whose judgment his knightly identity is valorized. The heroic motive has been subjectivized, then, in that it has been reoriented toward an internalized relationship invisible to the world. This change in the identity of the witnesses, from a warrior public to a personal beloved, signals a momentous shift in the warrior ethos and marks the development of romance out of epic.[52]

In Anglo-Saxon and Homeric epic, who are these witnesses, and what are their functions? They can be divided into three categories. First, in both traditions, divine agents of various types play the role of onlookers. Here, the relationship between mere witnessing and active supernatural meddling in the outcome of contests becomes blurred. It is clear to all concerned, for example, that combat in the *Iliad* and *Odyssey* transpires in the plain view of Olympus.[53] At the same time, Zeus's unruly children and consort show little bashfulness in promoting their favorites; impartiality and distance have no place here, except in the case of Zeus himself, whose will does ultimately hold sway. Thus, in the supreme conflict between Hektor and Achilles, fate is weighed literally in Zeus's scales (*Il.* 22.208–13); the outcome follows from this supernal determination. Although the ideological-theological setting of Old English poetry differs radically from Homer's—polytheism having given place to monotheism—this same association between divine witnessing and divine judgment figures significantly into the presuppositions of its warfare. Numerous passages in *Beowulf* implicate a transcendent God as the Judge and Determiner of events who watches over conflicts and is capable of overruling fate; indeed, the Geatish hero himself plainly acknowledges

the ultimate authority of such a deity.[54] Bloomfield has proposed that
Beowulf and *Maldon* provide an early form of the later medieval notion of the *iudicium Dei*, the "judgment of God," expressible through
"*unilateral* ordeals when fire, water swallowing, lots etc. are used on a
suspected violator and *multilateral*, when battle decides the issue"
(1969: 549). As Bloomfield observes, "trial by combat is surprisingly
not found in any clear-cut fashion in England before the Norman
Conquest" (554). One might suggest that this practice and notion of
the judicial duel, as elaborated in the context of later Christian law
and culture, rest psychologically on the contest structures that we
have been examining. Even better than Zeus, the Christian God Father satisfies the requirement that the witness be distanced, present
to the action in knowledge or seeing, and capable of effective judgment.[55] In sum, human conflict in both Homeric and Anglo-Saxon
narrative occurs in sight of the divine, and with this form of witnessing in both traditions basic notions of fate and supernal agency are
intertwined.[56]

Divine witnessing pertains more to the assignation of victory than
with the dissemination of *kleos*: Heroes labor not to impress God or
the gods but to secure victory through them. The shoring up of one's
reputation is accomplished through the other two types of witnesses,
both of them human. The most important of these—indeed, the paramount observers in the minds of Homeric warriors at least—are the
contestants' heroic peers of both armies. As I will stress in the next
chapter, one of the purposes of flyting is to establish an oral contract.
The rival warriors require external observers to provide a public
mnemonic record of their boasts, so that when they fulfill these boasts
militarily, their fame will be corroborated. Persisting into literate ages
in the requirement for signatures of witnesses on certain kinds of
documents (such as wills),[57] this functioning of witnesses as verifiers
and sealers of contracts allies flyting with the heroic oath.[58] Indeed,
the witnessing function is often actively structured into the oath-tak-
ing process as the oath taker swears "by" something. Flyting heroes
in Homer and *Beowulf* seldom refer to the witnesses explicitly;[59] yet
they are there, for heroic flytings regularly occur in established social
arenas. Their presence formalizes the stake of honor that each contestant pits on the outcome of the exchange.

The third kind of witnessing belongs to a different narrative level
than the others, for it transpires not within the narrative but in the
narrating.[60] I am referring, of course, to the epic poet himself as a
kind of witness, who enables his readers or auditors to give further
witness to the deeds of great heroes through the medium of his narrative rendering. This view emphasizes the eulogistic function of he-

roic poetry, a topic treated in recent studies by Nagy and Opland.[61] Alexander the Great's lament (according to Plutarch) that the perpetuity of Achilles' fame was due as much to his good fortune in having attracted the notice of a great poet as to his own accomplishments is merely one well-known illustration that the ancient Greeks were not themselves insensible to the value of epic poetic testimony in the propagation of one's reputation. Of course, the epic poets did not watch firsthand the heroic displays that they so graphically relate. Their sources were oral ones—the Muses, daughters of Mnemosyne, to Homer, or the oral tradition, which the *Beowulf* poet credits each time he says "I heard."[62] Yet heroes are in quest of honor-and-glory, and epic poets are leading traffickers in this commodity. Though standing apart from the field of battle both literally and in the layerings of narrative, the poet, whose perceptions inform the narrative everywhere, offers himself to us as the witness par excellence. Recent critical theory has, in my view, exaggerated the role of self-reflexivity in art. Nonetheless, this interdependency between heroic accomplishment and its poetic celebration signals an important self-reflexive dimension in the heroic epic genre.

So much for the human participants in heroic contests; let us now turn to the problem of settings. Pizarro takes up this problem in the course of his comprehensive review of the *senna* in early Germanic narrative.[63] Following Pizarro, Clover finds in Germanic flyting episodes "two standard settings, one outdoors over what Phillpotts called 'the sundering flood' (a body of water separating the contenders), the other indoors in the hall—at drinking, often at court (or, in Iceland, at the Alþing)."[64] Although both Clover and Pizarro are concerned with specifically Germanic flyting characteristics, certain core elements are in evidence outside the Germanic sphere. Most flyting in the *Iliad*, for example, occurs outdoors on the Trojan plain through which the river Skamandros flows, figuring prominently into the action of book 21. On the other hand, Odysseus's flyting with Euryalos occurs, if not indoors, at least in the context of Alkinoös's hospitality. As I argue in chapter 2, these episodes exhibit systematic parallels with comparably situated flyting exchanges in *Beowulf* and *Maldon*.

Yet a particularly striking corroboration for this twofold division of verbal contest settings as a cross-cultural pattern is found in Diodorus of Sicily's third-century A.D. description of the feasting and fighting practices of the ancient Gauls. After reviewing the manner of eating and drinking, Diodorus tells us that the Gauls

> invite strangers to their feasts, and do not inquire until after the meal who they are and of what things they stand in need. And it is their custom, even

during the course of a meal, to seize upon any trivial matter as an occasion for keen disputation and then to challenge one another to single combat, without any regard for their lives.[65]

Turning then to warfare, Diodorus tells us that, when the Gauls are in battle formation, it is customary

to step out in front of the line and to challenge the most valiant men from among their opponents to single combat, brandishing their weapons in front of them to terrify their adversaries. And when any man accepts the challenge to battle, they then break forth into a song of praise of the valiant deeds of their ancestors and in boast of their own high achievements, reviling all the while and belittling their opponent, and trying, in a word, by such talk to strip him of his bold spirit before the combat.[66]

The fact that these descriptions follow one another in immediately adjacent sections (5.28–29) suggests that the author recognized the common core activity—verbal contesting—of which these descriptions represent alternate forms. Also noteworthy are the broad similarities between the first description and the Odysseus-Euryalos encounter, or the Beowulf-Unferth flyting, or the bone-throwing episodes in *Hrólfs saga kraka*, chapters 30–36; likewise, the second description is clearly reminiscent of battle scenes in the *Iliad*, or even the *Heike monogatari*. All this is evidence for the generality of association between setting type and flyting pattern.

Of course, the scenic concomitants of flyting do not always fully match between one culture and the next. It would be difficult to sustain the Germanic "sundering flood" motif, for example, through most heroic literature. Given the seafaring habits of the early Anglo-Saxons and Vikings, this association of battle with bodies of water is hardly surprising. However, the "hall" seems to have distinct symbolic associations in the Anglo-Saxon world at least, as a recent article by Earl maintains.[67] The same does not hold true through heroic literature generally. And so flyting at the home court does not always occur indoors in the *Iliad*; nor, for that matter, does it do so at the Icelandic Althing. These particular scenic associations, then, are culture-specific.

Yet general patterns can nonetheless be identified. These are best described not so much in terms of physical environment as in terms of the social groups involved and the mode of relation between them. Three distinct possibilities here emerge. First, the flyters may represent two nations or communities at war with one another. This context governs most (though not all) of the flyting interactions in the *Iliad* and *Maldon*. As one might expect, the "setting" is typically a battlefield, or a beach, or some other site commonly used for purposes of warfare by the society in question. The second mode of interaction pits verbal contestants from distinct tribes that are engaged in a process of guest-host bonding. Action in such cases is usually set in the host's home hall or court, often in the context of feasting—the optimal environment for hospitality. Examples include the Beowulf-Unferth and Odysseus-Euryalos flytings, or the encounter between the young Alboin and his archenemy Turisind in Paul the Deacon's remarkable account in *Historia Langobardorum* 1.24.[68] The third pattern engages adversaries from the same tribe or nation. One would expect such encounters to occur where that community customarily convenes; thus a council provides the setting for the classic instance of this type of flyting in book 1 of the *Iliad*, whereas a superb Eddic example, the *Lokasenna*, takes place in the hall among the feasting Norse gods. Perhaps in this category also we might list flyting at the Althing, although these examples are made more problematic by the curious character of Icelandic "national" unity and its legal institutions.[69] Of course, other possibilities emerge from early literature. The quarrel in *Scél Mucci Mic Dathó*, for instance, blending elements of the first and second patterns, pits two enemy clans—the men of Ulster and Connaught—who are simultaneously the guests in the hall of Mac Dathó, king of Leinster (N. Chadwick 1927). The *Alliterative Morte Arthure* features flytings between Arthure and Lucius through the mediation of emissaries, who, from the standpoint of the flyting interaction, are both battlefield enemies and guests.[70] Despite such variations and embroiderings, however, the two fundamental distinctions, between the ingroup and the intergroup, and between the intergroup hostile and the intergroup hospitable, enjoy a primitive universality. No interaction in early epic can afford to ignore these fundamental conditions.

This concludes our discussion of the heroic contest per se. Let us turn now to the contest's verbal aspect. Viewing the dialogic encounter within the larger setting of the contest paradigm, chapter 2 will focus on the relationship between flyting and fighting, the contest's two facets. Chapter 3 will narrow its focus further to the flyting itself, analyzing the materials and interactional rhetoric of the agonistic verbal exchange.

CHAPTER TWO

Flyting-to-Fighting Pathways

THE ORAL CONTRACT

Flyting, in heroic epic and many other settings, seems to be associated with fighting. It would not be true, however, to characterize that relation as one of direct and necessary causation, as if to imply that every flyting must culminate in martial combat. Clover is particularly emphatic in disabusing scholars of their misconceptions on this point (1980: 459), citing episodes from the *Bandamanna saga*, *Magnússona saga*, *Örvar-Odds saga*, *Hárbarðsljóð*, and Saxo Grammaticus as just a few examples in which violence fails to eventuate. At the same time, martial overtones resonate unmistakably in many flyting speeches, and flyting exchanges do arise in settings where battles are conducted or brawls break out; frequently verbal combat precipitates fighting. Heroes in the *Iliad* consistently follow up their speeches with blows, as do Byrhtnoth and the Vikings in *Maldon*; Arthur and Lucius exchange threatening speeches through emissaries prior to their decisive engagement in the *Alliterative Morte Arthure*; the exchange of insults between Skarphedin and Flosi at the Althing in chapter 123 of *Njáls saga* terminates efforts to arbitrate the feud between their factions and leads in due course to the burning of Njál and his family; and even Hárbarthr and Thórr in *Hárbarðsljóð* and Siegfried in chapter 3 of the *Nibelungenlied* interject occasional threats of personal violence, although they fail to carry through on these. Then is it sufficient to conclude, as Clover does, that flyting represents a "verbal combat complete in itself" and that "if a loser decides to seek redress in battle, that is a new phase of the story and may be treated independently as a revenge episode" (1980: 459)? Do verbal and martial contests stand in a relationship of equivalency, that one could balance off another in a revenge sequence?

I must reemphasize that the following remarks apply to only that one specific genre of verbal contesting whose parameters I am now setting out to identify. There do, in fact, exist verbal contest modes that bring themselves to a certain closure without combat or any form of external testing. Success, in such contest genres, depends exclusively on one's facility in the verbal medium. Prime examples would include the "ludic" flytings of the Scottish makars, or "playing the dozens" among American teenage blacks (Labov 1972: 297–353), or the obscene exchanges among Turkish or Mayan adolescents described by Dundes, Leach, and Özkök (1972) and Gossen (1974: esp. 97–106). *Örvar-Odds saga*, *Hárbarðslóð*, and *Lokasenna* seem too to share some of these same ludic features.[1] The courtroom trial and the academic debate are examples of nonludic verbal contests that resolve "internally," within the verbal medium and without recourse to physical combat.[2] Further analysis of this diversity of verbal contest genres and the rules that differentiate them from "heroic flyting" proper will be reserved until chapter 5.

Yet in heroic flyting narrowly conceived, verbal and martial (or, more generally, nonverbal) contesting are bound together in an unequal relationship through what I will call the *oral contract*. In effect the flyting adversaries, through their verbal disputation, are negotiating the terms of a martial display that will determine which of them has won. Such "contract formation" can occur overtly or covertly; and the "trial of arms" can take several forms, as we shall see. Indeed, flyting heroes usually have the option of backing out and thus forfeiting the contest, just as many animal threat displays allow for resolution without injurious combat. Yet whether combat eventuates or not, these flyting heroes all recognize that the crucial test will occur in a nonverbal medium. It is this power of contract that links flyting and fighting in heroic epic. Although my analysis of the contest pattern in this chapter owes much to the tradition of Arend (1933) and discussions of "theme" and "type scene" in the oral-formulaic school,[3] I attach less importance to the surface narrative realization of the pattern than to the "ethical" and ideological assumptions from which it is generated. For it is the system of expectations that the flyting contact summons up, whether or not they are fulfilled, that provides the narrative driving force.

How is it possible for such venomous exchanges, as heroic flytings so often are, to be predicated on contractual processes? In fact, heroic rivalries are not typically animated by blind, unreasoning hatred. The previous chapter stressed that *kleos* (glory, reputation) implies a highly individualized display within a highly socialized setting. This brings us to the recognition of two fundamental motives in the deep structure of heroic contests. I will call them the *eristic* and the *contractual*. The importance of this dialectic cannot be overemphasized, for the life of the flyting exchange unfolds in the interplay of these polarities. On the one hand, each hero has embarked on a thoroughly individualistic enterprise—to defeat his opponent. On the other hand, the two adversaries collaborate in establishing the terms and meaning of the contest. The interdependency yet opposition between these two aspects yields a complexity in the motivational structure of contests that resists description in strictly formalistic and nonqualitative terms.[4]

Let us consider each of these imperatives more carefully. The eristic (querulous, disputatious, adversarial) impulse manifests in each contestant's attempt to force himself into a position of superiority to his foe and thereby to win *kleos* at his adversary's expense. The presence of this motive constitutes a defining characteristic of the flyting activity. The eristic character of heroic flytings is obvious and should require little demonstration. It appears in Unferth's and Euryalos's attempts to humiliate their new guests, and in Beowulf's and Odysseus's refusal to be "put down" (*Beo.*499–606 and *Od.*8.158–233); it emerges in the Viking messenger's and Achilles' attempts to intimidate their adversaries as well as in Byrhtnoth's and Aineias's refusal to be cowed (*Maldon* 25–61 and *Il.*20.178–258). We should recognize, however, that *eris* finds expression in different ways and to different degrees of intensity. Indeed, in the encounters between Diomedes and Glaukos (*Il.*6.119–236) or Beowulf and the Danish coastguard (*Beo.*237–319) an initial hostility has been entirely dissipated by the end of the interactions, which cease to be flytings at all. There are no simple formal criteria for quantifying the "eristic intensity" of any given exchange; only a sensitivity to intentional and tonal coloring will serve. In this respect flyting as a genre centers on an animating force rather than a structure.

While flyting interactions project eristic displays into the bold foreground, a process of contract formation, often "silent" in the sense that contestants overtly shy away from the language of collaboration, projects the future course of the exchange and sets forth the terms and significance of victory. For example, the Beowulf-Unferth "intermezzo" features a quarrel over Beowulf's adolescent swimming match with Breca and his forthcoming fight with Grendel. The contractual element of the exchange is minimal, in that neither disputant explicitly sets forth any proposal for his adversary's ratification. Yet in their quarreling the Dane and the Geat are tacitly establishing a ground of concord that is as significant as the disagreement. Unferth predicts that Beowulf will lose in his fight with Grendel (if he dares the venture), while Beowulf boasts that he will prevail. Both positions presuppose that this particular heroic exploit will provide the definitive measure of Beowulf's heroic greatness and thus will determine which of the two flyters has won the quarrel. In short, Beowulf and Unferth are contracting for a fight between the Geat and Grendel. In the Achilles-Aineias exchange (*Il.*20.160–352) the heroes contract to fight one another directly as Achilles first threatens his opponent

(195–98) and Aineias replies, in effect, "let's stop haggling and fight!" (250–58). In many cases the flyters negotiate among several contractual possibilities. In *Maldon*, for instance, the Viking messenger offers two alternatives: Byrhtnoth surrenders, or the Vikings attack; Byrhtnoth chooses the latter, and a fight ensues. In all these cases the essential ingredient, the feature that distinguishes heroic flyting from, say, academic debate, lies in this contractual link between the verbal duel and and a nonverbal "test," often though not always military in character. Heroic flyting can be defined, therefore, as an eristic verbal exchange in which the warrior rivals, even as they contend with one another for that glory or *kleos* on which their heroic identities are founded, are contracting on some future course of action from a range of possibilities, at least one of which entails a trial of arms or some other form of nonverbal manly display.[5]

In its commissive aspect,[6] flyting is much like boasting. Indeed, boasts often participate in the constitution of flytings; their larger narrative importance is brought out by Renoir (1963), who discusses the "heroic oath" as a major plot determinant in *Beowulf*, *The Song of Roland*, and the *Nibelungenlied*. Obviously central concerns in the Old English poetic consciousness, boasting, vowing, taunting, and like matters have been the subject of recent studies by Nolan and Bloomfield (1980), Conquergood (1981), and Murphy (1985).[7] Yet flyting comprehends far more than boasting does. For flyting requires two present adversaries directing their verbal attacks at each other; it is dialogic, whereas boasting is monologic. The projective "vow" and the retrospective "boast," to follow Murphy's distinction (1985: 105–6), are only two of the many moves available to the flyters, as we will see in chapter 3. Indeed, flyters may, if they choose, concentrate their verbal abuse on the defects of their adversaries and forgo boasts and vows altogether. In addition, although such great vows as that of Achilles in his quarrel with Agamemnon (*Il.*1.233–44) or those of Bhīma (van Buitenen 1975: 146, 151) during the celebrated dicing match between the Pāṇḍavas and the Kauravas in the *Mahābhārata* occur in obvious contests in which adversaries are present to each other and exchanging insults, in other notable instances, such as Beowulf's oaths prior to his fights with Grendel (*Beo.*677–87) and the dragon (*Beo.*2518–37), vows are addressed to comrades. Thus boasts and vows can find their home in many settings, of which flyting is just one.

The effectiveness of the flyting contract, like the power of the boast, depends on heroic willingness to honor its commitments. It is with respect to the contract, therefore, that contests are most vulnerable to "cheaters." Yet cheating is hazardous, for it jeopardizes the systems of reciprocity upon which relations even between war enemies to one degree or another rely, and thus it invites deception in return. In the animal and plant worlds, as Trivers points out (1985: 395–420), deception flourishes but only within limits, and the evolutionary process seems to have designed mechanisms for its control. And so we should not dismiss too quickly, for example, Beowulf's sense of fair play toward even his monstrous opponents, or the regard for code and formality prevailing in most Iliadic encounters. This Homeric attitude is well expressed by Hektor who, at the end of his flyting with Aias, explicitly rejects the sneak attack (*Il.*7.242–43):

> ἀλλ' οὐ γάρ σ' ἐθέλω βαλέειν τοιοῦτον ἐόντα
> λάθρη ὀπιπεύσας, ἀλλ' ἀμφαδόν, αἴ κε τύχωμι.

> But I do not wish to strike you, such a one as you are,
> By watching secretly, but publicly, if I might hit the mark.

It is through observances such as this that the scope of sheer violence can be controlled. In such insistences on honorable behavior—everrecurrent and unquenchable in heroic cultural expression however often violated in practice—we can see an incipient movement toward a law base and community that comprehends both warring factions. The flyting contract, like any other, presupposes bilateral "lawfulness." The orderliness of flyting-to-fighting sequences testifies to the contract's very real normalizing and legalizing influence. It may ultimately prove that war codes of the type epitomized in the flyting contract have contributed materially to the emergence of larger concepts of community that history has witnessed over the past several millennia.

Why, and how, does the flyting contract bind? It does so through what could justly be characterized as an ethical principle governing the relation between words and deeds. In brief, the heroic ethos requires that a hero's performance match his own report. The hero who succeeds in doing this wins *kleos*, whereas he who fails loses it. This powerful though implicit ethical imperative—which applies to monologic oaths and boasts as much as to dialogic flyting contracts— generates a tension of expectancies between episodes of saying and doing in heroic epic. Whether or not these expectations are ever fulfilled, their mere presence colors the action and redounds to the credit or discredit of the heroes concerned.

Words and deeds thus perform distinct though complementary functions. No doubt heroic narrative prizes proficiency in both media: ideally one should be both "a speaker of words and a doer of deeds."[8] Yet always the proof lies in action. Flyting episodes themselves acknowledge the primacy of heroic performance through their orientation toward the actions, past or future, of the contestants.[9] Further, one finds in *Beowulf* and Homer, and elsewhere in heroic narrative, many attestations to the inadequacy of unsupported words. Aineias touches upon this theme when he urges Achilles to give over his "womanish" haggling and to join in combat (*Il.*20.244–58). Beowulf similarly points out to Unferth that Grendel could never have continued in his depredations against the Danes "gif þin hige wære, / sefa swa searogrim, swa þu self talast" ("if your mind and spirit were as battle-fierce as you yourself say").[10] By contrast with the Danish *thyle*, Beowulf makes good his boasts: In the midst of his fight with Grendel, he explicitly recalls his "æfenspræce" (*Beo.*759), his speech of the night before, and goes on to deal with his enemy accordingly. We should note that the question here is not one of *veracity*. Flyting contracts are commissives, not assertives. Interest centers, therefore, on the courage and capacities essential to the fulfillment of such commitments.[11]

In fact, if I may digress briefly, this concern with substantiating words with deeds recurs widely, not only in heroic narrative but in many forms of cultural expression, and especially when macho conceptions come to the foreground. I will give two examples from highly diverse cultural settings. The first, surprisingly enough, comes from the *Parzival* of Wolfram von Eschenbach, a poem registering intensive spiritualizing and chivalric influences in a spirit generally remote from that of heroic epos. Nonetheless, speaking in his own person (or persona), Wolfram describes himself thus:

> Whichever lady cares to inspect my patent—and not only see but hear it— I shall not mislead her. My hereditary Office is the Shield! I should think any lady weak of understanding who loved me for mere songs unbacked by manly deeds. If I desire a good woman's love and fail to win love's reward from her with shield and lance, let her favor me accordingly. A man who aims at love through chivalric exploits gambles for high stakes.[12]

The second example derives from the present-day sports world, an arena rich in "heroic" attitudes and belief systems. The incident involves a verbal skirmish, carried out through the news media, between Mike Ditka, the coach of the Chicago Bears (a professional football team), and Buddy Ryan, formerly an assistant coach under Ditka but newly hired as the coach of the Philadelphia Eagles. Prior to a game between the Eagles and the Bears, Ryan and Ditka had been exchanging highly publicized unpleasantries, delivered in interviews and featured in sports columns. After Chicago's victory, *USA Today* (September 16, 1986, p. 3C) carried the following blurb:

> Chicago Bears coach Mike Ditka blasted Eagles coach Buddy Ryan Sunday night on Chicago's WGN radio. "He'll be lucky to have a job in three years," Ditka said after the Bears 13–10 win against Philadelphia. "If you're gonna pop off, back it up. We don't have to pop off. We won the Super Bowl."

While the idiom and level of artistic sophistication may differ, sentiments of this very type are voiced repeatedly by epic heroes.

This ostensible privileging of action over speech characterizes flyting in the heroic mode. At the same time, while heroic action provides the substance on which *kleos* feeds and the emblem with reference to which it defines itself, words constitute the medium in which it lives.[13] In an oral culture, communally determined value judgments are perforce transmitted through speech. Speech defines the interpretive context by which heroic action means. Thus verbal disputation brings definition and evaluation to contests: through their flyting, heroes are defining the terms and significance of their contest by propounding rival interpretations of personal merit. Speech proposes, combat disposes;[14] the verbal contest sets forth meanings that combat tests and then confirms or rejects. And when the issues that verbal combat has raised have been decided by arms, the results are published, once again, in words. Thus, speech initiates and completes the contesting process; it realizes and establishes as public fact those meanings that heroic action only adumbrates. If heroes did not feel themselves obligated to redeem their words through action, then this process by which the heroic ethos defines and reaffirms itself could not work. Only by the strength of those who honored oral contracts could heroic idealism wield its influence.

The notion of the oral contract as the bond between words and deeds, flyting and fighting, provides the foundation of my argument for this and the next two chapters. Let us now turn more specifically to the flyting-to-fighting patterns to which it gives rise.

THE CONTEST PATTERN

As suggested previously, the contesting hero's words usually relate to his actions in one of two ways: They project deeds to be performed in the future, or they comment on deeds accomplished in the past. Murphy has recently drawn this distinction, styling future-oriented speeches "vows" and past-oriented speeches "boasts."[15] The connotations of these terms are to a degree felicitous, to the extent that "vow" implies contract whereas "boast" implies self-display. In fact, the flyting contract is established through those speeches that project future action, whereas the hero's "boasts" (in Murphy's sense) summon past action as proof of his heroic standing (see chapter 3). Because it runs against the grain of common usage to restrict the word boast to this one meaning, however, I have designated orientation in speeches toward the future or the past through the words *prospective* and *retrospective*. Both orientations have a role in the generation of contests.

Specifically, in its fully developed yet simple form, a contest typically moves from prospective speech through a trial of arms to retrospective speech. Thus the first Achilles-Hektor encounter (*Il*.20.419–54) opens with an exchange of speeches that focus on the imminent combat, continues with a martial exchange that is interrupted by Apollo, and concludes with a speech by Achilles that comments on this escape that Hektor, with the god's help, has just effected. Now it is true that these prospective speeches contain retrospective elements, just as retrospective speeches sometimes contain prospective elements. In the prospective flyting just alluded to, Achilles recalls the killing of Patroklos (20.425–26), while Hektor, whose brother's slaughter has roused him into battle (419–23) despite Apollo's advice to the contrary (375–78), similarly "retrospects" (431–33) on the speech Achilles has just addressed to him. Beowulf and Unferth likewise devote much of their "prospective" flyting (*Beo*.499–610) to Beowulf's childhood swimming match with Breca. Yet in these and other cases, past incident is being summoned up not so much for its own sake as for its predictive value on the coming exchange. Achilles recalls Patroklos because now he intends to kill his killer; Hektor recalls Achilles' speech because he wants to demonstrate that he has not been "psyched out" for the fight; Beowulf and Unferth recall their differing versions of the swimming adventure because they think it reflects on Beowulf's likelihood of success against Grendel. Conversely, many predominantly retrospective, post-combat speech exchanges contain predictive or even contractual material of various types. Patroklos's dying words are a prophecy of death for Hektor (16.851–54; see also Hektor's response to this prediction, 16.859–61); Hektor similarly dies with a warning to Achilles (22.358–60; see Achilles' response, 22.365–66); Aias and Hektor conclude their fight with a compact of peace and gift giving (7.277–312). Yet all of these exchanges acquire their meaning in the context of what has occurred. Their primary purpose is to bring closure to the contest, both as incident and as narrative. The terms prospective and retrospective, then, when applied to complex interactions with movements of both kinds, refer to the *dominant* orientation. It should hardly surprise us if winners are more likely to concentrate their remarks on their recent victories, whereas losers are apt to deflect attention away from their own failures through curses, dire predictions, and similar rhetorical moves.

Although the term flyting might be used to designate all speech associated with heroic contesting, I limit it here to the prospective speech exchange, that is, the precombat dialogue in which contracts are established. The total contest pattern, in its simple form, might be described then as a movement through four stages:

A. *Engagement.* Two heroes and potential adversaries arrive or are poetically brought to the foreground at some typical contest site.
B. *Flyting.* The heroes engage in an adversarial verbal exchange that has two qualitatively distinguishable yet mutually interpenetrating aspects:
   1. *eris*—the heroes contend for *kleos* or glory; and
   2. *contract*—they implicitly or explicitly agree on a course of action from a range of possibilities, at least one of which entails a trial of arms or some other form of manly display.
C. *Trial of arms.* The heroes engage in the trial of arms or display specified in the contract (if the flyting did indeed resolve on a combative option); one of them wins.
D. *Ritual resolution.* The heroes terminate their contest through
   1. *retrospective speech*, sometimes accompanied by
   2. *symbolic action.*

For a simple and straightforward example of this pattern, let us review the Achilles-Asteropaios contest in *Il.*21.139–204. The Engagement (element A) occupies lines 139–48, which inform us that Achilles was advancing to attack this Trojan, who in turn was inspired by the river Xanthos to stand against him. Of course, Achilles by this time needs no introducing on Homer's part; Asteropaios does, however, and accordingly the poet inserts some minimal genealogical information (141–43) between a pair of statements to the effect that Achilles assaulted him (139–41 and 144).[16] Achilles initiates the Flyting (element B) with a terse, two-sentence question and threat (150–51):

τίς πόθεν εἰς ἀνδρῶν, ὅ μευ ἔτλης ἀντίος ἐλθεῖν;
δυστήνων δέ τε παῖδες ἐμῷ μένει ἀντιόωσι.

Who and from where are you among men, you who dare to come against me?
Children of unfortunate ones are they who oppose my strength.

The question, "Who are you?" arises from the need in heroic epic for the participants in contests to be named and identified, for only so can the significance of these encounters be fully assessed. The threat, while cast in the form of a generalized statement, implies that the Trojan—whoever he might be—will lose in the coming encounter. Although Achilles does not intend to give his enemy any real choice in the matter, he is nonetheless establishing the eventuality of a fight in contractual fashion. Asteropaios responds first to the question, describing his homeland (154–55) and lineage (157–60), both of which Achilles' inquiry seemed to call for. He concludes by an invitation to battle (160): "νῦν αὖτε μαχώμεθα, φαίδιμ' Ἀχιλλεῦ" ("Now, however, let us fight, shining Achilles"). By this exhortation Asteropaios demonstrates his refusal to be intimidated and ratifies the contract option (of fighting) that Achilles had intimated. After an exchange of spear throws, the Achaian cuts his adversary down with a sword (element C: 161–82). Achilles now leaps on his breast and strips his armor— the symbolic act (element D2: 182–83). In his vaunt (element D1: 186–99), Achilles stresses the superiority of his own ancestry, for although Asteropaios descends from a river god, "ἐγὼ γενεὴν μεγάλου Διὸς εὔχομαι εἶναι" (187; "I boast to be of the progeny of great Zeus"). This comment illustrates that Achilles had interpreted Asteropaios's earlier genealogical statements eristically: In his view they implied a boast (on battle proficiency) that he has now proved hollow. Withdrawing his spear, he leaves Asteropaios's corpse for the river and its carnivorous fish (200–204).

In fact, relatively few contests exhibit this pattern in so bald a form. In most cases, it has been elaborated or syncopated through a group of fairly standard operations. In one instance—the Alexandros-Menelaos duel in book 3—the "flyting" (in which contract formation almost entirely displaces quarrel) is conducted through intermediaries. More frequently, the prospective speech–combat–retrospective speech cycle is reduplicated, particularly when the first exchange of blows is inconclusive, with the result that speech precedes, follows, and is distributed through the course of a prolonged trial of arms. These intermediary speeches will often contain a retrospective element, as when a hero comments on the failure of his opponent to kill him, and a prospective element, as when he discusses his own planned attack.[17] Sometimes a hero, having killed his foeman, addresses his postbattle vaunt to some enemy witness who had just previously won a contest of his own; on other occasions each contestant in turn first speaks and then attacks, without allowing his adversary to interject a reply. All these and other forms of contest elaboration we will discuss more fully in the following sections.

Many contests, however, do not realize all of the elements in my four-step pattern. In some cases, contract negotiation leads directly to the termination of conflict. The flyting contractual process usually

John K. B.

allows for one party or the other to capitulate without a fight; among animals as well as humans, one of the major functions of threat displays is to allow for the circumvention of bloody combat. It is also possible for a contestant intimidated by his adversary's flyting to abandon the dueling altogether and try to escape through flight. The flyting process, through its heavy reliance on threat structures, implicitly acknowledges such options. Such premature terminations of the heroic contest at the flyting stage entail, of course, forfeiture of honor on the quitter's part.

Yet the contest process can be abridged or broken off in other ways. In special circumstances flyting negotiations can conclude in a peaceable settlement in which neither side wins or loses; we will review examples of this later in this chapter. Frequently, in the *Iliad* especially, gods terminate a conflict prematurely by delivering heroes from their peril.[18] Yet there are other instances in which the contest lacks prebattle flyting, or the postbattle vaunt; and some episodes feature "flytings" in which only one contestant actually speaks. At the "minimal extreme," we are confronted with contests of the bare "X killed Y" variety, in which the slaughter narrative is unaccompanied by speech of any kind. Such episodes obviously cannot provide us with any direct information about flyting. Nonetheless, contests that include flyting or postbattle vaunting sometimes use this same "X killed Y" motif to frame biographical or genealogical information, in much the same way as the unadorned killing episodes do.[19] Thus, viewing all these contests, from the most developed to the least, as members of a single continuum seems most plausible. The poet is free to use the "total" contest pattern to whatever degree best suits his purposes.

At this juncture I will need to raise a methodological question: How are we to respect the integrity of a pattern when, in the strict sense, it only describes a few members of what appears to be a larger family of episodes? For example, flyting is paradigmatically dialogic. Can we meaningfully discuss under this rubric exchanges that do not fulfill even this minimal requirement? A particularly fine example from the *Alliterative Morte Arthure* illustrates that silence does not always imply dialogic nonparticipation. King Arthur has just directed a particularly abusive speech at the Giant of St. Michael's Mount (1059–73). The poet describes the giant's reaction thus (1074–7):

Than glopned þe gloton and glored vnfaire;
He grenned as a grewhounde, with grysly tuskes;
He gaped, he groned faste, with grucchand latez,
For grefe of þe gude kyng þat hym with grame gretez.

Then that glutton gaped and glowered foully;
He bared his teeth like a greyhound with dreadful fangs;
He opened his mouth wide and growled savagely, with a dour
    expression,
In rage at that good king who greeted him with anger.

True, the monster never actually replies in words; yet the general import of his "body language" in this passage is unmistakable. His silence speaks indeed. Although Homer and *Beowulf* never illustrate the principle quite so graphically, here too we should recognize that the dynamics of human interaction can be in full force even when dialogue—literally, "speaking"—is absent. Single speeches in a contest interaction can articulate eristic and contractual themes in the same manner as full-fledged "flytings" do. Of course, actual dialogues express the contest situation more satisfactorily. Both rivalries and contracts entail bipartisan involvement; and dialogue calls explicit attention to the polarities of viewpoint. Nonetheless, any analysis failing to recognize the fundamental kinship of these dialogic and single-speech encounters would be a prisoner of its own superficial formalism.

In fact, the most important determinants in heroic contest narrative consist not in some fixed and preconceived "pattern" but in the forces that give rise to these contests in the first place. I am referring here to the glory motive, quarrel and contract formation, the bonding of words to deeds, and the other heroic values that we have been discussing. The four-element contest pattern outlined earlier provides a useful heuristic tool, in the same sense that the description of modern English sentences as progressing from subject to verb to complement alludes to real tendencies amid the multiformity of actual language use. If we were to insist that every sentence conform literally to this sequence, with no inversions, embeddings, coordinated reduplications of grammatical functions, and so forth, then the study of syntax could never progress beyond the mere listing of variant types in the surface structure. Discussions of "theme" and "type scene," while they have brought into view important characteristics of oral narrative, often suffer from an enslavement to narrative exteriors. Of course, methodological consistency and objectivity are often best served by starting with what is first and most superficially evident. Yet exteriors are usually generated from within—or, more accurately stated, exteriors and interiors are interdependent and mutually determining. Actual heroic narrative, not surprisingly, offers considerable variation in contest structure, reflecting the narrative context, "formulas" of the particular tradition, habits and aesthetic designs of the author, and so forth.[20] By referring these diverse expressions to a single pattern, I do not mean that they are derived from a fixed archetype. My aim is rather to highlight principles that the "pattern" illuminates with particular expository clarity.

Heroic contests in which fighting lacks some or all of the requisite verbal concomitants according to the four-element scheme are not somehow deficient or incomplete. John Foley has recently described the relationship between traditional structure and its performative actualization as one of "metonymy" whereby the "phrase or scene is always embedded conceptually in the wordhoard, the experience of tradition."[21] A formulaic expression such as "δῖος Ὀδυσσεύς," in other words, refers to the totality of experience associated with the character of Odysseus within the narrative tradition, at least to the extent that it has been accessed by the poet and audience concerned. In this sense a traditional depth underlies oral poetic expression, although the poet is free to bring this "depth" into the conscious foreground of narrative to whatever degree suits the artistic aims of the moment. By the same token, "contests" as a class belong to the experience that an oral-traditional audience and poet can bring to any particular instance. The poet may choose to develop a contest in a fashion that engages this experience profoundly, or he may let the opportunity pass with a bare allusion: "X killed Y." Yet even these minimally narrated fights contain those potentialities that are more fully expressed in the great contests with which the stories climax. A competent audience would be well versed in the larger spectrum of possibilities and would recognize the continuities that join its members.

In these respects the aesthetics of creation and response are conditioned by the poet's and audience's engagement with their own particular tradition. Yet the contest pattern—or rather, the motivational structures that underlie it—have a cross-cultural validity as well. Present-day boxing or professional wrestling matches furnish good analogues. A long build-up, featuring bragging and insults, culminates in a highly stylized combat, after which the victor proclaims his supremacy: "I am the greatest!" Similarly structured contests used to unfold week after week in the saloons of television and Hollywood Westerns of the 1950s and 1960s: cowboys insulting each other over whiskey, shooting it out, and bragging over the results before frightened bystanders. In various forms, garbed in the idioms of the cultures and traditions and media in which it appears, this sequence of events must indeed be one of the most universal patterns of human storytelling, at least in those genres of storytelling that concern themselves with physical combat. We should not overlook this dimension of significance and appeal in Homeric and Old English heroic poetry by attributing all features of their contesting to culture-specific circumstances.

I have deliberately defined the contest pattern in general terms applicable to a wide range of heroic contest material. However, this pattern has several forms corresponding to the types of social environment in which it occurs. As noted in the previous chapter, flyting interactions in the Greek and Old English traditions most often feature members of warring armies, warriors from communities engaged in guest-host interactions, or heroes from the same group. Different conditions obtain in each of these cases, which will be studied in the following sections in this chapter; the most dramatic point of variation distinguishing these patterns is in the Trial of Arms (element C). In certain circumstances flyting can modulate from one pattern to another; two possibilities to be examined are the modulation from the more bellicose battlefield pattern to its guest-host counterpart, and vice versa. All of these movements presuppose "serious," contractual flyting. The possibility of "ludic" verbal disputation (of the "playing the dozens" variety) needs to be considered, although this phenomenon has little importance in our focal texts. In any event, such exchanges represent a different genre of verbal contesting whose characteristics will be outlined in chapter 5.

THE BATTLEFIELD VARIANT OF THE CONTEST THEME

The battlefield setting sponsors the most eristic form of heroic flyting. Since the communities involved are bent on destroying one another, nothing restrains the contestants from following the most violent course. Thus, the battlefield Trial of Arms engages the heroes in direct mortal combat (unless one of them should flee or capitulate). Ritualization affects the manner in which the fight is conducted, not the bloodiness of the result. Of course, heroes may disregard the ritual norms and win in any way that they can, by hook or by crook. Such victories are not of the agonistic sort, however, and do not reap honor in the same way. In *Beowulf* and the *Iliad* heroes normally conform to the dictates of ritual propriety, though the same cannot always be said for the *Odyssey* and other works in the heroic mode.

The battlefield (bf) sequence runs as follows:

A[bf.] *Engagement.* Two armies, P and Q, are pitted against one another militarily at some typical battle site (whose exact characteristics are culture- or tradition-specific). Heroes p and q separate out for single combat.

B^bf. *Flyting.* Heroes *p* and *q* initiate an adversarial exchange that has two qualitatively distinguishable yet mutually interpenetrating aspects:

1. *eris*—the heroes contend for *kleos* or glory; and
2. *contract*—they implicitly or explicitly agree on a course of action from a range of possibilities, at least one of which entails direct, mortal combat between the two of them.

C^bf. *Martial combat.* Heroes *p* and *q* fight; *p* wins.

D^bf. *Ritual resolution.* Hero *p* declares his victory through one or both of the following:

1. *vaunting*—*p* boasts over his fallen enemy. In some cases, this element takes the form of an exchange between *p* and *q*. In this event, the interaction clearly presupposes the proven superiority of *p* over *q*, and it closes with a speech by *p*.
2. *symbolic action*—*p* performs one or more of the following: He puts his foot on *q*'s chest to pull out the spear, strips *q*'s armor, or tries to drag off *q*'s body for purposes of mutilation. These actions occur frequently in association with contests in Homer, but not in my limited corpus of examples from Old English.[22]

This pattern is subject to many forms of variation, which are best and most commonly illustrated in the *Iliad*. The Old English *Waldere* and the *Battle of Maldon* also provide examples.

Engagement, the first element in the pattern, comprises in effect the narrative introduction of two heroes in the battle setting. Homer finds many ways of doing this. A simple instance appears in *Il*.5.627–29:

> Ὥς οἱ μὲν πονέοντο κατὰ κρατερὴν ὑσμίνην·
> Τληπόλεμον δ᾽ Ἡρακλεΐδην ἠΰν τε μέγαν τε,
> ὦρσεν ἐπ᾽ ἀντιθέῳ Σαρπηδόνι μοῖρα κραταιή.

> So these [Aias and the Trojans] labored in the mighty conflict.
> But strong fate stirred up Tlepolemon, son of Herakles, brave and tall,
> Against godlike Sarpedon.

On the other extreme, almost two hundred lines in book 22 are devoted to Hektor's vacillations, escape attempts, the machinations of gods, and so forth, which culminate in Hektor's death struggle with Achilles; all this prefatory matter might be regarded as an immense elaboration on an element that the Tlepolemon-Sarpedon conflict dispatches in two lines. During the great *aristeia* or on other occasions when a particular hero's exploits have just been narrated, there is no need to identify him anew; thus, the passage that features Agenor's burgeoning resolution to take a stand against Achilles (21.544–81), does nothing to introduce Achilles himself as a contestant, since his ravages have occupied the last two books. Many contests, on the other hand, contain no lines devoted exclusively to engagement but plunge immediately into the encounter.

Element B, the Flyting, is examined intensively in the next chapter; my concern here is with its role in the larger contest setting. A classic example is the verbal duel between Sarpedon and Tlepolemos (5.633–54) that follows the Engagement just quoted. Tlepolemos opens with the assertion that Sarpedon, while held to be the son of Zeus, in no way measures up to the standards of Zeus's offspring of former ages. By contrast Herakles, Tlepolemos's own father, sacked Ilios, thus exemplifying, we are to gather, a heroic standard that Sarpedon cannot match. Indeed, Sarpedon's defense will not avail the Trojans: He will be vanquished by Tlepolemos and sent to Hades. In reply, Sarpedon acknowledges the Heraklean episode. Nonetheless, he, Sarpedon, will kill his enemy by spear, thus winning glory ("εὖχος," 654), and will send his soul to Hades. In this exchange, the quarrel-contract dichotomy stands in bold relief. The two men press their eristic assertions of superiority through genealogical retrospection and through predictions of success in combat. They contract through their implicit agreement that the imminent death struggle will provide the appropriate test of their heroic claims. Immediately after this flyting, the two warriors wound each other with their spears and have to be carried off by their companions.

Most Homeric flytings follow this pattern of two speeches, one by each of the contestants. The Pandaros-Diomedes encounter in *Il*.5.274–96 provides a rare example of a precombat flyting in which only one contestant speaks.[23] Pandaros's verbal assault (277–79) represents a typical flyting contribution, however:

> καρτερόθυμε, δαΐφρον, ἀγαυοῦ Τυδέος υἱέ,
> ἦ μάλα σ᾽ οὐ βέλος ὠκὺ δαμάσσατο, πικρὸς ὀϊστός·
> νῦν αὖτ᾽ ἐγχείῃ πειρήσομαι, αἴ κε τύχωμι.

> Stout-hearted, warlike son of good Tydeus,
> Indeed my swift missile, my bitter arrow, did not overcome you;
> Now again I will test you with my spear, to find if I might hit the mark.

The eristic tone, repressed in this speech, bursts out a few moments later in Pandaros's premature vaunt (element D1: 284–85); this leads in effect to a renewed Flyting (element B) in which Diomedes denies Pandaros's success and boasts of his own imminent attack (287–89). The Achaian's spear cuts through Pandaros's face and kills him.

Another variation on the usual (two-speech) pattern occurs in the Menelaos-Euphorbos Flyting (*Il*.17.12–42), a three-speech exchange that Euphorbos opens and closes. This asymmetry is due to the fact that Euphorbos's opening speech tries to intimidate Menelaos and so deter him from entering the fray; since the Achaian vigorously rejects this contract proposal, Euphorbos's second speech stresses his own warlike intentions. An interesting transformation occurs in the Sokos-Odysseus contest (11.426–58), in which flyting is distributed through the course of combat. First Sokos flyts, and then casts his spear; Odysseus in turn foretells his own victory and then kills Sokos, concluding the encounter with a particularly cruel Vaunt (element D1). Usually the precombat flyting is self-contained; yet on some occasions, such as this one, it is renewed, if an initial assault is unsuccessful.

All of these flyting episodes engage adversaries with a real interest in fighting each other. Yet the contractual process does not always focus exclusively on the bellicose alternative; on occasion the aggressor or his prospective victim tries to circumvent the fight altogether. One method consists in intimidation, such as when Achilles urges Aineias to withdraw from an encounter that would be his death (*Il*.20.332–39); Aineias refuses, and is eventually lifted out of the melee by Poseidon. The Vikings in *Maldon* similarly try to persuade Byrhtnoth and his forces to capitulate to their demands without a battle, as we shall see presently. Both Deïphobos and Diomedes, for variously legitimate reasons, find themselves unwilling to take up the challenges proposed to them by Idomeneus and Hektor (*Il*.13.446–59 and 8.161–71). Apollo likewise refuses an invitation to fight with his uncle Poseidon (21.436–67); and although his hesitancy seems motivated by respect for a close senior relative, his sister Artemis calls him a coward for it nonetheless (472–77). A particularly comic version of the intimidation motif occurs when Hermes concedes defeat to the goddess Leto before she has even offered battle (21.498–504). Themes of shame and dishonor reverberate through most of these episodes.[24]

Some warriors are simply outmatched. Those who cannot begin to meet the condition of "comparability" that contestants ideally ought to have sometimes try to beg for mercy, usually by clasping the knees of their adversaries and promising ransom from their fathers in exchange for their lives.[25] In this way they are trying to use the negotiatory aspect of the flyting process to terminate contestation. Although the *Iliad* alludes to previous occasions in which this strategy worked (interestingly, cognate practices are ordinarily successful in intraspecific male contests among animals), in every Iliadic episode belonging to the narrative present (rather than a digression or flashback) the aggressor insists on fighting—that is, on continuing in the contestation mode of interaction—and simply slaughters his supplicant.[26] Menelaos, for his part, seems to have been initially well disposed toward the prayers of Adrestos but, prompted by Agamemnon, chooses in the end to kill him (6.37–65); Agamemnon in turn rejects the petitions of Peisandros and Hippolochos, who unlike all the others in this group supplicate not at their enemies' knees but from their chariot (11.122–48). The slaughter that Odysseus and Diomedes mete out to Dolon (10.369–468), from whom the crafty Ithakan first extorts intelligence on the disposition of the Trojan forces, smacks of treachery and can hardly be called a heroic contest. The most dramatic episode of supplication, however, involves Achilles and Lykaon.[27] This contest is indeed a highly developed one. The Engagement (element A), occupying thirty-three lines (34–66), includes an anecdotal-biographical digression on Lykaon framed by elaborate ring structuring; following an aborted fight (67–70), the Flyting (element B: 74–113), composed of Lykaon's petition and Achilles' pitiless rebuttal, is highly developed and particularly pathetic; the renewed Combat (element C: 114–21) is narrated briefly but graphically; and Achilles' vaunt and abuse of the body (element D: 120–35) exhibit the same spirit that his treatment of Hektor's corpse does later. This case illustrates unmistakably that supplication exchanges represent a variant of flyting: If the petitioner prevails, the contest might be resolved prematurely, but if he fails, it follows its bloody course. Lykaon tries to promote the contractual and repress the eristic movements of the flyting; but Achilles cannot be persuaded. Perhaps no moment in the *Iliad* displays Achilles' alienation from human sympathies more drastically than this one does.

In many contests, however, including a number with the postbattle vaunt (element D1), the flyting element is lacking. As we have already noted, nothing compels Homer to develop this aspect of contesting in every case. In fact, several exchanges that contain element D open immediately with a narration of combat according to the highly typical "X killed Y" pattern. For example, in *Il.*13.363–84, Homer tells us that Idomeneus killed Othryoneus, describes Othryoneus's background and wooing of Kassandra, narrates the killing in greater detail, and reproduces Idomeneus's postbattle vaunt (element D1). This device—two "X killed Y" frames encasing a brief biographical digression—occurs by my count in more than thirty-five episodes that lack precombat flyting discourse.[28] In the Idomeneus-Othryoneus episode and others like it, Homer seems quite simply to have added a vaunting speech (from the element D) to what began as a typical killing incident.

Because Combat, element C in the contest pattern, comprises a highly involved subject in its own right, I do not discuss this facet of Iliadic battle narration in any detail. It is worth observing, however, that most martial encounters in the *Iliad* which contain much typical and formulaic material,[29] result in death to one contestant or another. According to Mueller (1984: 82), some "170 Trojan and fifty Achaean named warriors lose their lives in the *Iliad*; another dozen, evenly divided between the two sides, are injured." This remarkable disproportion suggests death's thematic importance in the epic. Yet death follows less regularly in the exchanges that we are concerned with—that is, contests with either speech element B or D, or both. Out of thirty-four "legitimate" battlefield contests between human beings in the *Iliad* (and I am excluding the "analogical" exchanges to be discussed later), only twenty are mortal, a far less overwhelming majority than one finds in instances of combat unattended by speech. It would seem that in these more developed and personalized exchanges Homer was less willing to kill off his prime actors.

Element D, composed of vaunting and symbolic gesture, is a form of resolution that eventuates only if Combat (element C) has produced a killing. When they have felled their enemies, however, winners at combat rarely hesitate to taunt their victims cruelly. Idomeneus, for example, mocking Othryoneus's wooing of Kassandra that Homer told us of a few lines before, offers his dying enemy an Achaian bride (13.374–82); Poulydamas calls his spear the walking stick that will help Prothoënor to Hades (14.454–57); the "gentle" Patroklos characterizes Kebriones, who has just tumbled in death from his chariot, as a skillful diver (16.745–50); Achilles verbally consigns the bodies of Iphition and Lykaon to the waters and its fish (20.389–92 and 21.122–35). All these speeches recapitulate the eristic movement of precombat flyting; yet these vaunts are functional as well, reminding the victim and witnesses of the contractual significance of victory. Thus Achilles (21.184–99) describes his own genealogy to the disadvantage of that of his dying enemy Asteropaios, confuting the Trojan's prior genealogical "boast." Athena, for her part, trumpets her recent victory over Ares as proof of her greater strength (21.410–14). To Menelaos, the killing of Peisandros augurs more such just punishment for the Trojans who so impiously stole away his wife Helen (13.620–39). Thus, vaunting stamps the verbal seal on victory in combat and in some fashion rationalizes the heroic standing of the victor.

Frequently the winners will use the vaunt as an occasion to fling insults at the larger enemy force. Menelaos's remarks just alluded to are, in fact, addressed to the Trojans as a group. In a string of duels in books 13 and 14, heroes undertake battle specifically to avenge fallen friends; their vaunts, accordingly, are addressed to the opposing army, or to the particular warriors responsible for those killings that so offended them. For example, after slaying Hypsenor, Deïphobos boasts that Asios has been avenged (13.414–16). In response, Idomeneus cuts down Alkathoös; and addressing Deïphobos by name, in his vaunt he compares his three recent killings with that of Deïphobos and challenges that Trojan to combat (446–54). Here vaunting merges with the initiation of a new flyting exchange—one that Deïphobos, after internal debate, shies away from. Similarly, in response to Poulydamas's success against the Achaian Prothoënor, Aias, aiming for that Trojan culprit, instead strikes Antenor; Aias then points out (14.470–74) that this was a worthier victim than Poulydamas's was. Immediately after this, however, Akamas spears Promachos and boasts to the enemy Achaians that his brother's death has been avenged (14.479–85). In response, Peneleos, missing Akamas, stabs Ilioneus; and in a vaunting speech addressed to the Trojans, he compares the grief of Ilioneus's parents with that of Promachos's wife (14.501–5). In all these cases vaunts are being used as contributions to dialogue in revenge contest doublets. I would not call these flytings, since the vaunters are celebrating their recent triumphs rather than contracting for new fights. The exception is Idomeneus's speech already alluded to; and his enemy Deïphobos, as we have seen, does not pick up the gauntlet.

In these contest pairs, the vauntings participate in incipiently dialogic structures. In several D1 sequences within single contests, however, the vaunting is explicitly elaborated into full-fledged dialogues between the contestants (usually victor and victim). Minor instances include the Diomedes-Pandaros (5.284–89) and Diomedes-Alexandros (11.380–95) encounters, to which I will advert shortly, as well as the postcombat taunts between Aineias and Meriones (16.617–25). This latter exchange is remarkable in that Patroklos interrupts it, castigating his companion Meriones for trying to let words substitute for action (16.627–31). Since Patroklos himself does not shrink from verbal abuse on suitable occasions, perhaps he finds this "vaunting" on the part of a fellow Achaian who has only avoided an enemy's assault and not launched one of his own to be too much in the character of Flyting (element B) without the contractual orientation toward a sequent Trial of Arms (element C).

The most dramatic postcombat dialogues, however, occur in association with the two most crucial fights in the *Iliad*; and the degree to which they mirror each other suggests that Homer recognized these D-element dialogues as belonging to a common type. The Patroklos-Hektor vaunting (16.830–61) contains three speeches: a retrospective taunt by the Trojan who points out that Patroklos has failed in his martial ambitions, a self-justification by Patroklos who denies Hektor credit for the deed and predicts his death at Achilles' hands, and, after Patroklos's death, Hektor's response that the outcome of the anticipated fight with Achilles remains in doubt. In his exchange with the dying Hektor (22.331–60), Achilles in turn begins by pointing out that his enemy's hopes have cheated him. Hektor then begs his enemy not to abuse his body, and Achilles refuses. The Trojan concludes with a warning about the wrath of the gods, and dies; Achilles responds with an imperative, "τέθναθι" ("Lie dead!"), and expresses willingness to accept his own coming fate (365–66). In both of these exchanges the winners concentrate on the fact of victory as a heroic judgment, whereas the losers try to relativize their murderers' accomplishments through gloomy prognostications. For both parties the dialogic venture is an interpretive one, to define and contextualize the significance of the recent martial test.

Of course, in some instances the results of combat are not so clearcut. Both Hektor and Aineias are at different times lifted by a partisan deity out of a fight with Achilles. And although Achilles is frustrated by these failures to consummate his victory with a corpse, his speeches—delivered in his adversaries' absence—point out that the tide of arms had been flowing in his direction and that his enemies were lucky to escape.[30] After Agenor has been similarly rescued by Apollo (21.596–607), and the god, pursued by Achilles who has mistaken him for his delivered enemy, has disabused the Achaian of this confusion (22.8–13), Achilles retorts angrily that Apollo has cheated him of glory (15–20). Although this last "vaunt" is particularly atypical in that Achilles addresses the god rather than the victim, all three postbattle speech or dialogue episodes bring their contests to a close and allude to the themes of victory or battle glory, whether or not the speaker has gained these to his own satisfaction. Vaunting at these moments has been justified at least in the sense that Achilles has won the battles by default. Paris similarly tries to boast over an adversary whom he has injured but not killed (11.380–83); Diomedes rejects his claims vigorously, however, comparing his enemy to a woman or child, denying the severity of the wound, and pointing out that Paris had not taken him on in man-to-man combat (385–95). Like Patroklos, who insists that he was subdued by others and not by Hektor (16.844–54), Diomedes is concerned to deny Alexandros any glory from the encounter. Twice Pandaros vaunts over Diomedes prematurely (5.102–5 and 284–85), thinking that he has killed his great adversary. On the first occasion Diomedes is magically healed of the arrow wound by Athena; the second time Diomedes retorts that Pandaros's spear throw missed him (287–89) and goes on to cut him down with a spear cast of his own. We have already noted the Aineias-Meriones vaunting (16.617–31), engaged in by heroes who had failed even to injure each other and interrupted by Patroklos probably for this reason. All these examples suggest that vaunting is subject to the ethical constraints discussed earlier in this chapter, relating to the imperative that words should be substantiated by deeds. Just as a hero is disgraced if he does not try to fulfill his flyting contract, so he has no right to brag about the fighting afterward if his performance did not justify it.

Stripping an enemy's armor and mutilating his body—element D2—are themes adverted to over forty times in the *Iliad*. In fact, the greater part of book 17 is devoted to the struggle over the corpse of Patroklos (who wears Achilles' armor); and Zeus seems to be far more offended by the abuse that Achilles inflicts on Hektor's dead body in book 24 than he was by that hero's mistreatment of any number of living men. The significance of armor need not be dilated on, especially in view of the number of lines that Homer sees fit to devote to it in book 18. The acquisition of an enemy's body and armor functions as such a potent symbol of victory and battle glory that heroes repeatedly risk their lives for it. These motifs mark the closing of a contest with particular effectiveness. Sometimes the armor-stripping or body-abusing motifs accompany vaunting, as in the Menelaos-Peisandros encounter (13.618–42). More often Homer contents himself with just one aspect of element D—either the speech or the symbolic action. And in a few cases, particularly when no one has been killed, he drops the element altogether. Yet even when explicit body abusing and armor stripping are absent, Homer often alludes to these motifs indirectly. For example, the Achaian and Trojan forces fight over the "body" of Hektor, who had been stunned in a battle with Aias but who eventually escapes both in his armor and unmutilated (14.421–39). After Tlepolemos and Sarpedon have injured one another, Homer mentions that their respective armies carry them off (5.663–69). The traditional poet and audience evidently found references to vaunting, armor, or bodies (whether living or dead) fitting at the conclusion of contests. Having reviewed some of the forms that individual elements of the battlefield contest pattern assume in the *Iliad*, we can now consider contests as a whole to determine some of the characteristic variations on the basic pattern.

One means of narrative elaboration consists in the reduplication of speech-to-fighting sequences. Something of the kind occurs in the Diomedes-Pandaros contest discussed previously. After a one-speech monologic flyting, Pandaros hits Diomedes' shield with a spear and vaunts prematurely; Diomedes retorts by denying the injury, projecting success in his own assault, and killing Pandaros with a spear throw (5.274–96). The contest might be analyzed thus: A-B-C-D-B-C. The Odysseus-Sokos exchange, as reviewed earlier, progresses through monologic flyting speeches separated by combat: A-B-C-B-C-D (11.426–58). The most developed and intricate example, however, occurs in the climactic Hektor-Achilles encounter in 22.248–369. After Hektor has finally given up on escape, he tries to engage his enemy in a contractually oriented flyting, but Achilles will agree to fight and nothing else. After Achilles' first attack has proved ineffective, Hektor addresses to him a speech (279–88) with both retrospective and prospective elements. First, he notes that the spear throw missed and condemns Achilles' attempt to daunt him through words in their earlier flyting. Finally, he refers to his own prospective attack, wishing it the best. Missing for his own part and finding that pseudo-Deïphobos (Athena) has abandoned him, Hektor engages in an interior monologue (297–305) with retrospective and prospective segments: He recognizes that the gods have cheated him, but resolves to die bravely. This monologue, while standing outside the normal pattern, mirrors his previous speech. Finally, he attacks with his sword, is cut through the neck, and engages in the dying exchange with Achilles analyzed previously as a case of Vaunting (element D1). In its overall outlines, then, this contest follows the classic A-B-C-D pattern, with the two additional speeches by Hektor—one vocalized, the other interiorized—breaking up the combat. Yet since each of these speeches begins with a retrospective and closes with a prospective element, the combat sequence itself (the C element) might be analyzed as follows: combat-retrospective speech-prospective speech-combat-retrospective speech-prospective speech-combat. Even this highly elaborate contest, then, becomes more intelligible in the light of the principles that we have been reviewing.

Although all of these contests are implicitly ritualized to varying degrees, the *Iliad* features monomachies that both armies formalize with special ceremony.[31] In the first, the Menelaos-Alexandros contest that occupies most of book 3, the two principals never directly address each other at all. In their stead, their brothers have taken over the flyting and vaunting functions. Thus Hektor, after having engaged in one of his several reproach-and-apology exchanges with Alexandros, presents to the Achaians his brother's challenge for single combat, which Menelaos enthusiastically accepts. After due rites, vows, and preparations, Alexandros and Menelaos match off; but when the fight has turned to the Achaian's advantage, Aphrodite lifts her darling out of battle. In the book's concluding speech, Agamemnon claims victory and demands that the Trojans fulfill their contract. In its broad outlines, then, the episode follows the standard contest pattern with speeches (the B and D elements) reassigned to noncontestants: an initial Engagement (element A), from which Paris flees (15–37); a mediated Flyting (element B: 86–110) repressing the eristic (abusive) strain and foregrounding the specialized contract; a fight (element C); and a proclamation of victory (element D1). This type of mediated flyting-by-proxy is illustrated in a far more developed form in the embassies between the emperor Lucius and Arthur in the *Alliterative Morte Arthure*.[32]

The second specially ceremonialized duel—between Hektor and Aias in book 7—begins similarly but develops along new lines. Again, it is Hektor who sets forth the challenge, now on his own behalf; yet on this occasion the Achaians seem to have been intimidated, and only after Nestor's reproaches do respondents emerge. Chosen by lot out of a group of nine, Aias now engages Hektor anew in a classic contest of the "modulating" variety to be discussed later in this chapter; the two heroes flyt, fight, and resolve their exchange peaceably. Kirk (1978) has treated these two dueling episodes in much greater detail than I can undertake here. These two duels are in many respects cases apart, for their contracts, solemnized through bipartisan ratification, contain special provisions binding not just the individual contestants but their armies as well; indeed, the Alexandros-Menelaos duel is proposed to stand in place of further warfare. On the other hand, they are distinguished from each other, in the first instance, by use of proxy speakers, and in the second instance, by the incorporation of a full contest sequence (elements A through D) as one part of a larger duel. In short, these two monomachies entail far more than most contests do, but they are based on the same fundamental principles.

We have already noted how vaunts are sometimes used to set one contest against another, and I would like here to reiterate that contests are frequently employed as parts of larger structures or sequences. Seriatim killings—whether by one hero, or by heroes in opposing armies—fill long stretches of battle narration, not only in the *Iliad*, but in other such works in the heroic mode as *The Song of Roland* or the *Alliterative Morte Arthure*. This is less often the case in Homeric contest sequences with B and D speech elements; yet there are several notable exceptions. The Deïphobos-Hypsenor and Idomeneus-Alkathoös contests (*Il.*13.402–59) are linked not only through the revenge motives and explicit mutual address in the vaunting, but in a mirroring in total design—both lack flyting, and thus take the form A-C-D. The Akamas-Promachos and Peneleos-Ilioneus contests (14.476–

507) enjoy this same relationship, a common A-C-D structure and interactive vaunting. Such contest doublets or series linked by speeches appear profusely in other heroic poems.

I will conclude discussion of battlefield contests in the *Iliad* with passages that do not, strictly speaking, contain patterns of this type but that register its influence. Several episodes exhibit what we might call structural analogues to flyting, as two heroes, instead of quarreling directly, in turn exhort their own forces into battle.[33] In book 15, for example, Hektor encourages the Trojans, and Aias the Argives (486–513); Hektor prods on Melanippos, and Aias again exhorts the Argives (553–64); Hektor calls for fire, and Aias appeals for defenders against the destruction of the ships (718–41). Although Hektor and Aias do not at this stage separate out into single combat, Hektor spearheads an attack against which Aias provides the chief resistance. I could not label this a contest of the type that the contest pattern defines, yet it exhibits similar adversarial structuring tendencies.[34] Later, when Achilles and Hektor alternately exhort their forces (20.354–72), they are prevented from fighting one another directly only because Apollo advises Hektor to retire (376–78). If this exchange had contained true flyting, it would provide an excellent example of a contest aborted because of flyting intimidation. On the other hand, the Hektor-Lykophron episode (15.422–41) contains a traditional (ring-structured) killing. The flyting, however, has been replaced by another of Hektor's exhortations (425–28), while Aias's commentary to Teukros (437–41) stands in place of Hektor's vaunt.[35] We find a fairly classic contest in the Automedon-Aretos episode, capped with arms stripping and a boast (17.536–39); the flyting slot, however, has been filled by Hektor's and Automedon's speeches to their comrades (485–90, 501–15; note especially that 514 is repeated verbatim in 20.435, in the course of Hektor's flyting with Achilles). In the Diomedes-Hektor encounter in 11.343–68, a contest with traditional A, C, and D elements, an appeal by Diomedes to Odysseus (347–48) substitutes for the usual flyting. At the end of the Patroklos-Sarpedon exchange (16.419–505), instead of narrating the usual armor stripping and vaunting on the part of the victorious Achaian, Homer presents us with Sarpedon's dying speech in which he urges Glaukos to rescue his body from the ravages of his enemies (492–501). All these examples reveal a variation from the normal pattern through the insertion of different (though usually traditional) varieties of speech matter in the B and D slots. The fact that speech seems appropriate at these moments, however, arises out of the same logic as that which created the A-B-C-D pattern in the first place.

All of these contests pit human adversaries, and I conceive this to be a defining characteristic of the type of heroic contest I am examining. Struggles between the gods in Greek mythology or the Norse *Edda* fall into a separate category. Nonetheless, the *Iliad* does feature several contests between gods or between gods and men that resemble the battlefield heroic exchange. For example, after he has prevailed over Aineias, Diomedes stabs Aphrodite, who is in the process of carrying her favorite out of battle, and vaunts in fairly typical fashion (5.311–51). Achilles similarly engages in an exchange with the river Xanthos that has structural correlates of the major contest elements: Engagement (element A: 21.1–33, 136–38, 211–13), as the river becomes increasingly disturbed over the slaughter; a kind of Flyting (element B: 214–26), as the god and hero exchange threats and contract projections; a prolonged Combat (element C: 227–355), mythic rather than heroic and altogether unlike other fights in the poem; and a form of Resolution (element D: 356–82), as the river sues for peace. Actually, this exchange modulates from the man-versus-god to a god-versus-god pattern; for while the flyters are Achilles and Xanthos, combat pits the river's flood against Hephaistos's fire. In any event, both of these man-god contests are highly unusual and made possible only through the partisanship of the heroes' divine allies. For the most part, the *Iliad* attests to the impropriety of such conflict and the general powerlessness of man before the gods.

The Xanthos episode nonetheless launches a series of contests among the gods (21.383–513): between Ares and Athena, Athena and Aphrodite, Poseidon and Apollo, Hera and Artemis, and Hermes and Leto. Most of these have been discussed previously, even though they clearly lack essential battlefield characteristics. For example, combat between deities cannot be "mortal," either in intention or effect; it takes place in ambiguous relation to a recognizable battle site; and it joins members of a single community—indeed, close kin. Nonetheless, the exchanges proceed for the most part along lines that the battlefield contest pattern would predict. The reason is contextual: The gods are aping the style of conflict they have been watching on the earth. Through this displacement Homer hits an incongruous and comic note; at the same time he may be signaling the breakdown of order even in the heavens and thus building toward his epic climax. This parodic use of a traditional pattern illustrates the variety of effects and "artistic freedom" available to a bona fide master in a traditional medium.

Battlefield contesting—verbal and martial—is abundantly represented in the *Iliad*. Unfortunately, the far more limited corpus of Anglo-Saxon battle narrative provides us with only two examples, both of them fragmentary. From the incomplete flyting speech in the second, thirty-one line fragment of the Old English *Waldere* we can do no more than draw a few inferences. The flyting and combat in *The Battle of Maldon*, however, provide a valuable analogue for the Homeric battlefield contests. It too is broken off before completion; moreover, it contains several new features. Nonetheless, the basic flyting-to-fighting process is depicted in a clear and powerful form.

The *Waldere* fragments pick up the action at a climactic juncture of what was clearly a much longer poem.[36] The story, as gathered from analogues (especially the tenth-century Latin *Waltharius*), runs thus. Waldere of Aquitaine and his sweetheart Hildegyth, escaping from captivity, are waylaid by Guthhere, king of the Burgundians, and his men. After killing the Burgundians one by one, Waldere finds himself facing only Guthhere and his unwilling liege man, Hagen. The flyting speech in the last eighteen lines of the second Old English fragment fits at this juncture. In its opening passage Waldere, the speaker, dares Guthhere to attack him and try to strip the corselet from his shoulders (2.14–17). Here Waldere is simultaneously contracting for a fight and implying that his adversary could not win it; and he aggravates this insinuation of Guthhere's martial inferiority by characterizing himself as "heaðuwerigean" (2.17, "battle weary"), as well he might be after having defeated the Frankish king's entire force single-handedly. In a mere three lines, then, Waldere has set forth both the quarrel and contract. Now he chooses to dilate for another seven lines (18–24) on the virtues of that corselet that would stand, for Guthhere, as the prize of victory; since Waldere is implicitly denying that his opponent can succeed against him, this flaunting of his armor amounts to a taunt. The passage as a whole corroborates my speculation earlier that armor stripping may be integral to the Old English flyting-fighting contest, as it plainly is to the Iliadic. The final lines before the fragment ends (2.25–31) provide one of the best expressions in Old English poetry of the theme that God presides over contests and can grant victory where he likes. It is a pity that the fragment does not contain the remainder of Waldere's speech and Guthhere's reply, if there was one. Yet the little that we have shows the flyting process plainly at work. Further, if the Latin analogue can be trusted on this point, Waldere's battle contract was ratified and honored in the deed, for he, Guthhere, and Hagen fought until all three were wounded. In the end, however, like Hektor and Aias in *Il*.7.206–312, they made their peace.

The contest pattern is represented in *Waldere* in only a brief moment of its flyting phase. *Maldon*, however, while incomplete at its beginning and end, nonetheless depicts the contest process more fully. Let us review the progress of this encounter, which centers on the contractual interactions between Byrhtnoth and the Viking invaders.

The Engagement element (A) is set forth in 25–28, as the Viking messenger advances to address Byrhtnoth, with whom the poem's no doubt partisan English auditors are already familiar. There follows a Flyting (element B: 29–61) that illustrates the eristic and contractual movements particularly well. Trying like many of the Homeric heroes to intimidate his adversaries, in this case the English, the Viking messenger urges them to abandon resistance and to buy peace; for (31b–33b)

> . . . eow betere is
> þæt ge þisne garræs   mid gafole forgyldon
> þon[ne] we swa hearde   [hi]lde dælon.

> . . . it is better for you
> that you buy off this rush of spears with tribute
> Than that we, as fierce [as we are], should engage [you] in battle.

The eristic motive manifests in the messenger's representation of his own force as superior in battle: The English, so he implies, could not match them there. Yet his overt aim is contractual—to induce Byrhtnoth to capitulate to the Vikings' terms of tribute. Thus he is extending two contract possibilities, a preferred option (an English surrender) and a default option (battle). In a speech far more eristically toned than that of his adversary, Byrhtnoth vigorously rejects the former alternative, for such a course of action would be "shameful" ("heanlic," 55), and endorses the second contractual option with a grim metaphor: Spears are the only form of payment that the Vikings can expect (46-48). This sequence resembles the first two speeches of the Euphorbos-Menelaos exchange (*Il*.17.12–32), in which the Trojan first tries to discourage his enemy from interfering with his attempt to strip Patroklos's armor, while Menelaos refuses to be intimidated. As in the *Maldon* episode, Euphorbos's speech is more contractually and Menelaos's more eristically toned.

There is a sequel, however. Finding themselves unable to advance across the channel, the Vikings request free passage, which Byrhtnoth in his *ofermode* grants them (93–95):[37]

> "Nu eow is gerymed: gað ricene to us
> guman to guþe.   God ana wat
> hwa þære wælstowe   wealdon mote."

> "Now it is made clear for you; go quickly to us,
> [you] men to battle. God alone knows
> who may be allowed rule the slaughter-place."

In effect, the Vikings have requested a codicillary contract provision—that the contest be fought on "equal" terms through English forfeiture of a tactical advantage; to this Byrhtnoth agrees.[38] His decision accords with the heroic insistence on openness and fairness in contests. Whether heroic considerations ought to have been paramount at this juncture is, of course, another question altogether.

While the *Maldon* exchange illustrates the eristic and contractual principles of flyting, it lacks the personal orientation of its Homeric counterparts. The messenger, for example, is never identified by name; further, both he and Byrhtnoth represent themselves as speaking not personally but on behalf of their forces. In the following battle, the two of them, so far as we know, never square off against one another; thus the flyting has not projected any single combat but rather a mass encounter. The fighting, however, is narrated largely in terms of individual attacks: Byrhtnoth's death struggle begins with a single encounter (130–48), and the warrior who subsequently deals him his next blow is in turn killed by Wulfstan (149–58). Yet the style of combat—or combat narrative—that we find in *Maldon* does not seem to provide the same scope as Homeric narrative does for flyting-to-fighting encounters involving just two men. Further, the emerging sense of English nationhood by the late tenth or early eleventh century may have invested the idea of honor with a larger communal content. Thus, flyting with its contractual entailments would be more *ad gentem* than *ad hominem*.

At the same time, the idea of honor continues to carry major personal entailments, as *Maldon* repeatedly emphasizes. For immediately after the death of Byrhtnoth, Godric and his brothers flee from battle, an act the poet explicitly condemns, pointing out that it belies earlier boasts made in the mead hall.[39] There follows a series of speeches by Ælfwine, Offa, Leofsunu, and Dunnere that reaffirm martial commitments; Ælfwine in particular stresses the need to fulfill mead-hall promises to the lord (212–15). As has often been noted, these same themes appear during the dragon episode in *Beowulf*, in the exhortation and later reproach that Wiglaf addresses to the aging Geatish king's unfaithful retainers (2633–60 and 2864–91). We cannot, of course, assume that mead-hall boasting necessarily constitutes a form of flyting. The drinking contest in *Örvar-Odds saga*[40] exemplifies mead-hall flyting, but of a ludic sort that does not bring with it martial entailments. In the *Alliterative Morte Arthure*, however, Arthur's vassals reaffirm their willingness to fight for him in a series of speeches that, while they engender martial commitments, do not in any direct way imply mutual competition. The precise relationship between mead-hall boasting and flyting merits closer study. Yet the boasting and allusions to boasting in *Maldon* do clearly attest to the force of the moral imperative that words be substantiated by deeds, a force out of which, as I have argued, the contest paradigm arises.

The element of postcombat vaunting (element D1) is missing from *Maldon* as we now have it. Because the poem is incomplete, it is always possible that a literary termination to the battle could have featured boasting, vain defiance, armor stripping, corpse mutilation, and other motifs that we have seen in the *Iliad*. Nonetheless, Byrhtnoth does offer a prayer to God (173–80) just before dying, at the moment that, in an Iliadic contest, we might have expected to find a vaunting exchange between victor and vanquished. Several reasons for this substitution might be proposed. First, the *Maldon* poet is far more partisan than Homer; consequently, he and his audience might have been repelled by the prospect of verbal abuse added to military defeat. More significant, the poem registers a clear strain of Christian piety. The habit of boasting over dying enemies represents a particularly virulent breed of vengefulness that is difficult to reconcile to the principle of Christian *caritas*. Accordingly, one might expect to find this element in the heroic pattern softened and eventually displaced in the evolution of the Anglo-Saxon poetic tradition. The substitution of a prayer to God in lieu of a vaunting exchange would, however, situate Byrhtnoth creditably in a Christian salvific context. In the same stroke it would provide an interpretive comeback to a defeat that must have grated on the sensibilities of a residually heroic society and that any hero would have to answer in some way.[41]

As a group, these battlefield episodes illustrate a common system of relations: prospective flyting that proposes a martial test; combat of a lethal variety that carries through on the flyting contract; and postcombat speech that provides interpretations of what has just occurred. In fact, it is through this battlefield variant that heroic contesting finds its freest and most uninhibited expression. Let us now turn to a form of contesting in which the heroes' movements are more circumscribed.

THE GUEST-HOST VARIANT OF THE CONTEST THEME

Heroic contests, despite the individualistic movements that they accommodate, belong to a highly socialized mode of behavior, and different social environments impose different sets of restrictions. Contestants in battlefield settings are free to give full expression to aggression and violence—indeed, they are constrained to do so—for shirking from battle counts as a serious offense. Yet when flyting breaks out between warriors representing different communities that are engaged in guest-host bonding, the scope of the conflict is far more circumscribed.

Hospitality is a major theme in its own right, not only in ancient Greece and England, but in many early societies, for in a world without advanced communications, peaceable intertribal relations depended on the guest-host bond. *Beowulf* brings this relationship into prominence in the interactions between the Geatish hero and the Danish king Hrothgar. In the *Odyssey*, the guest-host exchange comprises one of the central paradigms: Odysseus tries to engage in it in almost all of his island encounters and even accosts the pseudohost suitors in this way.[42] In fact, numerous episodes in both narrative traditions suggest that the power of guest-host bonding compares with that of an agonistic relationship. Because hospitality demands peace while flyting tends to war, verbal dueling in guest-host settings brings out deep tensions that the bonding communities need to defuse. Thus guest-host flyting generally observes conventions designed to contain contestational aggression.

Superb examples of this specialized guest-host contesting are found in the encounters between Odysseus and Euryalos on the island of the Phaiakians and between Beowulf and Unferth in the court of the Danes. Each of these interactions is permitted to take its course, but only within limits—for the contesting cannot be allowed to jeopardize the larger process of guest-host bonding. In its abstract outlines, the guest-host (gh) contest pattern proceeds thus:

A$^{gh.}$ *Engagement.* G, a visiting party of one or more warriors, engages in guest-host interactions at the home of *H*, the hosting tribe. Hero *g*, the leader of *G*, and *h*, the leader of *H*, are marked out as principals.

B$^{gh.}$ *Flyting.* Hero *h′* provokes *g* into a flyting exchange. Hero *h′* is a member of the hosting party (*H*) yet nonconsanguineous with *h* himself. The flyting has two aspects:

1. *eris*—*g* and *h′* contend for *kleos* or glory; and
2. *contract*—*g* and *h′* implicitly or explicitly agree on *X* as the test for their quarrel. *X* is a trial of arms or other manly enterprise that does *not* entail direct, mortal combat between *g* and *h′*.

C$^{gh.}$ *Trial of arms.* Warrior *g* proves his superiority to *h′* with respect to *X*.

V$^{gh.}$ *Vaunt.* Hero *g* boasts of his victory.

D$^{gh.}$ *Ritual resolution.* Heroes *g*, *h*, and *h′* terminate the quarrel and renew guest-host interactions through:

1. *verbal contracts of friendship*: *h′* tries to restore peace by (directly or indirectly) apologizing for his earlier affront and by offering *g* a gift; *g* verbally accepts the offer of friendship.
2. *symbolic action*: *h* and *h′* give *g* gifts (as corporal acts).

This contest pattern, in overview, introduces four new features: h', X, V, and the gift-giving resolution. The articulation of an h' distinct from h helps to establish a ritual distance between the host and the contest. The *Odyssey*, in fact, provides an explicit statement concerning the impropriety of contests between host and guest. Odysseus, having just defeated the Phaiakians in the discus throw, offers to compete in boxing or wrestling or running with any one of them—except for Laodamas, the son of Alkinoös (*Od*.8.208–11):

ξεῖνος γάρ μοι ὅδ᾽ ἐστί· τίς ἂν φιλέοντι μάχοιτο;
ἄφρων δὴ κεῖνός γε καὶ οὐτιδανὸς πέλει ἀνήρ,
ὅς τις ξεινοδόκῳ ἔριδα προφέρηται ἀέθλων
δήμῳ ἐν ἀλλοδαπῷ· ἕο δ᾽ αὐτοῦ πάντα κολούει.

For he is my host; who would fight with a friend?
Indeed, foolish and worthless is that man
who promotes strife [ἔριδα] at contests with his host
among a foreign people. He denies himself all things.

Even though Odysseus in this speech seems to confer the title of host upon Laodamas, clearly the presiding host figure is Alkinoös himself; Odysseus evidently feels that the ban on guest-host fighting should extend to members of Alkinoös's family. Because Euryalos, the h' figure in this flyting episode, is never represented as consanguineous with the royal family, Alkinoös need not personally be implicated in the Odysseus-Euryalos quarrel except in his broader function as king and upholder of the law.

The other distinctive guest-host features likewise serve to distance the contest from its social environment. For example, the indirect character of the Trial of Arms helps to free both the hosting and visiting parties from serious embroilment in a hostile exchange: Because g and h' do not kill each other, G and H will not need to exact vengeance. Of course, the test X that the flyters propose might involve considerable hazard; yet neither g nor h can be held directly responsible. The victory boast, a provocative element in the battlefield pattern, remains vestigially. Yet now as V^{gh} it has been extracted from the ritualized closing sequence, since its presence there would make it difficult for G and H to resume their guest-host interactions; its new purpose is not to terminate the contest but, more narrowly, to establish g's victory as spoken public fact. The new gift-giving resolution (D^{gh}) symbolizes the termination of adversarial relations and the reinauguration of friendship between g/G and h/H. When the guest-host contest ends, it ends.

The examples of guest-host contesting in our focal material, though few in number, are both distributed between the two traditions and highly developed; the parallels between them are too extensive to be attributable to mere coincidence. The episodes center on the two guest-figures, Beowulf and Odysseus, who, after sea voyages, reach shore and travel inland to the homes of their prospective hosts, the Danes and the Phaiakians (A^{gh}).[43] Beowulf arrives at the head of a band of retainers. Odysseus travels alone; yet he remains still the prince of his kingdom, and the Phaiakians recognize and entertain him as such. Thus the G (guest party) element persists at the generic level even though Odysseus's companions have perished in fact.[44] These episodes of the hero's arrival and progress through encounters with his host belong to the guest-host exchange and do not in themselves carry any agonistic implications.

But now the quarreling (B^{gh}) begins. In scenes of feasting and entertainment, two new men from the hosting parties, Euryalos and Unferth (the h' figures), are brought into the foreground. Unferth is the Danish *thyle*, apparently a noteworthy role or office whose precise nature has been much disputed.[45] Euryalos is a Phaiakian youth who has recently distinguished himself by surpassing all his fellows in wrestling (8.126–27). Unferth, evidently disgruntled, is moved to "unbind his battle-runes" ("onband beadorune," 501) by his displeasure that "any other man should ever carry out more glorious deeds [*mærða*] in the middle-earth than he himself" (503–5). Euryalos is drawn into the interaction by his friend and Alkinoös's son Laodamas, who extends to Odysseus the initial invitation (8.145–51) to join in the athletic competition that has been in progress for some time. Although Laodamas speaks in fair terms, Odysseus construes this invitation as mockery ("κερτομέοντες," 8.153); yet later on, as we have seen, he explicitly refuses to compete with Laodamas, his host and host's son. In both poems, then, the distance between the principal host and the competition in which his guest engages has been maintained.

In their subsequent flyting speeches, Euryalos and Unferth explicitly question their guests' athletic-martial competence and cast aspersions on their abilities to perform the test (X) that the present situation seems to designate (*Beo.*506–28 and *Od.*8.158–64), while in reply Odysseus and Beowulf defend themselves on both accounts (*Beo.*530–606 and *Od.*8.166–85).[46] Thus the flyters in both episodes have contracted on X as a test for their quarrels: g will try to surpass h' with respect to his ability to perform X. In the Odyssean example, of course, X is the athletic competition initiated by Alkinoös the host. In *Beowulf*, X is the fight against Grendel, an enterprise dictated by the Danes' recent misfortunes; we are given to understand, more-

over, that Hrothgar, like Alkinoös, has authority over the contest in
that warriors must apparently secure at least his tacit consent before
undertaking it.[47] Neither of these tests will pit the g and h' figures
against one another in direct combat; yet the competitive dimension
to both enterprises is made plain. For Euryalos, having recently displayed his own athletic prowess, implies a personal comparison when
he remarks that the visitor does not have the appearance of an athlete
(8.164); and Odysseus, after proving his skill in the discus throw,
claims that he could defeat present company (including, of course,
Euryalos) in archery and spear throwing as well. Similarly, Beowulf's
intention to overthrow Grendel is construed by Unferth as a personal
insult ("æfþunca," 502); Beowulf, in turn, points out that Grendel
could never have ravaged Heorot as he has done "if your valor were
. . . as you yourself report" ("gif þin hyge wære . . . swa þu self talast,"
593–94). In point of fact, Unferth has made no explicit verbal claims
for himself; yet his very willingness to flyt with Beowulf implies a personal challenge and comparison, as the warrior witnesses know full
well. Thus the eristic and contractual motives of flyting are in full
force, even though the test is outwardly directed and less visibly man-
against-man than is the case in the battlefield contest pattern.

Beowulf and Odysseus undertake the martial or athletic trials that
they had contracted on, and both men prevail (C^{gh}). Yet the two episodes differ appreciably in their scale and importance. On the one
hand, Odysseus's victory—a relatively minor incident in the *Odyssey* as
a whole—requires no more than the toss of a discus, narrated in eight
lines (8.186–93) that follow immediately after the flyting. Beowulf's
struggle with Grendel, on the other hand, is separated from the flyting by more than one hundred lines, occupies over one hundred lines
in itself, and constitutes one of the three great climaxes of the epic.
Further, whereas Odysseus was drawn into the competition solely by
Euryalos's goading, Beowulf's flyting with Unferth created merely
one of the several "weaves" that bound him to this heroic undertaking; for Beowulf had already committed himself, through his
speeches to the coastguard and Hrothgar, and through his very journey to Denmark in the first place. In other words, the contest pattern
can be developed to various degrees and its elements worked individually to suit the poet's larger designs. This is possible because the root
principle that deeds should match words, which creates the force
binding the B and C elements, defines a flexible relationship that can
be shaped to suit particular plot circumstances.

In the Odysseus-Euryalos episode the victory boast (V^{gh}) receives
considerable foregrounding as the Ithakan in a thirty-two-line speech
(8.202–33) asserts his superiority to all of the Phaiakians in archery

and discus and spear throwing (though not, he concedes, in running). Beowulf, for his part, avoids comparing himself, in the wake of his victory over Grendel, with his less successful Danish rival. Nonetheless, Beowulf does rehearse to Hrothgar a brief account of his triumph (958–79), and the *Beowulf* poet follows up this speech immediately with the comment:

> Ða wæs swigra secg,   sunu Ec[g]lafes,
> on gylpspræce   guðgeweorca . . . (980–81)

> Then was that man, the son of Ecglaf, more silent
> in the boasting of battle-works . . .

In short, the poet himself has made the comparison from which Beowulf has tactfully refrained. Later, in the gift-giving scene (element D), the poet reinforces this comparison when he indicates that Unferth has forfeited glory ("dome forleas," 1470) through his unwillingness to brave the perils of the "waves' turmoil" (i.e., Grendel's Mere) as Beowulf was at this moment about to do (1468–72). These narratorial intrusions, I am suggesting, arise from the structural need to realize the V^{gh} element in some form: The fact that Beowulf has prevailed not only over Grendel but also over his Danish flyting adversary has to be declared in speech, established as spoken fact. Since Beowulf himself is keeping silence on the matter—no doubt in the interests of good relations with his Danish hosts—this victory boast, reduced out of direct discourse, has reverted to the poetic narrator.

The Beowulf-Unferth and Odysseus-Euryalos episodes end with another striking set of parallels. Some seven hundred lines after the conclusion of his fight with Grendel and immediately after the displaced vaunt (V^{gh}), while Beowulf is in the process of arming for combat against Grendel's mother, Unferth offers him a precious heirloom, the sword Hrunting (1455–64). The poem does not refer to any speech of gift giving on Unferth's part, although clearly the situation would have required something of the kind; it does, however, quote Beowulf's speech of thanks and acceptance for this and Hrothgar's assorted gifts (1474–91). Nor does Unferth apologize for his earlier affront; however, the *Beowulf* poet rationalizes this, pointing out that the Danish *thyle* cannot remember his own previous insults spoken under the influence of drink, even though the contest had cost him glory (1465–72). This detail of Unferth's "forgetting" the flyting exchange (as the narrator quite pointedly refuses to do) may reflect at a surface level an underlying structural event—ritual closure of the contest. For the Danes and Geats need to "forgive and forget," leaving verbal disputation behind them. In the parallel Odyssean sequence, D^{gh} begins (some one hundred fifty lines after the conclusion of the athletic competition) with Euryalos's apology and offer—once again—of a sword (8.401–11); Odysseus accepts this gift (as he had already accepted those of Alkinoös) and affirms friendship (413–15). In both episodes, then, the contesting has been brought to a close and the relationship reestablished on their earlier, guest-host grounding.

MODULATIONS FROM BATTLEFIELD TO GUEST-HOST PATTERNS

The battlefield and guest-host patterns provide the two dominant pathways in the realization of epic contests, at least in the material under review. Yet the Homeric and Old English heroic traditions both seem to have recognized within the logic of the battlefield pattern itself the possibility of modulation into the guest-host channel. In this section we will examine three cases of such track shifting, two from the *Iliad* and one from *Beowulf*. Modulation in the opposite direction, from the guest-host to the battlefield modes, seems to represent something of a breach of good faith and thus does not belong to the category of legitimate, "contractualized" contesting. The phenomenon does occur nonetheless; we will consider examples in the next section.

The comparative methodology underlying this study is again, in my view, vindicated by the parallels between the two most outstanding instances of this shifting from the battlefield to the guest-host modes, the Glaukos-Diomedes exchange in *Il*.6.119–236 and the encounter between Beowulf and the Danish coastguard in *Beowulf* 229–319.[48] In both cases the interaction hinges on flyting contract. At the opening of the Iliadic flyting exchange (B^{bf}), Diomedes in an eristic address demands that his opponent identify himself, proposing to kill him if he is mortal but refusing to fight if he is a god (6.123–43). The principle of comparability is asserting itself here, for the Achaian, as advised by Athena earlier (5.124–32), will not commit himself to a hopeless mismatch of mortal versus immortal.[49] Accordingly, he has extended two contractual possibilities, one combative and violent, the other irenic; nonetheless, he arrogates to himself the right to choose which it will be, although this choice will be based on the information that his adversary gives him. Glaukos, in the way of self-identification, supplies an extended review of his own ancestry (145–211). Diomedes now realizes that they are bound by ancestral friendship ties, since his own grandfather, Oineus, had for twenty days hosted Glaukos's grandfather Bellerophon, to whose doings most of Glaukos's genealogical account had been devoted. Accordingly, Diomedes sets aside his spear and proposes a new contract of friendship, which Glaukos accepts (212–36). The flyters have thus bypassed the Trial of Arms, progressing directly from B^{bf} to D^{gh}. What legitimates this short-circuiting of the contest process is the power of the ancestrally descending friendship bond; although the present exchange occurs in the battlefield setting, it evokes the imagery of hospitality through allusion to successful guest-host relations between grandfathers in the past (215–23) and through explicit reference to the possibility of guest-host relations between Glaukos and Diomedes themselves in the future (224–25). The interaction concludes (D2) with an embrace and an exchange of gifts—in this instance armor rather than swords. Thus, as in the guest-host pattern, the quarrel has been ritually and symbolically set to rest.[50]

This same movement directly from flyting to a compact of friendship appears in Beowulf's encounter with the Danish *weard*. Like the Diomedes-Glaukos encounter, this episode locates itself in a suitable battlfield setting, the beach. Like Diomedes, the Danish coastguard opens the exchange by demanding who his potential adversary might be (237–40). Although in the speech that follows he does not spell out the contractual alternatives as explicitly as his Achaian counterpart had done, the gist of his message could not be plainer: The Geats must accede to Danish authority or prepare to fight (240–57). Like Glaukos, Beowulf incorporates genealogical information into his reply (260–85): He is a Geat and a son of the well-known "ordfruma" (leader) Ecgtheow, who, as we later discover, had reason to be grateful to Hrothgar, the coastguard's master. Out of this background of intertribal friendship, Beowulf comes to Hrothgar with friendly intention ("holdne hige," 267) to offer counsel with respect to the "sceaða" (enemy) now afflicting the Danes. At this juncture the coastguard, like Diomedes, feels prepared to abort the contest, skipping the Trial of Arms in a movement directly from B^{bf} to D^{gh}. As only a deputy for Hrothgar, he lacks the authority to seal friendship with an exchange of gifts; instead, he guides Beowulf and his companions to Heorot and promises to guard their ship—gift giving, we might say, according to his role and capacity. The power of diachrony in Beowulf's ancestral reference reemerges in the following scene when Hrothgar, recollecting the timely protection and support that he had extended to Ecgtheow during his (Ecgtheow's) difficult feud with the Wylfings, expresses the expectation, based on Ecgtheow's oaths ("aþas," 472) which apparently in some fashion devolve upon his son, that Beowulf comes to aid him in his struggle with Grendel (372–89 and 457–72); and he welcomes and entertains Beowulf accordingly.

Thus *Beowulf* actualizes within its own narrative that guest-host exchange that the Diomedes-Glaukos dialogue had only proposed.

Both of these encounters modulate from the battlefield to the guest-host patterns at the contractual stage. However, the first Hektor-Aias contest (*Il.* 7.219–307), embedded within the larger structure of a formally negotiated single combat between champions of the two armies, progresses fairly conventionally through the flyting (element B^{bf}, 7.226–43), in which the two heroes contract on direct combat, to an extensively developed and even sanguinary fighting exchange (element C^{bf}, 244–73). At this juncture, however, Zeus's heralds intervene, instructing them to stop fighting for the night (274–82). The two heroes agree to this, and of their own initiative exchange gifts (a sword for a warbelt) and part "in friendship" ("ἐν φιλότητι," 302) to fight again at a later occasion ("ὕστερον αὖτε μαχησόμεθ'," 291). Thus again the D^{gh} resolution seems to provide the best mechanism for resolving contests in which the two contestants are still alive and hale. This type of movement from the battlefield to the guest-host pattern while combat is in midcourse occurs rarely and, when it does, requires strong motivation if the heroes are to escape the charge of having weakened and succumbed to cowardice. In some cases, as the encounter of Gawain and Priamus in the *Alliterative Morte Arthure* (2513–2669), fine performance in battle engenders a mutual respect that culminates in friendship (and, in Priamus's case, defection to the Briton cause). Perhaps we would have found the same thing in the Old English *Waldere* if its fragments had included the fight between Waldere, Guthhere, and Hagen. In any event, the reconciliation in the Hektor-Aias episode is directly dictated from on high, by Zeus who holds both men dear (*Il.*7.280). Here as in many other cases in the *Iliad*, the normal progress of contesting is altered by the meddling of the gods.

MODULATIONS FROM GUEST-HOST TO BATTLEFIELD PATTERNS

As we have seen, contests in the battlefield pattern can modulate fairly easily and naturally into the guest-host mold, if the contestants discover grounds to justify this movement. The reverse, however, is not true: The shift from guest-host to battlefield contesting seems ordinarily to represent a breakdown in relations rather than a socially legitimated flyting-to-fighting pathway. This asymmetry is due to the greater fragility of the guest-host relationship, for it is possible for heroes in a battlefield situation to negotiate a peaceful settlement without harm to their armies, as long as no serious forfeiture of honor or strategic advantage is involved. Fighting, after all, can always be resumed on another day, as Hektor points out to Aias (*Il*.7.288–92). Guest-host interactions, on the other hand, transpire in someone's immediate home environment, where an outbreak of armed conflict would be particularly ruinous. As we have already observed, it is in the long-term interest of communities such as are represented in *Beowulf* or the Homeric epos to insist on the sacredness of the guest-host trust, for otherwise foreign relations would be difficult to sustain. And so intertribal flytings, reeking of xenophobia and nursing old grievances, must be suppressed; or if this proves impossible, their conventions must ensure the inviolability of a ritualized distance between the contesting and the guest-host bonding, each to proceed in its sphere.

Nonetheless, ancient societies were fully aware that old feuds or newly budding quarrels might defy such containment; and their literatures often dramatize this problem. We have already noted Diodorus of Sicily's account of the ancient Gauls, who, he said, would entertain strangers at their feasts and then afterward quarrel and challenge them to single combat, often with sanguinary results (5.28.5–6). Diodorus does not suggest that the Gauls felt in any way inhibited about killing off their guests in this manner; his history may be less than fully reliable on this point, however, since he is engaged in describing some of the more colorful habits of a foreign people and might not have appreciated or felt himself obligated to represent the subtle systems of social control usually operative in such situations. Also bearing on the Celtic world (though from a much later period), the *Scél Mucci Mic Dathó* (in N. Chadwick 1927) narrates a highly flamboyant flyting that culminates in a battle between members of two rival groups of guests, the men of Connaught and the men of Ulster, who are both enjoying the hospitality of Mac Dathó. Other examples could be cited to illustrate the intrusion of full-scale, deadly combat in guest-host settings. Nonetheless the general observation holds, that this type of environment discourages such violent exchanges; and when they do break out, they are usually deficient as formal contests, on one account or another. Thus the Old Eddic *Atlakviða*, which tells of the visit that the Burgundians Gunnar and Hogni pay to the court of Atli the Hun and their subsequent betrayal and murder there, does not contain what we could properly call a contest, despite the gruesome action and fierce dialogue. The subject rather concerns the Burgundians' defiance and fearlessness in the face of torture. The same might be said of those other instances of treachery in the *Edda* and elsewhere in which victory is secured more through cunning and deceit than through open heroic display in the contesting mode.

One of the most fascinating early Germanic dramatizations of the tension between the codes of hospitality and vengeance appears in Paul the Deacon's *Historia Langobardorum* 1.23–24. Here Alboin, son of Audoin of the Langobards, pays a visit to Turisind of the Gepidae, in accordance with Audoin's insistence that his son receive arms from the king of a foreign nation. The complication lies in that Alboin had recently killed Turisind's son Turismod in battle; exacerbating the problem, Alboin, when he arrives with forty retainers at the court of the Gepidae, chooses to occupy Turismod's former seat at the banquet. An exchange of insults breaks out between the two parties; but before the argument can come to blows, Turisind interrupts it, vowing the death penalty for any of his own following who resort to violence, and stressing that guest killing is displeasing to God. After what then becomes a friendly and high-spirited feast, Turisind confers on Alboin the arms of his son and sends him home unharmed. Both men, we are told, won high praise for their behavior in this encounter. Thus the figure of greatest authority and responsibility— the equivalent of Alkinoös in book 8 of the *Odyssey*—squelches what he recognizes as a virulent battlefield form of flyting before it can have deadly issue; although Alkinoös did not feel himself thus obligated to circumvent a contest that was in that instance merely athletic rather than martial and that lacked the prior history, like Turisind he does act to uphold the peace by insisting that Euryalos apologize after the fact (*Od*.8.396–97; cf. 8.236–40). What makes Paul's account particularly remarkable, however, is its stark clash of obligations yielding a judgment in favor of the guest-host bond. Whatever may have been the usual practice of early Germanic kings, the mere existence of such a story illustrates the esteem in which this relationship was held.

Surviving Old English heroic narrative does not, unfortunately, provide us with any fully told breakdowns in the guest-host process, though allusions and legends suggest that the problem interested Anglo-Saxon storytellers. The closest approximations of modulations between guest-host and battlefield patterns occur in the Finnsburg Episode in *Beowulf* (1066–1159) and in *The Fight at Finnsburg*.[51] Unfortunately for my purposes, the *Beowulf* poet tells this story synoptically, offering relatively few details about the fighting and no dialogue, flyting or otherwise. Also *The Fight at Finnsburg*, while narrated directly and scenically, survives only as a forty-eight-line fragment with the antecedents and upshot of the struggle left untold. Yet despite the ambiguities a common story line emerges, beginning with the surprise nighttime attack that the Frisians, under the leadership of Finn, unleash on their Danish guests.[52] Neither poem provides us with an unambiguous narratorial judgment on the ethical propriety of such behavior,[53] though both points of view seem sympathetic to the Danes. Clearly, nonetheless, the Frisian tactics were designed with a massacre, not a ritual contest, in mind. At this juncture the fragment breaks off, with this first (five-day) battle still in progress; yet the episode traces the story on through the subsequent uneasy truce between the two parties, confirmed by oaths ("fæste frioðuwære," 1096), to a resumption of hostilities in which Finn is killed and the Danish injuries avenged. Of course, this synopsis glosses over many problems of detail engendered by the highly allusive style at this turn of the *Beowulf* narrative.[54] Nonetheless, we can assert with some confidence that the larger story in both versions turns on themes of treachery rather than the establishment of heroic identity through open, public contesting.

The Fight at Finnsburg does nonetheless crystallize into what we might call an incipient flyting moment. At the beginning of the attack a Frisian named Garulf, against the advice of Guthere, calls out to the Danish opposition within the hall, asking who holds the door against him. The reply, unlike his inquiry, is presented in direct discourse (24–27):

> "Sigeferþ is min nama,"   (cweþ he,) "ic eom Secgena leod,
> wreccea wide cuð;   fæla ic weana gebad,
> heordra hilda;   ðe is gyt her witod,
> swæþer ðu sylf   to me secean wylle."

> "Sigeferth is my name," he said, "I am a man of the Secgans,
> an exile widely known; I have endured many woes
> and hard battles; it is already here ordained for you
> which of two things you will gain from me."[55]

By the analysis to be set forth in the next chapter, this address contains three elements characteristic of flyting speeches: the speaker's self-identification; his recollection of past heroic accomplishment; and his projection concerning an anticipated martial test. Both the eristic and contractual motives come into play: The Dane is bringing his heroic identity into view so that it can be measured in battle against that of his adversary. The flyting is incompletely developed in that Garulf's speech is not given in direct discourse, and thus his participation in the quarreling and contracting must simply be inferred. Although the ensuing battle is narrated with a minimum of detail, we do learn that Garulf was the first to fall. Sigeferth has not been identified as his killer, it is true. Yet the fact that the poet chooses to supply us with this one name from what was apparently an extensive death roll (see ll.33–35) probably reflects the influence of an underlying battlefield flyting-to-fighting movement: Since battlefield flyting proposes the comparison of the two heroes through direct combat, their subsequent fortunes of war would naturally come to the foreground of narrative interest, even when (as in this case) the precise agents of success and downfall are left unspecified. In summary, then, *The Fight at Finnsburg* seems to instantiate a movement from an initial betrayal of guest-host bonds into a martial encounter in which battlefield contesting can begin to take place. Yet since this movement is incompletely represented in our fragmentary text, it is difficult to ascertain precisely what mechanisms of social control—inhibitory or otherwise—might have been involved.

In the Homeric material, however, the evidence is much richer. This is particularly true for the *Odyssey*, in which the guest-host exchange, whether honored or abused, provides the basic framework for most of Odysseus's island encounters.[56] Whenever feasible, Odysseus usually tries to uphold guest-host proprieties, since it is clearly in his best interests to do so; and thus his contesting with Euryalos on the island of the Phaiakians takes a form compatible with this mode of exchange, as we saw earlier. His encounter with Circe does not qualify as a heroic contest, as I have defined it here, but as a covert struggle waged within the context of guest-host formalities. On the other hand, his encounters with the Kikonians and the Laistrygonians are not so much agonistic as marauding or, in the latter case, downright predatorial (the Laistrygonians, Odysseus tells us, speared his men like fish and carried them off for their feasting, 10.124). Neither of these episodes depict flyting or single combat in any form. In general, most Odyssean encounters are defined in terms of either the successful establishment of guest-host relations or their failure. The ascendancy of the guest-host paradigm often limits aggression; when guest-friendship breaks down, uncontained violence erupts. In neither case is aggression structured along formal, agonistic lines.

In the Polyphemos episode, on the other hand, we do find the real beginnings of a movement from the guest-host to the battlefield mode, although this movement never completes itself and finishes on a confused and ambiguous note. Through the earlier part of the encounter, nonetheless, Odysseus—as on other occasions—assiduously avoids contesting. Even after Polyphemos has expressed open contempt for Zeus, the gods, and all claims of hospitality (*Od.*9.273–80) and has eaten several of Odysseus's men, the calculating Ithakan persists in defining their relationship in guest-host terms, offering a gift of wine and revealing his name to be "Nobody" ("Οὖτιν," 9.369) in exchange for a "guest-gift" ("ξείνιον," 365). Until this point, then, the impulse toward flyting and open agonistic display has been muzzled, despite the violence that is in fact taking place.

After Odysseus's escape, however, a curious contest ensues. Odysseus initiates this dialogic sequence (9.473–542) by taunting his former host, now blind at his cave door. In reply Polyphemos casts a stone that misses Odysseus's ship narrowly; and this leads to a kind of pseudoflyting (500–35) in which the adversaries work at cross-purposes in their rival interpretations as to where in the contest process they currently are. Odysseus begins again by naming himself, accurately this time. The Cyclops, after lamenting the fulfillment of an old prophecy, now tries to lure his crafty foe back by offering to renew guest-host relations. The Ithakan rudely and eristically rejects this offer; Polyphemos prays to his father Poseidon and throws another stone, which misses once again. As a formal contest, this episode is defective on several accounts. Despite the fact that his "martial victory" over the Cyclops was not achieved in the formalized heroic manner, Odysseus evidently conceives this exchange as an occasion for boasting over his accomplishment (D^{bf}), as Hektor did over Patroklos or Achilles over Hektor; certainly he does not wish to contract for a new battle. Polyphemos, however, wants to construe the verbal exchange as prebattle flyting (B^{bf}) to be consummated by martial display (stone throwing); yet hedging his bets, he tries deceitfully to contract for a modulation from a battlefield to a guest-host pattern: Let's quit fighting and be friends. His prayer and curse, finally, could be interpreted as a loser's malediction within the D^{bf} dialogue, such as the dying Patroklos addressed to Hektor and Hektor in turn to Achilles. Thus, the Cyclops has capitulated in the end to the definition that Odysseus in his earlier "postbattle" vaunt has given to the interaction. So the contest theme has at last emerged into the foreground, if only in its final stage; yet because of the ritual violations producing it, its expression is confused and unsatisfying. Of course, this very lack of closure serves the larger designs of the poem, since most of Odysseus's subsequent difficulties result from this unfortunate meeting.

After Odysseus has landed in Ithaka, fitful and usually abortive movements out of the guest-host toward the battlefield contest mode begin to compose an important motif. In fact, this emergence is motivated by the deeper structural exigencies of *return song* sequence, one of the major mythic patterns in world literature of which the *Odyssey* represents an outstanding instance.[57] In its barest outlines, the story runs thus. A hero and ruler in his own district becomes separated from his young bride (or bride-to-be) by a summons to battle and subsequently languishes in captivity in some foreign land. Liberated at last, he embarks on his *nostos* (return) and arrives after an indeterminate period at the boundaries of his kingdom.[58] Assuming a disguise, he returns home and tests the loyalty of his wife, his household, and the ruler-substitute who has usurped his role during his absence. At length he declares himself, vanquishes the imposter king, and reunites with his consort. The dynamics of this myth arise from a tension of identities: The hero has long been alienated from his proper role of ruler and householder and thus has become, from the generic standpoint, "nobody" indeed. How is he to regain his public identity, particularly since his office has been usurped? The *Odyssey* further complicates this already ambiguous situation by establishing a collective body, the suitors, in the role of ruler-substitute and by figuring the returned and completed Odysseus into the action proleptically in the person of his son, Telemachos. This instability of roles contributes to the mood of ambivalence that gets dispelled only when Odysseus finally declares himself and enters into open combat.

Yet throughout the second half of the poem Odysseus keeps prodding the action toward this moment. This process was, in fact, initiated earlier by Telemachos in his various verbal sparrings with the suitors. These are not yet heroic flytings, since neither side is yet willing to break the peace. Odysseus takes the process further, however. In what is the only clear contest between himself and another man during the Ithakan's adventures prior to the showdown in books 21 and 22, Odysseus, for the moment conforming to the principle of "comparability of adversaries," takes on his prime competitor for the role of official banquet beggar, Iros. The episode opens, in what could be construed as a parody of the Odysseus-Euryalos guest-host contest exchange, in a feast presided over by Antinoös, the acting host. Iros arrives (element A^{gh}) and through his insults initiates the flyting with Odysseus (element B^{gh}, 18.10–31), which proceeds in an appropriately eristic manner. The suitors, functioning as witnesses and combat officials, now sponsor a wrestling contest (element C^{gh}, 40–104), which Odysseus wins. In a manner appropriate to this pattern, the episode distances Antinoös as host (*h*) from Iros as active combatant (*h'*); and though Antinoös in no way exhibits the impartiality that his Phaiakian counterpart did, in its externals the nonlethal guest-host contest pattern has been followed. We should note, however, that immediately before combat, Odysseus deliberates whether to kill his adversary, in a moment of introspection recalling the first book of the *Iliad* (188–92) when Achilles similarly contemplates killing Agamemnon. Like Achilles, Odysseus finally opts for the nonlethal alternative (C^{gh}) and merely stuns what has by this time become a thoroughly intimidated opponent. The contest closes with a post-battle vaunt (V^{gh} or D^{bf}? [105–7]); no reconciliation (D^{gh}) follows. Although this contest does not succeed in breaking out of the guest-host mold (since Odysseus is not yet prepared to weather all the difficulties of battlefield relations), it comes dangerously close to doing so, both in the near-killing and in the omission of the reconciliatory resolution, and thus it anticipates the denouement in book 22.

The Odysseus-Iros exchange is encapsulated by two others, between Odysseus and Antinoös (17.414–91) and Odysseus and Eurymachos (18.346–421), that take further steps toward the battlefield encounter mode. In both episodes a quarrel breaks out at a scene of feasting, in the first instance when Antinoös rudely refuses Odysseus's solicitation for food, and in the second when Odysseus rejects Eurymachos's ironically intended offer of employment. These quarrels are deficient as flytings in that neither Antinoös nor Eurymachos is prepared to admit Odysseus as a worthy adversary, while Odysseus for his part is ostensibly accepting his role as a beggar and therefore admits to a lower rank; yet across this gulf of heroic impropriety the two suitors sense the stranger's challenge nonetheless. In consequence, each of them, losing his temper, embarks into an injuriously intended yet nonlethal combat (C^{gh} or C^{bf}?) by hurling a footstool at the unduly presumptuous beggar. Odysseus does not respond, further underscoring the questionable standing of these "contests." Both episodes conclude nonetheless with tenuous and externally imposed "reconciliations" (D^{gh}) as outside parties try to cool off the tempers. Once again, the modulation from the guest-host to the battlefield pattern has been stopped short of its terminus, although the tensions by this stage clamor for some more satisfactory resolution.

These last few abortive "contests" all suffer from the same structural flaw, in the suitors' reluctance to admit adversarial comparability. Of course, many bona fide contests—such as those between Achilles and various of his lesser Trojan victims—involve extreme mismatches; yet Achilles has been willing to put this point to the test, indeed, he insists on doing so. Odysseus's alleged unworthiness to serve as a contestant, however, is tied to the fundamental existential problem of the nobody-hero of the return song. For the right to engage in contesting has to be earned; this in turn requires that the hero win some measure of social recognition. Yet the dominant hierarchy among the suitors resists this process, intuiting that it will challenge the status quo.

The peculiar predicament of the return-song protagonist resembles that of many initiatory heroes. An interesting comparison might be drawn here between Odysseus and two major characters of *Hrólfs saga kraka*, one of the major *Beowulf* analogues.[59] The relevant portion of the narrative runs thus. Arriving at the court of the renowned

Danish king Hrólfr, Bǫthvarr, the son of Bjǫrn ("Bear"), encounters the pathetic Hǫttr, the son of a peasant couple whose hospitality Bǫthvarr had recently enjoyed. It would seem that Hǫttr, unable to fend for himself, has become the butt of abuse for Hrólfr's retainers, who each evening bombard him with the bones of their feasting. Thus, when Bǫthvarr first encounters him, Hǫttr is building a "shield wall" of old bones to protect himself from the evening's anticipated onslaught. Bǫthvarr takes up Hǫttr's cause, kills a retainer who tries to attack them in the usual manner, claims seats of honor for the two of them at Hrólfr's table, and, with the assistance of his timorous friend, kills the troll that has been poaching on Hrólfr's cattle. These two characters correspond structurally to the two aspects of Odysseus's identity. Hǫttr, on the one hand, represents what, in the suitors' perception, Odysseus *ought* to be—the fool, coward, and scapegoat; Hǫttr's unworthiness as a contest adversary is suggested by his ludicrous idea of what comprises heroic self-defense (his "shield wall"). On the other hand, Bǫthvarr, like the real Odysseus hidden in the beggar's garment, takes up the heroic challenge and wins glory and recognition for himself and his friend. This process culminates symbolically in episodes of *naming*, when Odysseus declares his identity before the suitors, and when Hrólfr decrees that, in light of his accomplishments, Hǫttr should be known hereafter as Hjalti. (Hjalti is a shortened form of Gullinhjalti, "Goldenhilt," the name of the sword the king had previously loaned Hǫttr after warning him that it was for heroes only.) Both Odysseus and the Nordic pair have progressed from a state of exclusion from the company of worthy warriors through the establishment of the right to be tested to an eventual triumph.

In fact, the denouement of this process in the *Odyssey* arrives not in a single martial encounter but in a pair of contrasting tests. The first of these takes the indirect—C^{gh}—form, as Odysseus and the suitors vie with one another in a noninjurious archery contest. Antinoös, Eurymachos, and the other suitors vehemently object to Odysseus's participation in this competition, and only through the persistence of Penelope and Telemachos is it allowed (21.275–353). Odysseus's success in stringing the bow and hitting the twelve axhandles, where all before him had failed, leads directly to his self-identification and the massacre of the suitors, a C^{bf} contest episode that occupies most of book 22. This reduplication of the Trial of Arms (C) element, which incorporates the movement from a martial contest of the guest-host variety directly to a contest of the battlefield type, recapitulates the entire modulatory process in miniature: Having established his qualifications through contesting under a false identity within the guest-host mode, Odysseus reveals and establishes himself in the role of host and proprietor through contesting in the battlefield mode. At last the transformation has been completed, contesting has been recognized and brought into the open, and the tensions of identity have been resolved.

INGROUP CONTESTING

The patterns studied to this point have all implicated two distinct communities.[60] Yet the occurrence of flyting and fighting between warriors of a single tribe or *comitatus* remains a logical possibility. How is this problem treated in the traditional heroic narrative under review?

Before embarking on this inquiry, I will need to stress again the generic specificity of "heroic flyting"—that is, flyting that projects martial resolution. Most societies have devised formats for verbal contesting, because it would be neither possible nor desirable to curb this tendency altogether. The modern academic and political worlds, for example, are suffused with *agonia*, though perhaps less overtly so today than a century ago.[61] Yet these demilitarized debate forms do not jeopardize community survival to the extent that those contest forms do that serve as a prelude to a fight; and this danger is accentuated when codes of vengeance must be reckoned with. Not surprisingly, true full-blown heroic flyting within single communities is a relatively rare occurrence. Hostility is usually rerouted, often by senior members of the community, out of the more violent tracks. Nonetheless, breakdowns do occur, especially in the course of dominance struggles, and both the Anglo-Saxon and Homeric worlds were intensely aware of the trauma that could be engendered by these episodes, which explains their great narrative and thematic importance.

Unfortunately the Greek–Old English comparison, which has by and large served this exposition well to this point, now fails us altogether: Old English poetry does not directly narrate any examples of ingroup flyting of the "heroic" type. Debates such as are found in *Andreas, Juliana, Elene, Genesis B*, and elsewhere must be excluded from this category since they do not project martial resolutions in the heroic manner. *Beowulf* gives several ironic intimations of eventual strife within the Danish royal family, particularly in Wealtheow's speech to Beowulf in 1169–87; yet the tale of Hrothulf's subsequent usurpation remains untold in *Beowulf* and must be inferred from Norse analogue material.[62] Thematically related are motifs of cowardice and betrayal that appear in the desertion of Odda's sons in *Maldon* or in the failure of Beowulf's retainers to assist their lord during his fight with the dragon. Yet none of these acts emerge into open contesting—indeed, the failure to engage in contesting is exactly the problem. A greater plenitude of examples could be found in such works of Norse literature as the Eddic *Lokasenna*[63] or in the feuds of Icelandic saga (on which see Byock 1982). Yet the conditions of community and the legal institutions connected with feuding in medieval Iceland were unique, as Byock stresses; to extend my comparison into this domain would require more methodological adjustments than can be undertaken in this space.[64] In short, I will be obligated to skip over the Germanic leg of this comparison for lack of relevant material falling within my purview. In any event, ingroup verbal contesting in all its manifestations defines a broad subject area that would require its own, extended treatment.[65]

Homeric epos, on the other hand, offers several minor and one monumental instance of verbal combat among fellow warriors. Of course, mere disagreements of viewpoint in consultatory situations— as in the exchanges between Hektor and Poulydamas in *Il*.12.211–50 or between Agamemnon and Odysseus in 14.65–108—cannot qualify as heroic flytings for the obvious reason that the disputants are not contracting for a martial test; the same holds true for the various spats between Hektor and Alexandros or between Alexandros and Helen. A marginal contest flares up in the ludicrous encounter between Odysseus and Thersites in 2.211–77. In fact, Thersites intends merely to abuse, not at all to contract for heroic exploit; thus, the comparison his speech sets forth is not between himself and Agamemnon, the butt of his invective, but between Agamemnon and Achilles.[66] Odysseus likewise refuses to engage Thersites as a heroic adversary but insists that he does not qualify to be judged by the heroic measure. Thus, Odysseus's blows do not constitute a martial contest (the C element) but a simple beating by which an authority figure puts a fool and braggart back in his place. Nonetheless, following close on the heels of the Achilles-Agamemnon quarrel and making explicit allusion to that event, the Thersites-Odysseus exchange clearly does define itself by relation to the contest pattern that it parodies. Its parodic quality derives from the fact that the condition of comparability has not been remotely satisfied; by heroic standards Thersites' aspirations to warriorhood are as laughable as those of Hǫttr in *Hrólfs saga kraka*. Odysseus's authoritarian response, even while occasioning what Homer's audience evidently took to be a comic moment, simultaneously checks the movement of the epic toward parody and highlights the singularity of the ingroup flyting between Achilles and Agamemnon.

Yet before we turn to that critical episode, several other instances

merit consideration. The series of flyting-fighting encounters between various pairs of gods and goddesses in *Il*.21.383–513 have
been already treated in the section on battlefield flyting. It should
recalled, however, that while these exchanges follow the "direct combat" pathway, they do not qualify as true battlefield contests—first,
because the gods, being immortal, cannot kill each other, and second,
because they do not represent separate communities but, to the contrary, are joined by familial ties. As I suggested earlier, these aberrant
conflicts are best explained as styling themselves after the human
warfare on the plains of Troy below. The gods' descent into such behavior introduces, once again, a comic note even as the heroic action
is swelling toward its apex.

Two books later, and just prior to the denouement in book 24, we
find a body of evidence that is remarkable precisely for its lack of
bearing on our theme, for the funeral games following the cremation
of Patroklos contain virtually no true flyting at all. The only real instance occurs in 23.667–75 in which Epeios asserts his supremacy in
wrestling. His speech is both eristic—he promises to break the skin
and bones of any challenger—and contractual, since his boasting is to
be borne out in athletic competition. Euryalos, his challenger, offers
no verbal reply and is roundly defeated. No vaunting follows the
match. This contest seems to follow the guest-host pathway, in that
the "Trial of Arms" is of a nonlethal (though, evidently, personally
injurious) variety. As a flyting-to-fighting contest it has been minimally developed. Yet it is the only ingroup flyting exchange in scenes
of athletic competition in Homer.

The other quarrels that break out during the games—between Idomeneus and Aias Oïleus's son (23.450–98) and between Menelaos
and Antilochos (420–41, 540–611)—fail to qualify as heroic flytings
on various accounts. In the first instance the heroes are pitting not
rival claims concerning their own heroic merit but merely rival opinions on who is winning the chariot race; they do not project a Trial
of Arms but merely a wager concerning the outcome. These are
quarreling fans, not contestants. The dispute between Menelaos and
Nestor's son, however, concerns itself with whether Antilochos won
the chariot competition fairly. Either of these quarrels might have
gone the way of the Agamemnon-Achilles conflict in book 1, but in
both cases this is prevented by Achilles' own timely intervention.
Achilles' new role as judge and peacemaker has an ironic appropri-
ateness: Having promoted schism in the first place through ingroup
flyting, he now heals the injuries he has wrought by heading off any
repetition of such an incident as the poem winds to a close.[67] Significantly, both of the major athletic competitions in Homer—here, and

on the island of the Phaiakians in *Od.* 8—are presided over by strong authority figures who act at different times to resolve verbal disputation. Alkinoös seems to have allowed more scope for such activity than Achilles does. Perhaps his disinvolvement registers the cultural perception that carefully controlled *agōnia* comprises an inevitable and even healthy element in relations between friendly communities. On the other hand, the lack of such agonistic *verbal* displays among Achaian or Phaiakian confreres, despite ample opportunities to engage in such, may reflect a realistic apprehension of the dangers of such disputation among men who might need to collaborate with each other on a daily basis in conditions of war.

In any event, all of these rather minor Iliadic ingroup quarrels have been subordinated to the initial contesting exchange between Achilles and Agamemnon, ingroup flyting par excellence.[68] The proem itself locates this quarrel at the root of a line of causation from which the entire narrative derives—for the quarrel engendered Achilles' wrath, which in turn brought "countless sufferings" ("μυρί' . . . ἄλγε'," 1.2) for the Achaians. The wrath that derives from quarreling ("Μῆνιν" and "ἐρίσαντε," 1.1, 6) is Homer's theme; and the fact that it is the Achaians who suffer (1.2), not the Achaians and Trojans, underscores the ingroup character of the conflict. Yet to dramatize this theme in narrative terms, Homer has elaborated on those contesting structures that we have been uncovering in such fashion as to draw all of the major threads of action into its web. Achilles' fight with Hektor, for example, does not represent a departure from the Achaian's initial agonistic stand, but, to the contrary, is as firmly incorporated into his contract with Agamemnon as the fight with Grendel was into the contract between Beowulf and Unferth. Thus a clearer perception of the architectonics of the *Iliad*'s plot line is one of the happy fruits of the recognition of its contestation underpinnings.[69]

The quarrel begins in a type of setting that usually resists eristic dialogic turns. The council and assembly in Homer are deliberative in function. Differences in viewpoint often emerge, yet the aim of participants in such exchanges is to establish a consensus that can serve as a basis for united action. Thus it is a practical issue pertaining to the collective welfare of the Achaians that initially divides Agamemnon and Achilles, rather than a preconceived intention to fight with each other. Most heroic flytings originate in direct challenges on heroic identity, as when Unferth publicly doubts Beowulf's heroic competence, or when Achilles asserts his own martial superiority to Aineias. For the two Achaians, however, the dispute centers on rights to battle spoils, essentially a legal problem that ought to have been negotiated through nonviolent recourse to the system of reciprocal bonds that tie Agamemnon and Achilles together. In short, heroic flyting violates the norms of the deliberative mode. Nonetheless, both Achilles and Agamemnon interpret their differences agonistically: The battle spoils (in this case Chryseis and Briseis) stand for heroic honor, and their redistribution cannot be accomplished without one or the other of these men losing face. Thus a contest has sprung up in a place and fashion where a contest should never have been.

The irregularity of this flyting is reflected in several ways. To anticipate briefly in a topic that we will treat more fully in the next chapter, one device by which flyters usually develop their material involves "retrojection"—the casting back in time and the recollection of martial accomplishment and genealogical information bearing on present states of honor. Achilles and Agamemnon, while they do retroject, choose to concentrate on moral deficiencies pertaining not to the agonistic but to the collaborative sphere: Achilles has hubristically refused to acknowledge Agamemnon's authority as *basileus*, whereas Agamemnon has divided battle spoils without duly recognizing those labors by which it was gained. Agamemnon construes Achilles' behavior as a challenge to his dominance; Achilles construes Agamemnon's as a violation of the codes of ingroup reciprocity that it ought to have been his part to uphold. It is true that Achilles moves in the direction of bona fide heroic comparison when he points out that his own accomplishments in the winning of these spoils far surpass those of his chief (1.165–68). Agamemnon's reluctance to broach heroic themes can be attributed to his obvious inferiority in this domain. In short, then, this flyting is "mixed"—only partially heroic—in its retrojective subject matter.

Another indicator of the anomality and inappropriateness of this flyting exchange appears in the intrusion of Nestor.[70] In most flytings contestants monopolize the dialogue while outsiders play silent witness. Even Alkinoös and Hrothgar allow the Odysseus-Euryalos and Beowulf-Unferth quarrels to run their courses before intervening. Exceptions to this rule are few.[71] Nestor, however, tries to shut the flyting down, and his strategy in this attempt reveals many of the cultural assumptions pertaining to this crisis. First, he reaffirms the corporate character of the present military expedition against the Trojans, pointing out that Priam and his sons would rejoice at the present quarrel. Next, by asserting the heroic superiority of his own generation to that of the present disputants, he is both grounding his own authority as the senior participant in this exchange and casting cold water on the heroic pretensions of his junior colleagues. Boasting is not appropriate here—not at any rate on the parts of Achilles and

Agamemnon; it should be reserved for encounters with the enemy. Finally, he stresses what he construes to be the just claims of each man, and thus reaffirms the system of bonds and reciprocity that ought to prevail. The burden of all of these arguments is the same—that disagreements among the Achaians should be negotiated nonagonistically. Of course, Nestor always enjoys these opportunities for lengthy digressions on his youth. Nonetheless, the situation has called for his intervention, since Agamemnon, who ought like Alkinoös or Hrothgar to have been upholding the peace, has himself become embroiled in the quarrel.[72]

Yet the most remarkable turn in this flyting occurs in 1.188–244, comprising Achilles' moment of introspection, the epiphany of Athena, and his great vow[73] declared before Agamemnon and the Achaians. Homer here describes Achilles' division of mind, whether or not to kill his leader.[74] In a dialogic exchange, Athena advises against this divisive alternative. Obediently Achilles refrains, but instead sets forth a flyting contract of another type. Now he proposes to deny the Achaians his assistance against Hektor. Agamemnon, for his part, tacitly concurs in this contract and thus becomes party to the form of contest that Achilles has set forth. What form is this? Initially, Achilles had contemplated a Trial of Arms (element C) of the battlefield variety. Dissuaded from such extreme recourse, he now resolves on the guest-host form: Achilles will surpass Agamemnon with respect to an outerdirected measure, X. In this instance, of course, X is combat with Hektor; if Achilles proves that he can defeat Hektor where Agamemnon had failed, he has won the contest. The parallels with the Beowulf-Unferth flyting, which proposes the fight with Grendel as its martial test (C^{gh}), need no elaboration. It is also worth noting that in moving from the battlefield to the guest-host contest patterns, Achilles reverses in his mind a process that Odysseus enacts on the physical plane in books 21 and 22 of the *Odyssey*, when he first surpasses his suitor rivals in the nonlethal archery contest (C^{gh}) and then fights with them directly (C^{bf}). Interestingly enough, then, these two contests of Achilles and Odysseus both arise out of settings (ingroup or guest-host) that are apt to resist those verbally agonistic displays that carry martial entailments. Yet they comprise two of the three most foregrounded contests in Homer, the one setting forth the basic problem in the *Iliad*, the other culminating Odysseus's return. One would have to gather that Homer and his tradition were much preoccupied with such problematic encounters. At the same time, surprisingly, Achilles proves himself more willing to pursue the more conciliatory pathway with respect to his community than does the less temperamental, far-sighted Ithakan.

Thus having pledged himself, Achilles, the very exemplar of commitment to the heroic principle that words should be substantiated by deeds, fulfills his contract to the last clause, long after it has ceased to matter to anyone but himself. The first eighteen books are devoted to the first half of the demonstration, that Agamemnon and all those under him cannot avail against Hektor. Agamemnon himself was prepared to concede defeat long before this; yet as we see dramatized on numerous occasions, Achilles is of a type reluctant to disengage from a contest until it has been carried to its logical end. This heroic value, deeply internalized in Achilles' case, underlies his refusal to accede to the pleas of Odysseus and Phoinix in book 9. The flyting contract has projected a course of action that at this point is only in its beginning stages. Because, in Achilles' perception, his honor has been insulted and his heroic merit called to the proof, he will not drop the issue until every term of that proof has been satisfied. Achilles remains always true to his concept of heroic honor, and so the norms of the heroic flyting genre are thoroughly observed.

The subsequent development of this contest does contain an unusual twist, in the metathesis of the C^{gh} and D^{gh} elements. Or perhaps we might rather describe the events in book 19 as a proleptic Resolution (element D), in which Agamemnon—much like Euryalos and Unferth—apologizes, admits defeat, and seals the renewal of friendship with the offering of gifts. Achilles at this juncture has renounced his wrath against Agamemnon, since it has now turned against a new target, the killer of Patroklos. Yet we should not undervalue the original flyting contract as a determinant of this new plot turn. Achilles had bound himself to the killing of Hektor from the outset; the death of his friend has merely allied the new demands of vengeance with those of his own prior word. I do not mean to imply that Achilles is inwardly unchanged—that is a separate question—but only that he is heroically consistent in his actions. The martial demonstration (C^{gh}) does not arrive until book 22; here it is developed as a complete contest in its own right. By defeating Hektor where Agamemnon and his forces had failed, Achilles has at last fulfilled the flyting contract and won the contest. The resolution between the two Achaians had already been effected; yet the athletic competitions in book 23 seem to represent a completion of this process, as Achilles—through contest established, temporarily at least, in a position of superiority to Agamemnon, just as Odysseus and Beowulf found themselves with respect to Euryalos and Unferth—promotes friendly sportsmanship and discourages those ingroup quarreling tendencies that he himself so recently displayed. The "reconciliation" between Achilles and Priam in the final book, although it has been carefully prepared for through the ordering of events in the books preceding, nonetheless falls outside the logic of those two contests that have dominated the epic. For it has no bearing on the Achilles-Agamemnon quarrel at all. Although it does pertain to the Hektor-Achilles rivalry, it represents a form of resolution radically apart from that which the battlefield contest pattern anticipates. At this juncture Homer seems to be privileging a new, pacific outlook that the agonistic mind-set cannot adequately comprehend.[75] Appearing as it does, this perspective limits and relativizes the path of heroic endeavor and the contesting that is its outcome.

CHAPTER THREE

The Flyting Exchange

METHODOLOGICAL PRELIMINARIES

Heroic flyting in its larger contexts has been my concern thus far. Chapter 1 expanded on the underlying aims and constituting structures of the heroic contest, there conceived in reified and static terms. Chapter 2 redefined the contest as an unfolding event and outlined the pathways by which contesting moves through its verbal and martial aspects. In this chapter I shift my orientation from the level of the whole contest to verbal dueling per se. By what principles are flyting matches organized? What are the dynamics of the flyting exchange?

Because verbal disputation is an oral genre par excellence, oral-formulaic research could offer guidance. In oral-formulaic theory, repeating narrative episodes have usually been conceived as themes or type scenes. The traditional poet spins out his narrative with the assistance of formulas that serve not as fixed set pieces to be repeated verbatim but as generative kernels variously realizable. The long and complex history of scholarship in this subject would take us back through the contributions of such scholars as John Foley, David Bynum, Alain Renoir, Jeff Opland, Carol Clover, Mark Edwards, Gregory Nagy, Michael Nagler, David Gunn, W. F. Hansen, Bernard Fenik, Barry Powell, Donald Fry, Robert Creed, Robert Diamond, David Crowne, Francis Magoun, Albert Lord, and many others, to Milman Parry's 1936 review (M. Parry 1971: 404–7) of Walter Arend's *Die typischen Scenen bei Homer* (1933) in which Parry recognized the role that Arend's "type scenes" could play in an oral poetics.[1] It would lead us, at the same time, from Propp (1968), who has exerted continuing influence on folkloristics and other areas, through Levi-Strauss and the structuralist explosion of the 1960s and 1970s. Further, we would need to take into account the contributions of narratologists such as Gérard Genette, Seymour Chatman, Gerald Prince, and Susan Lanser, who have brought the study of narrative to an incomparably higher degree of development, but who have not, in general, recognized the bearing of oral tradition on their subject.

While my present aims cannot permit an extended detour into these treasure mines, I would like to single out two principles that often come into play in the analysis of traditional narrative units: the syntagmatic and the scenic. On the one hand, formulaic episodes are often constituted of recurring strings of narrative elements.[2] Propp (1968) has provided magnificent testimony to the descriptive power of this method.[3] My own breakdown of the heroic contest into four stages (Engagement, Flyting, Trial of Arms, and Resolution) is an analysis of this type. On the other hand, "scenic," as I intend it here, refers to to the environment of action. I am admittedly visualizing and spatializing the term more than, say, Arend (1933), Fry (1968), and Clover (1974 and 1980) do, who think of scenes and type scenes (*typischen Scenen*) more as scenes in a drama.[4] Yet one of the most famous oral-formulaic themes, Crowne's "hero on the beach," in which a hero finds himself *on the beach* with retainers *in the presence of a flashing light* at the outset or completion of a journey, features two scenic images in its catalog of four defining elements (1960; for a revisionary view of theme, see Richardson 1987). Thus both narrative-syntagmatic and scenic-environmental principles have been recognized in the formulary constitution of traditional episodes. In any event, I am struck by the extent to which these two (the sequential and scenic) principles correspond to the two modalities, the visual (or spatial) and the linear (or episodic), posited by what A. Paivio and other cognitive psychologists have called the "dual code theory."[5] Because both spatial and sequential principles are integral to the operation of human memory, it should not surprise us if recurrent tendencies in these two areas manifest in oral or oral-derived traditional narrative in whose composition memory is so crucial. Obviously scene and the sequential ordering of incident need not conflict—formularized incident might logically select a formularized setting. In fact, our analysis in the previous two chapters, which treated flyting as one constituent in a larger, *whole contest*, relied heavily on both scenic and sequential analytic methods. But at this point in our investigation we will need to ask to what extent these principles, individually or in conjunction, can serve us in articulating the structure of *flyting dialogues* themselves.

Naturally these problems have not gone unattended to in the scholarship on verbal contesting. Kirk (1978), for example, finds a common (though slightly disordered) thirteen-motif sequence in the formal duels of books 3 and 7 of the *Iliad*.[6] Working with Nordic material (from the *Poetic Edda*, Saxo Grammaticus, and three sagas), Harris describes the "structural framework of the *senna*" as "a Preliminary, comprising an Identification and Characterization, and then a Central Exchange, consisting of either Accusation and Denial, Threat and Counter-threat, or Challenge and Reply, or a combination; these

structural elements are realized through a more or less regular alternation of speakers, first in question and answer, then in comment and
reply" (1979: 66). Clover, in her seminal study, argues that the structure of flyting "is conditioned by the terms of debate and has as a
standard sequence a Claim, Defense, and Counterclaim" (1980: 452);
elsewhere she holds that saga scenes have a tripartite structure, composed of a "preface," "dramatic encounter," and "conclusion."[7] While
there is a general truth in these observations, they do not take us very
far into the dialogic process (since that is now our concern). The same
is true of investigations into flyting's scenic entailments.[8] The notion
of "scene" must always be basic to the narrative process, as one finds
in the narratological studies of Genette (1980: 109–12) and others;
this is especially so in the case of dialogue, which normally requires a
stable setting. Pizarro (1976) and Clover (1980) have studied this
problem in connection with flytings, as we reviewed in chapters 1 and
2 in the course of establishing the relationship between social environment and the choice of flyting-to-fighting pathway. In an especially fascinating study of Örvar-Odds saga, Lönnroth argues for the
pertinence of what he calls the "double scene" in the mannjafnaðr
(verbal contest) in the thirty-seventh chapter; a double scene occurs
"whenever the narrative appears to be enacted by the performer and
his audience on the very spot where the entertainment takes place"
(1979: 95). This scholarship as a body has immensely enriched our
understanding of heroic flyting in ways that I have not indicated
here; and I do not wish to criticize it for having failed to answer questions that it did not raise. Yet because the subject here is heroic flyting
as a cross-cultural genre in its own right, I should note that these
studies have not revealed much about the dialogic interactivity of flyting exchanges.

More dialogically oriented, Bax and Padmos (1983) analyze the
Hárbarðsljóð, one of the outstanding Eddic instances of verbal contesting, on *pragmatic* grounds, treating speeches in their situation contexts as speech acts opening fields of possible responses.[9] One of their
aims is to uphold the generic integrity of the native Nordic terms
senna and the *mannjafnaðr*, thus challenging the existence of a category of "flyting" that Clover posits and that I have assumed in this
study. Since the Icelandic material is outside my purview, my contribution to this debate must a be limited one. I do feel nonetheless that
"flyting," which I define as verbal contesting with an ad hominem
frame of reference, and the subclass of "heroic flyting," or flyting
with martial entailments, have psychological groundings and exhibit
consistencies that justify the categories. There is no reason, however,
why a tradition should not develop more particularized genres with

their own, culturally specific set of conventions, although I do not wish to argue as to whether this has happened in the Nordic material. This generic problem aside, the pragmatic approach is a promising one, since, by recognizing speech as action, it opens a window to dialogue as dynamic interplay.

In what follows I propose to examine flyting as a dialogic expression of a contest's motivational structures; it is formulaic in the sense that the principles underlying it are consistent, and as such it may be treated as a traditional oral modality. My analysis will work on two levels: that of the individual speech, and that of the dialogue as a joint enterprise. The second section will study interplay between the twin aims of contest—the eristic and the contractual; although both movements are essential to the realization of any flyting exchange, contestants enjoy considerable latitude in negotiating which of them will emerge into expression and which will remain latent at any given time. Scaling down to the individual speech, the third section will enumerate and describe those characteristic mental operations by which flyters fulfill these contest aims. The fourth section will return again to the larger scale, studying this time the interaction not between contestational motives but between speeches as contributions to a dialogic sequence. We will conclude this analysis of heroic flyting, in the last section, with a close reading of a classic flyting episode that will draw on the formulations developed here and in the previous two chapters.

QUARREL AND CONTRACT: PRINCIPLES OF FOREGROUNDING

Flyting heroes are jointly engaged in two activities: quarreling and contracting. The first two chapters studied how these antithetical yet curiously interdependent motives inform the heroic contest in its fuller realization as flyting-and-fighting. Now we will need to consider the same problem within the narrower compass of the verbal exchange alone.

This dialectic between the querulous and the contractual is best conceived here in terms of a relationship between rhetorical foregrounding and backgrounding. Both motives are essential: For simple, unsocialized hatred would not gravitate toward the formal contest medium; however, without the eristic motive, heroes would not want to fight with each other in the first place. Yet because the surface dispositions of quarreling and contracting are opposed—the one conducing to collaboration and the other to strife—at a given moment, one or the other is liable to predominate in the foreground of encounter and the other to lie in potentiality. The balance between the two roughly correlates with the matter of speeches. At predominantly eristic moments speeches are typically filled with boasts and insults, whereas at contractual junctures the contestants are apt to make peace offers or otherwise limit the scope of the fighting. In short, flytings fluctuate between the polarities of the "purely" eristic (quarrel foregrounded, contract latent) and the "purely" contractual (contract foregrounded, quarrel latent). If the eristic element ceases to hold its place in the general balance, however, flyting has modulated into some other form of interaction. I should stress that throughout this analysis of foregrounding and backgrounding I will focus primarily on *structure* and only incidentally on *tone*. A speech that treats contractual matters has, by this analysis, foregrounded negotiation, however great might be the animosity that really inspires it.

Let us review examples that illustrate different "ratios" in the quarrel-contract balance. Curiously enough, despite the many courtesies exchanged between the Geats and the Danes, the Beowulf-Unferth flyting illustrates, in the structural sense, *eris* in a virtually unalloyed form. For from the time of his first arrival in Denmark Beowulf has been trumpeting his intention to fight Grendel; in the flyting he and Unferth implicitly acknowledge that he has bound himself to undertake this exploit, and accordingly the negotiation of the contract concerns them not at all. Rather, they use their contract—that Beowulf's fight against Grendel will measure the comparative merits of the two human heroes—as one of the grounds of their verbal competition. Thus the eristic element predominates from the structural point of view, even though the two heroes, and especially Beowulf, exhibit a certain amount of restraint in the tone of their speeches, avoiding, for example, a descent into the scurrilous.[10] The *Iliad* features numerous episodes of this kind, such as the exchanges between Tlepolemos and Sarpedon (5.632–54) and Odysseus and Sokos (11.428–55). All four of these heroes have determined in advance that they will fight with each other, and in the course of their flyting they never swerve from this resolve. Instead, they vie through words with claims for heroic superiority, using methods that will be set forth in the next section. Freed from the "burden" of explicitly making a contract, that is, they can indulge their proclivity for insulting, threatening, and boasting, in the knowledge that the significance and measure of this interaction has already and tacitly been agreed upon. Such high-visibility-*eris*, low-visibility-contract exchanges cloak the socialized and collaborative underpinnings of their own enterprise.

Nonetheless, they are fundamentally akin to those other contests in which the participants seriously propose and deliberate contracts; and to the extent that this happens, the contractual element displaces the eristic in the surface of dialogue. In *Maldon*, for example, the Viking messenger, by threatening Byrhtnoth, is, despite the hostile impression that his speech conveys, initiating a contractual exchange, in that he is trying to induce the English to abandon resistance and to accede to the Viking demands. In his reply Byrhtnoth, preferring a battle, rejects the Viking offer and so brings explicit contracting to a halt. Intimidation strategies such as the Viking's, while they are designed to avoid battle and engender peace, are eristically toned, in that both the warlike and peaceable contract options are characterized as contests that the intimidator wins. For the basic presupposition in intimidation is that the bully is the better fighter, in view of which the peace that the victim can secure by acceding to his demands is tantamount to an admission of defeat. Thus, the intimidator reaps the glory either way. Probably a universal pattern among men at war, such attempts at intimidation appear several times in the *Iliad*, with various results. Achilles, for example, so threatens Aineias, who responds in much the same that Byrhtnoth did (*Il.*20.178–258); Euphorbos likewise tries initially to scare off Menelaos in order to claim Patroklos's body and war gear (17.12–42). One is reminded of the battle boasts of the Gauls who, according to Diodorus, try through insults, genealogical boasts, and battle display to daunt their adversaries (5.29.2–3). In some cases, among our Iliadic heroes, these tactics are successful. Hektor, for example, taunts a fleeing Diomedes, and thus wins glory through the latter's unwillingness to turn and fight (8.161–66); the Achaian evidently feels sufficiently stung to need to redeem himself against the Trojan in a later encounter (11.343–67). In fact, these flytings that make visible use of the intimidation pattern are merely foregrounding contractual options implicit in any heroic flyting exchange. For the defender has always the choice of fighting or fleeing; and any aggressor will be conscious of these possible responses and his own role in influencing his respondent's selection.[11]

While heroes of the bullying variety will often try to contract their way out of fighting by means of threats, inferior fighters on occasion try to secure the same end by suing for mercy.[12] The most dramatic instance is the Achilles-Lykaon exchange (21.34–135); other examples include the encounters between Menelaos and Adrestos (6.37–65), between Diomedes and Dolon (10.370–464), and between Agamemnon and the brothers Peisandros and Hippolochos (11.122–48). Whereas bullies, capitalizing on their presumed martial superiority, emphasize the destructive consequences of a battle that they are encouraging their adversaries to avoid, supplicators downplay all belligerence and try to turn the minds of their adversaries away from contesting. Toward this end they use appeasement behavior (such as clasping the knees) whose effect is to redefine the relationship as that between master and servant. Thus, intimidation and supplication foreground the same contract alternatives in the same order of preference—that is, a peaceful course, secured through the capitulation of one party, is being preferred to a martial one. They differ in whether the initiator of the contract proposal characterizes himself as winner or loser and in the eristic intensity of his speech. In fact, neither kind of attempt meets with much success in our texts. Of all the supplicants who voice their pleas in direct discourse, for example, only the immortal Hermes (21.497–504) actually succeeds by these means in fending off an attack.

Both intimidators and supplicants are trying contractually to circumvent the Trial of Arms. The final Achilles-Hektor contest, however, illustrates another type of contract making. In an interior monologue just before the encounter (22.99–130), Hektor deliberates and dismisses outright surrender to Achilles on grounds that the Lykaon-Achilles episode amply substantiates. Instead, at the outset of the flyting, he proposes that, with the gods as his witnesses, each of them should agree to return to the bereaved kin the body of his enemy, should he win in battle (254–59). This contract assumes that direct combat has already been agreed upon (cf. 250–53), and in this assumption his speech follows the usual eristic pattern. Nonetheless, he sets forth his proposal with a minimum of insult and boasting, since, like Lykaon, he is trying to yoke to some form of agreement an enemy who has the better prospects of winning in battle. In a highly eristic response (261–72), Achilles bitterly rejects all codicillary noncombat contracts ("συνημοσύνας," 261) and so terminates overt contractual negotiations; characterizing their relationship in interspecific and even predatorial terms (as between lions and men, or between wolves and lambs), he further predicts that he will kill his Trojan enemy and so avenge the death of his friends. Thus, Hektor's attempt to negotiate limitations on battle conduct has failed.

Another instance of negotiating a "codicillary contract" in the course of a flyting exchange appears in *Maldon*, though here it enjoys a more favorable reception. For the Vikings, finding themselves unable to launch an effective attack across the river Pante, petition Byrhtnoth for the right of access to the shore held by the English (84–88). Byrhtnoth in his "ofermode" (89) accedes to this request, thus recognizing that basic contest principle that adversaries should fight on equal terms.[13] Although one may legitimately question whether Byrhtnoth at this juncture should have been thinking of himself as a heroic contestant rather than as a general or guardian of his people, his gesture has an appeal of nobility about it; and this derives from its connection with the agonistic paradigm that most warriors, by the nature of their vocation, internalize. Having thus adjusted the precise terms of combat, the two armies now engage in that battle to which both sides had contracted in the first phase of their flyting (29–61) and concerning which, as Byrhtnoth has just pointed out, only God knows the outcome (94–95).

For a final episode, let us consider once again the Diomedes-Glaukos exchange (*Il.*6.119–236). In the opening speech, after asking who his opponent might be, Diomedes proposes two courses of action: If his adversary is mortal, Diomedes will kill him; but if his adversary is divine, he will refuse to fight. Here we see a contractual array not unlike the threat structure of the *Maldon* exchange: two contractual possibilities, one violent, the other not; in this case, however, the choice of pathways will depend on who the opponent is, not what he prefers. (Diomedes has not proffered capitulation as one of his addressee's alternatives.) As we have seen, Glaukos's genealogical narration diverts the encounter into a purely noneristic, guest-host channel. Thus the contestants have contracted their way out of the Trial of Arms. Yet while Lykaon and the Viking messenger try to do this simply by advancing the contest directly from its Flyting (B^{bf}) to its Resolution (D^{bf}) through a concession of defeat by one side or the other, Diomedes and Glaukos have redefined their relationship in a way that makes further contesting impossible. There will be no winner or loser, since they are friends now. The characteristic tension between the eristic and contractual motives has been dissipated, and flyting has come to an end.

Let us now draw some general conclusions concerning the quarrel-contract dichotomy. First, it must be recognized that the preponderance, or at least the forceable presence, of the eristic motive constitutes a precondition of flyting exchanges; without this, they become something else. Yet as the complementary aims of this dialogic genre, the eristic and the contractual both influence all flyting interactions to some degree. When quarrel rules "completely," contract making continues tacitly at the base of encounter: Thus Beowulf and Unferth are contracting on the Beowulf-Grendel fight, even though ostensibly they propose nothing but devote themselves exclusively to attack-and-parry. More frequently, however, contract formation emerges with various eristic undertones into the surface of interaction, directing for various durations the thread of dialogue. As a general rule, an eristic tone prevails when the speaker judges himself as a warrior to be either superior to or equally matched with his adversary; even contractual propositions in such circumstances take on strongly eristic overtones. Inferior warriors, however, prefer irenically disposed contractual speeches, even when they are proposing to fight.

Speech Functions

Quarreling and contracting are inherently collaborative activities. It takes two to quarrel, it takes two to agree. Although the individual can *participate* in these speech events, he himself cannot perform them. Subsisting on interaction, requiring bilateral ratification, quarreling and contracting remain nonetheless qualitatively distinct from the individual speeches that bring them about. And yet flyting dialogues are, in the literal sense, constituted of speeches. How should we conceive these, viewing them now as individual rather than collaborative productions? What is the structure of the individual speech performance that, in its interaction with other speech performances, results in the flyting match?

My objective here is to identify and define those characteristic moves or mental operations by which the contestants develop their matter and bring the contest's motives into expression. I am trying to describe, in other words, the logical structure of the flyting speech—not in the sequential ordering of its materials, but in the relation and integration of those acts by which contestation, in the context of the heroic ethos, finds words. I do not mean to imply that these movements can be characterized psychologically as steps through which flyters trace their way, at a conscious or preconscious level, in the process of generating speeches; nor do I claim that all of these movements find expression in every flyting speech, since they clearly do not. But as a group, they seem to me to represent the set of operations or lines of development best suited to the advancement of the individual's participation in the flyting enterprise through the generation of discourse, given what has been set forth about that enterprise in the preceding chapters. Perhaps they might be called the core topoi in an implied rhetoric of the heroic flyting genre.[14]

With these specifications in mind, let us now consider the five following such movements or "speech functions": the identitive, the retrojective, the projective, the attributive-evaluative, and the comparative. The typical flyting speech will develop by these parameters, performing some and sometimes all of these acts. In other words, the flyter identifies himself or his adversary; retrojects or refers back to some fact or event; projects some future chain of actions or state of affairs; evaluates or attributes (implicitly evaluative) qualities to himself or his adversary; and indulges in a heroic comparison, to his adversary's disadvantage. Of these five functions, the first serves to fix the act of contesting on a specific pair of contestants, the second and third generate speech content, and the fourth and fifth determine the use to which this material is applied.

Identification

With considerable frequency flyters open their speeches by naming their rivals or otherwise adverting to the topic of their identities.[15] Though at first blush there may appear to be nothing noteworthy in such practice, we should bear in mind flyting's *personal* orientation. To land an ad hominem attack satisfactorily, the contestant must know with whom he is dealing. Naming designates a specific target and establishes a particular human frame of reference for the flyting as a generic act.[16]

In the most common form of identification, contestants simply name each other, using the nominative or vocative cases. Thus, Unferth initiates his attack with the question "Eart þu se Beowulf" ("Are you that Beowulf," 506); in the first line of his reply the Geat inserts appositionally the ironic vocative expression, "wine min Unferð" ("my friend Unferth," 530). Similarly Aineias opens his verbal assault with the vocative "Μηριόνη" (*Il.*16.617), and Meriones counters with his own act of naming, "Αἰνεία" (16.620). Often, contestants prefer patronymics or combine these with personal names: " Ἀτρεῖδη" ("son of Atreus," 2.225), "Πηλεΐδη" ("son of Peleus," 20.200), "Τυδεΐδη" ("son of Tydeus," 8.161), "Αἶαν διογενὲς Τελαμώνιε" ("Aias, Zeus-sprung, son of Telamon," 7.234), "'Ατρεΐδη Μενέλαε διοτρεφές, ὄρχαμε λαῶν" ("son of Atreus Menalaos, reared by Zeus, leader of the people," 17.12). Sometimes heroes resort to simple terms of abuse, or combine these with naming: "κύον" ("dog," 11.362 and 22.345), "ἆ δείλ'" ("ah coward," 11.441), "νήπιε" ("O fool," 21.99), "Τοξότα, λωβητήρ, κέρα ἀγλαέ, παρθενοπῖπα" ("Archer, slanderer, beautiful of hair, ogler of girls," 11.385). On other occasions, surprisingly, they accord to their opponents what in a martial context seems to constitute praise: "Πηλεΐδη μεγάθυμε" ("great-souled son of Peleus," 21.153), "Θεοῖς ἐπιείκελ' Ἀχιλλεῦ" ("O Achilles like unto the gods," 22.279), "Ὀτρυντεΐδε, πάντων ἐκπαγλότατ' ἀνδρῶν" ("O son of Otrynteus, most frightful of all men," 20.389), "καρτερόθυμε, δαΐφρον, ἀγαυοῦ Τυδέος υἱέ" ("O stout-hearted, war-minded son of proud Tydeus," 5.277), and so on. Some of these accolades, of course, may be ironical. At the same time, and on a deeper level, these alternating movements of praise and blame seem to me to express formulaically the underlying contestational motives: By abusing, a hero eristically asserts his own superiority, whereas by praising, he ennobles the enterprise and thus magnifies the stakes.[17]

Most of these identitive movements contain themselves within a brief compass. On several occasions, however, the problem of identity comes in for a more expansive review. At the outset of his first and unsuccessful encounter with Hektor, Achilles briefly characterizes the Trojan as Patroklos's killer (20.425–27)—the aspect of Hektor's identity animating him at the time. Later, upon encountering Lykaon, Achilles reflects at some length (21.54-63) on a previous encounter in which he took this Trojan captive. Both of these identifying movements qualify as "retrojections," which we will be discussing shortly.

But the significance of the identitive function is perhaps best illustrated in several episodes in which the initial naming is absent. Intending to lead the Frisian attack against the Danes fortified within the hall, Garulf of the Frisians calls out to the opposition, asking who guards the door (*The Fight at Finnsburg* 22–23). Sigeferth responds to this ostensibly simple question with a flyting speech (24–27): He names himself ("Sigeferþ is min nama"), boasts of his experience in battle by claiming "fæla ic weana gebad, heordra hilda" ("I have endured many miseries, many hard battles"), and indirectly alludes to the coming fight. This exchange is unmistakably agonistic in its intention and import. In the battle that follows, we learn that Garulf dies first among the assailants, though his killer is unnamed. Two other flytings open with the same question of identification but yield quite different outcomes. At the outset of their encounters with Glaukos and Beowulf, Diomedes and the Danish coastguard do not know whom they are addressing. Here again, flyting prefers known quantities; the quarreling and contracting heroes can only fire blindly until identities have been publicly established. And so Diomedes and the *weard* open their speeches with the question "Who are you?"—"Hwæt syndon ge" (*Beo.* 237), and "τίς δὲ σύ ἐσσι" (*Il.*6.123). In both cases the respondents identify themselves through crucial genealogical information that allows the modulation of flyting into a kind of guest-host bonding. Thus the role of identity in the flyting exchange is not only deictic but dynamic as well.[18]

Retrojection

In their eristic aspect flytings are battles of personal honor. A hero's present state of honor derives from his past and extends into the future. Whereas the retrojective act tries to establish what a man is by "casting back" and summoning into the homeostasis of the present that man's deeds and ancestry,[19] the projective act proposes trials by which this retrojectively established state of honor might be further tested. The retrojective and projective acts together generate much or most of the explicit "matter" of dispute.

The retrojective review usually takes one of two forms: the narration of an event or events in the life of one or both of the contestants, or a genealogy. In a classic example of narrative retrojection, the Beowulf-Unferth exchange devotes much of its bulk to the rival versions of a particular episode in Beowulf's career—the swimming match with Breca—on which each flyter imposes his own interpretative bias.[20] In *Il*.17.12–42 Euphorbos and Menelaos ground their flyting assertions on their own killings: Euphorbos claims credit for the slaughter of Patroklos, Menelaos counters by recalling his own slaying of Euphorbos's brother Hyperenor, and Euphorbos declares his intention now to avenge himself. Other flytings dredge up histories of prior martial encounters between the two present flyters. Achilles' narration of the previous encounter between them in which Aineias turned tail and ran is plainly designed to embarrass the Trojan (*Il*.20.178–98). Lykaon similarly recalls a prior meeting with Achilles but with the opposite motive—to remind Achilles that he spared his (Lykaon's) life once before in hopes that he will do so again (*Il*.21.74–96). All of these examples point to the centrality of action in the establishment of heroic identity. It is only natural that flyters should focus much of their discursive energy on those past heroic performances on the strength of which their present reputations are founded.

When heroes retroject into the sphere of action, usually they concentrate on the martial domain. Yet there is no reason in principle why heroes should not refer to other deeds that reflect creditably or discreditably on themselves or their adversaries. One would expect the strategies of attack and defense to register situationally appropriate ideologies. Because heroic flyting by definition concerns itself with combat, competence in this sphere is usually of prime interest. Yet Beowulf levels against Unferth the accusation of fratricide, a particularly heinous crime in an early Germanic society that accorded supreme value to loyalty and kinship. In his quarrel with Agamemnon (though not elsewhere), Achilles is concerned with iniquities in the distribution of battle spoils, a subject with particular bearing in an exchange between a ruler and his leading warrior. In the decisive struggle between Arjuna and his archfoe Karṇa in the battle of Kurukṣetra in the *Mahābhārata*, the doomed Karṇa and Krishna, here speaking on Arjuna's behalf, center their mutual appraisals on the theme of warriors' *dharma*; this focus is in keeping with the central thematic preoccupation of this epic. Concerns with overlordship, vassalage, and feudal rights figure largely in the flytings in *The Song of*

Roland and the *Alliterative Morte Arthure.* In short, we should expect a good measure of divergence, particularly between epic traditions, on the selection of focal flyting topics. What remains constant is the use of this material for the purposes of appraisal. Moreover, amid the variety, the interest in manly strength and prowess is likely to remain constant. For as we saw in the review of sociobiological backgrounds in chapter 1, these concerns are directly related to the evolution of such agonistic behavior.

In addition to the recollection of the personal accomplishments of the contestants, flyting affords another retrojective pathway through genealogical narration.[21] In response to the question "Who are you?" posed by Diomedes and the Danish coastguard, Glaukos (*Il.*6.145–211) and Beowulf (260–85) introduce genealogical information as the crucial component in their self-identifications, as we noted earlier. Asteropaios likewise answers Achilles' query as to his identity with a genealogical history (*Il.*21.153–60); and that Achilles gives an eristic construction to what many of us might have taken to be a rather neutral and nonbelligerent recital is shown by his postbattle vaunt in which he proclaims the superiority of his own lineage (184–99). Tlepolemos doubts that Sarpedon really is, as report would have him, the offspring of Zeus, and compares him unfavorably with Herakles, Tlepolemos's own father, whose sack of Troy he pointedly recalls (*Il.*5.633–46). In his reply Sarpedon admits the truth of this latter tale, though he predicts his own victory anyway (648–54). In *Il.*20.200–58 Aineias answers Achilles' taunting reference to their previous fortunes in battle with a genealogical retrojection; and the fact that Achilles pauses to reflect on this speech after the fight (344–52) bespeaks once more his recognition of the power and relevance of genealogical claims. Thus ancestry and deeds seem to contribute equally to heroic identity—the hero must defend both.

It would be worthwhile at this juncture to recall our previous discussion of the evolutionary backgrounds of intraspecific contesting, because in their selection of retrojective subject matter flyting heroes have with startling acuity singled out aspects of the heroic identity that correspond to major evolutionary determinants. A central purpose of agonistic displays in the animal world is to prove one possesses those qualities (such as strength and size) that promote adaptiveness. Yet far more important than survival of the individual is survival of the bloodline or, more precisely, the genes; thus many species adapt their behavior in the light of kinship, as we have seen earlier. By concentrating on martial prowess and personal ancestry, flyting contestants are foregrounding exactly these aspects of who they are: fitness and bloodline. This selection of topics seems to me to represent the refraction of evolutionary themes into this domain of human discourse.

In accordance with the aims of this chapter, my examples so far have derived from precombat flyting; yet some attention is due to postcombat vauntings as well, since the recollection of heroic incident (and, occasionally, genealogical information) plays a major role in these. Yet regularly it is the Trial of Arms immediately preceding to which the contestants are alluding. Thus, after killing Promachos, Akamas boasts to the listening Argives that hereby he has avenged the death of his brother (*Il*.14.479–85). Hektor similarly crows about his victory over Patroklos, while his dying foe tries pathetically to interpret the episode in such fashion as to minimize his own loss of glory (*Il*.16.830–54). On other occasions killers mockingly represent their victims' recent battle performance in terms of some other, nonmartial activity. Thus Patroklos praises Kebriones as a diver on account of the manner of his death fall (*Il*.16.745–50); in a similar spirit Poulydamas characterizes his spear as the staff on which his recent victim, Prothoënor, can lean during his descent to Hades (14.454–57). Although these cases do illustrate the marshaling of heroic accomplishment in support of present claims, I would nonetheless reserve the term retrojection for verbal acts that span outside the boundaries of the present contest.

There are, in fact, a few of these true retrojections in the postbattle vaunting material, such as Achilles' allusions to adversarial ancestral claims in *Il*.20.347–48 or 21.184–99. Other retrojections allude to matters neither primarily martial nor genealogical. Idomeneus, for example, mocks his dying victim Othryoneus with references to that Trojan's previous arrangements to marry one of Priam's daughters (*Il*.13.374–82). Menelaos similarly sets his own killing of Peisandros against the wrong that the Trojans did to him when they stole his wife Helen (*Il*.13.620-39). Both of these instances, it is worth noting, center on women. This subject matter seems in general to be excluded from the "serious," precombat flyting in the *Iliad*; the major exception, the Achilles-Agamemnon quarrel, is rather anomalous in other respects as well, as we saw in chapter 2. Yet postcombat vaunting evidently grants Homeric heroes greater lattitude in the expression of feelings and concerns pertaining to the nonmartial domain.

Projection

In their flyting, contestants regularly project future courses of action. I here intend "projection" or "casting forward" to designate the propositional substance in a sentence that refers to a future state of affairs; it is the pure, extracted content of future eventuality, divested of illocutionary overtones such as threatening, proposing, and commanding.[22] For example, when Beowulf *boasts* that he will kill Grendel, he is projecting (Beowulf kills Grendel); when Aias *challenges* Hektor to join in battle "ἀλλ' ἄρχε μάχης ἠδὲ πτολέμοιο," *Il*.7.232) or when Waldere *dares* Guthhere to strip the corselet from his back (*Waldere* 2.16–17), each hero is projecting an action that entails combat; when Lykaon *begs* Achilles for mercy (*Il*.21.94–96), he is projecting (Achilles does not slay Lykaon); when Meriones *speculates* that he would win glory ("εὖχος") if he could only hit Aineias with his spear (*Il*.16.623–25), he is projecting a possible two-step pathway to success in the form of a condition. Single speeches can project a multiplicity of possibilities; indeed, threats regularly do so. Thus when the Viking messenger in *Maldon* threatens Byrhtnoth (29–41), he is projecting the two mutually exclusive options of an English withdrawal and capitulation or a battle. Here again, the projective act comprises exclusively the mental or imaginative constitution of hypothetical futurity.

In that they are individually generated, unratified projections as such cannot constitute flyting contracts. Nonetheless, projecting is the usual mechanism by which contracts are developed. The validation that transforms projections into contracts results from a complex interactional process. For example, Unferth projects that Beowulf will lose to Grendel, whereas Beowulf projects that he will prevail. Their projections contradict each other on the matter of the outcome but coincide in the nature of the test: "Beowulf fights Grendel." This area of agreement, this projection overlap, comprises the contract. At no point during this structurally eristic flyting is this agreement set forth and approved as such; it remains a domain of tacit concurrence. Yet it is nonetheless binding for having been only partially articulated. Its binding power is rooted in the fact that heroic flytings as a genre exist precisely for the purpose of providing an interpretive verbal setting for such martial tests.

Attribution-Evaluation

Flyting exchanges backtrack and cast ahead in time largely for the purpose of evaluating the contestants. The retrojective and projective acts are involved with the marshaling of narrative matter, past and future. The chief task of the attributive-evaluative function is to bring this material to bear on the hero's present state of honor. Thus attribution and evaluation serve more to channel speaker attitudes toward incident than to represent and concretize it.[23]

Attribution and evaluation are two aspects of the same act. When

Sarpedon accuses Hektor of shying away from battle (*Il*.5.472–92), he is evaluating his companion-in-arms unfavorably by attributing to him the negative quality of cowardice.[24] Similarly, when Unferth through his narrative account attributes to Beowulf the quality of inferiority at swimming, this attribution implies an evaluation of Beowulf's heroic competence. In an eristic exchange, the attribution of qualities either increases or decreases honor. Attribution refers to the quality, evaluation to the augmentation or loss.

In a few cases, as we saw in the earlier discussion of the identitive function, contestants attribute and evaluate through terms of abuse or self-praise. Like contract formation, however, this function can—and often does—take place silently, in the sense that a narrative account can in itself attribute and evaluate without that quality or judgment being stated overtly. Unferth's speech, for example, contains virtually no explicit attributions; even his most condemnatory term, "dolgilpe" ("foolish boast," *Beo*.509) implies a lack of judgment and mental control rather than a lack of prowess. Yet the real point of the story is not that Beowulf was foolish in undertaking this swimming exploit, but that he *lost* at it; the incident can serve, accordingly, as the basis for the Danish *thyle*'s prediction, that Beowulf will perform even more poorly in his contest against Grendel than he did in his contest with Breca (525–28). For in this latter enterprise it is clearly brawn and not brains that will determine the winner. Thus, the major attributive-evaluative intention underlying Unferth's speech is not adequately represented by its only explicitly attributive-evaluative term.

William Labov, in his splendid analysis of "sounding" or "playing the dozens," develops a linguistic-semantic model that may be of use here (1972: 297–353). Ritual insults, Labov hypothesizes, have in their deep structure a clause of attribution, usually deleted in performance, that underlies stated insult propositions. Labov argues the point as follows:

> If sounds are heard as one kind of utterance, there must be a uniform mode of interpretation which shows all of these forms as derived from a single underlying structure. We propose that this structure is
>
> T(B) is so X that P
>
> where T is the target of the sound, X is the attribute of T which is focused on, and P is a proposition that is coupled with the attribute by the quantifier *so . . . that* to express the degree to which T has X.

B is here to be understood as the actual addressee; T(B), the target of the insult, is someone closely associated (normally consanguineous) with B, most often his mother. The attribute X is drawn from a range of characteristics (old age, obesity, blackness, etc.) viewed pejoratively by the sounder's social group. The surface syntax deletion of "T(B) is so X that P"

> is recoverable in the interpretation of the listener, who has the competence to know what attribute is being sounded on. For example, *Your mother look like Flipper* must be understood as "Your mother is so ugly that she looks like Flipper," whereas *Your mother name the Black Boy* will be interpreted "Your mother is so black that she is named 'Black Boy.' "[25]

It would not be difficult to imagine a similar process at work in heroic flyting. For example, if we condense Unferth's narration of the Breca episode into the proposition "Breca defeated you [Beowulf] at swimming," the total insult with its underlying attributive structure reinstated would be "you are so lacking in heroic prowess that Breca defeated you in swimming." Other flyting insults could be reconstructed in like fashion, with different heroically appropriate epithets of attribution. Of course, heroic flyters do not concentrate on the same qualities or sphere of competence as sounders do; as we saw earlier, heroes are most often concerned with battle proficiency and lineage, though other topics sometimes arise.[26] In fact, the differences between heroic flyting and playing the dozens are far-reaching: In chapter 5 I will argue that they represent two distinct genres of verbal contesting.[27] Yet despite the differences, *attribution* seems to be accomplished by a process common to both.

The intensity of attribution and evaluation typically correlates with the intensity of the eristic motive in the flyting exchange. For in those sections of flytings that foreground the contractual process (such as Hektor's speech to Achilles in *Il*.22.250–59), contestants will be most interested in negotiating courses of action; aggrandizements of the self and denigrations of the other would be liable to impede this process. But it is precisely through such evaluations that the eristic motive in verbal contests fulfills itself. Highly eristic flyting speeches, therefore, are evaluation-maximal; contractually oriented speeches tend to be evaluation-minimal.

Comparison

The retrojective, projective, and attributive-evaluative acts provide the chief mechanisms of articulation and judgment on matters of heroic identity. But whose histories, futures, and qualities do the flyters argue about? For the flyting match features *two* heroes, not one. What principle regulates the selection of and alternation between human targets?

This dichotomy in the structure of contests is negotiated through the operation of the comparative function; a hero in an eristic encounter tries to win *kleos* for himself and to discredit his opponent. Such comparisons can use matter generated through any of the processes examined so far. When Beowulf remarks that his struggle with the sea monsters surpasses any reputed deed of Unferth's, he is indulging in retrojective comparison. When he boasts that he will kill Grendel as Unferth and the Danes have failed to do, he is engaged in projective comparison. To the extent that his entire speech proves that he has more courage and martial capability than his Danish rival, he has performed an attributive-evaluative comparison. Thus, the comparative act establishes the *contestational relevance* of other discursive materials.

Sometimes heroic comparisons are plainly put forth, as in the previous examples. On other occasions, however, they are rendered with considerable indirection; yet they are nonetheless potent for their subtlety.[28] Waldere, for example, invites Guthhere to strip off his (Waldere's) corselet. The implication, of course, is that Guthhere will be unable to do this; and the insinuation that he could not despite the fact that Waldere is war-weary (*heaðuwerigan, Waldere* 2.17) from killing most of Guthhere's companions further suggests that in arms Guthhere must be very inferior indeed. Thus Waldere's projective comparison works through several levels of implicature. When Idomeneus mockingly congratulates the mortally wounded Othryoneus on the bridal compact he had previously negotiated with Priam and offers to find another bride from among the daughters of Agamemnon (*Il.*13.374–82), he is underscoring his (Idomeneus's) own victory in battle that has made all these things impossible. Yet at other times, especially when a contestant is trying to persuade a superior adversary to agree to some contractual provision, he suspends comparison and concentrates on projective exhortation. Thus, the speeches that Lykaon (*Il.*21.74–96) and Hektor (*Il.*22.250–59) address to Achilles reduce comparison to a minimum. In general, the degree to which heroic comparisons emerge into the surface of discourse varies in proportion to the dominance of the eristic over the contractual motives. For heroes engage in comparisons if they are planning to defeat each other, not if they wish to reach some accord.

It is worth noting, finally, that comparison plays a larger role than any other of these functions in the interrelating of flyting speeches. For a respondent is naturally inclined to reply to an eristic comparison with a comparison of his own. For example, Tlepolemos invigorates his attack on Sarpedon through a *retrojective* comparison: His adversary lacks the heroic qualities that his (Tlepolemos's) own progenitor, Herakles, displayed in his sack of Troy (*Il*.5.633–46). In answer, Sarpedon switches to a *projective* comparison: For while Tlepolemos's story of Herakles cannot be denied, speaking to the upcoming contest, "under my spear subdued you will surrender to me the boast, and your soul to Hades famed for his horses" (*Il*.5.653–54). The Achilles-Aineias flyting features a comparably motivated modulation from narrative to genealogical retrojection (*Il*.20.179–258), as we will study in detail in the last section in this chapter. In these and similar examples, it is the comparative motive that has singled out the grounds of attack and response.

Speech Linking

How does one flyter respond to another? What binds one speech to the next? What are the rules of interchange?

Comparing the principles of flyting with those of "sounding" or "playing the dozens," as Labov (1972) explicates them, offers a useful entry to this problem. Sounding, Labov argues, is based on the presupposition that none of the participants believe the insults to be true; indeed, some of these insults propose physical or biological absurdities ("Your mother's a duck," Labov 1972: 352). As a structural consequence, sounding moves from insult to insult. The game forbids self-defense, since such would undermine the "contract" of propositional nonreferentiality. This principle of nonresponse would, in the absence of a countervailing generic convention, result in simple disjunction between successive insults. Yet the connection is reestablished in another way: "A sounder opens a *field*, which is meant to be sustained. A sound is presented with the expectation that another sound will be offered in response, and that this second sound may be built formally upon it. The speaker who presents an initial sound is thus offering others the opportunity to display their ingenuity at his expense."[29] "Good" sounds are variations on the sound before. The constant feature can be either the target ("your mother") or some element of the proposition.

The notion of "field" pertains to heroic flyting as well as sounding. Yet heroic flyters, unlike sounders, intend their speeches as true statements, and so their flyting addressees cannot, when their turn comes, dispense with the self-defense. Thus, Clover characterizes the standard movement in flyting as a sequence of "Claim, Defense, and Counterclaim" (1980: 452). Because not all flyting speeches are attacks, a more comprehensive reformulation might propose a relationship of initiation and response, with the possibility of the respondent reinitiating and thereby provoking a further response, and so forth.[30] This initiation-response coupling represents a minimal bond of interchange, linking the speeches into continuing chains. I do not mean to imply that each speech centers on a single initiation to which the following speech immediately responds before turning to its own initiation. Obviously heroic flyting speeches are often complex affairs, initiating and responding in varying rhythms and in different topic areas. The precise manner in which a flyter spins these themes out discursively owes more to his personal rhetorical abilities and general rules of conversation than to universal principles of the heroic flyting genre.

Of what do these speech pairings consist? How do we know that one flyter has "responded" to another's "initiation"? What is the common substance that joins the initiation with the response?

Let us consider this problem of correspondence under two aspects: content and use.[31] In both of these areas the initiator marks out some topic of interchange (similar to a sounder's "field") to which the respondent is expected to address himself. This principle is everywhere operative in flyting exchanges. For example, in the Beowulf-Unferth encounter, the *thyle* designates two incidents as debate topics: the Breca-Beowulf swimming match and the Geat's prospective fight with Grendel. Beowulf responds in each of these two areas and initiates two attacks of his own, the first concerning Unferth's own dubious history as a brother-slayer, and the second concerning the failure of Unferth and the Danes generally to cope with Grendel's assaults. Thus, a retrojective and a projective assault have provoked, in the responding speech, rebuttals in the same retrojective and projective subject areas, and these rebuttals have served as the foundation for retrojective and projective reinitiations. For another illustration, consider the precombat flyting of Euphorbos and Menelaos in *Il.*17.12–42. Euphorbos initiates by retrojectively boasting of his role in the killing of Patroklos and by (projectively) warning his new adversary to back off or risk being cut down in turn. In the course of his reply, Menelaos retrojects on his own successful heroic exploit in the killing of Euphorbos's brother Hyperenor and counters with the same threat as his adversary has used—retreat or perish. Now Euphorbos expresses rage over the death of his brother and resolves to fight. Thus the topics that Euphorbos introduced in his first speech have, with certain transformations, persisted through to the end of flyting. The one heroic retrojection is matched by the other; and this retrojective interactivity is increased by the fact that each killing—and particularly Menelaos's killing of Hyperenor—not only reflects creditably upon the heroic competence of its author but stands as an insult to the flyting adversary who has not yet avenged it. Through their projections, however, these heroes are negotiating between a pair of options (fight or flight, reiterated by each contestant) in order to arrive at a martial contract. Thus the speeches are highly interactive and the flyting exchange as a whole remarkably coherent.

Yet flyting exchanges exhibit other copulative tendencies resulting from the interaction of speech illocutions.[32] The process I am referring to is in fact quite commonplace and not unique to flyters. For a question, such as that which the Danish coastguard addresses to Beowulf, calls for an answer; a command or exhortation, such as those that Achilles addresses to Aineias or Lykaon to Achilles, expects either acquiescence or refusal; an assertion, such as those that Unferth sets forth to Beowulf, implies a need for affirmation or negation.[33] Of course, interactions need not follow such straightforward pathways. A respondent to an inquiry, for example, does not *have* to answer; he can pretend that he has not heard, change the subject, ask his inquisitor to clarify his meaning, deny felicity conditions, and so forth.[34] Nonetheless, whatever his response, he must cope in some way with the expectation of an answer that the initiator's request has placed upon him. He cannot speak freely but must respond to certain constraints.[35]

In general, one can distinguish between speech act pairings in predominantly contractual versus predominantly eristic interactions in that the former conclude in a condition of relative closure whereas the latter leave off unresolved. For example, Diomedes asks a question and Glaukos answers it (*Il.*6.123–211); this unit of exchange has resolved what it raised and does not in itself require continuation in the same field or topic area. Diomedes reinitiates with a proposal that Glaukos accepts, and so, once again, closure has been attained. Contractually oriented speeches thus aim to produce terminal couplings, or units of interchange that resolve what they propose; a contestant can, of course, reinitiate, but the logic of the terminal unit does not itself insist on this. The eristically oriented speech, by contrast, generates open (continuing) speech pairings. Unferth accuses, Beowulf defends; although the Geat's response has been adequate to the attack, the discord projects some sequel. Beowulf now reinitiates with charges of his own; and while Unferth offers no reply, we as an audience know that the issue has not come to rest and that some further struggle is in store. They are indeed able to terminate their verbal exchange only on the strength of their contract: Now the fight with Grendel will judge between them. In fact, heroic flytings are usually able to close themselves within a relatively brief compass because contracting plays such a major and visible role. In other verbal contest genres (such as playing the dozens) that do not project any sequent combat, and which accordingly give full play to the eristic expression without any concomitant explicit contract negotiation, the verbal exchange continues until one of the contestants gives out and thereby concedes defeat. Thus contracting concludes while *eris* perpetuates itself. Contract making, on the one hand, occurs for the sake of that which is external to the verbal duel. Verbal *eris*, on the other hand, exists for its own display.

A SAMPLE EPISODE

Until this point our inquiry into the abstract principles that underlie flyting speeches has required that incidents and examples be stripped from their narrative contexts and juxtaposed one beside the other for the sorting out of similarities. In adopting such methods, however, one runs the risk of reducing all episodes to a generalized model, obscuring the fact that flyting belongs to the domain of behavior, or in our case, behavior fictionalized in epic representation. Contesting heroes are certainly not mere poetic instruments mechanically acting out a system of prescriptive epic laws. Their ability to hold the interest of listeners and readerships derives in some measure from the fact that they represent people, and like people, their behavior unfolds with a kind of holistic unpredictability. "Flyting" as a system of abstractions emerges only from specific actions, and in order to appreciate the real meaning of the abstract principles, we need to view them again clothed in the dress of their natural narrative environments.

The Achilles-Aineias encounter in *Il.*20.158–352 serves exemplary purposes well because it is highly developed both as a whole contest and as a flyting exchange. The episode runs as follows. In a scene of martial combat on the day of Achilles' greatest rampage, two eminent heroes are singled out from their embattled armies (element A^{bf}, 158–77) and engage in a nominally contractual yet eristically toned Flyting (B^{bf}, 178–258) in which they compare their merits retrojectively and contract for a fight. The actual Combat (C^{bf}, 259–340), intensively pursued and expansively narrated, is broken off in midcourse as Poseidon lifts the Trojan out of battle. Achilles, although cheated of the kill, nonetheless proclaims his victory (D^{bf}, 344–52). The contest lacks "correct" Resolution in that the Achaian does not cut down his enemy and boast over the corpse. Yet, as the modern military strategist and Homer both know, the progress of battle is subject to unpredictable external influences, chief among which, for Homer, is the intervention of gods. Heroic contests cannot claim absolute autonomy and insulation from the outside world. "Real"-life vagaries repeatedly impinge upon the course of heroic endeavor in the *Iliad*; and the battlefield contest pattern, here as elsewhere, exhibits the flexibility to accommodate this.

Let us now examine individually the two precombat flyting speeches and the postcombat "victory boast." The actual fight will receive only summary consideration since our primary interest lies with the verbal rather than with the martial aspect of the contest. Achilles opens the exchange (B^bf) in *Il.*20.178–98:

"Αἰνεία, τί σὺ τόσσον ὁμίλου πολλὸν ἐπελθὼν
ἔστης; ἦ σέ γε θυμὸς ἐμοὶ μαχέσασθαι ἀνώγει
180 ἐλπόμενον Τρώεσσιν ἀνάξειν ἱπποδάμοισι
τιμῆς τῆς Πριάμου; ἀτὰρ εἴ κεν ἔμ᾽ ἐξεναρίξῃς,
οὔ τοι τοὔνεκά γε Πρίαμος γέρας ἐν χερὶ θήσει·
εἰσὶν γάρ οἱ παῖδες, ὁ δ᾽ ἔμπεδος οὐδ᾽ ἀεσίφρων.
ἦ νύ τί τοι Τρῶες τέμενος τάμον ἔξοχον ἄλλων,
185 καλὸν φυταλιῆς καὶ ἀρούρης, ὄφρα νέμηαι,
αἴ κεν ἐμὲ κτείνῃς; χαλεπῶς δέ σ᾽ ἔολπα τὸ ῥέξειν.
ἤδη μὲν σέ γέ φημι καὶ ἄλλοτε δουρὶ φοβῆσαι.
ἦ οὐ μέμνῃ ὅτε πέρ σε βοῶν ἄπο μοῦνον ἐόντα
σεῦα κατ᾽ Ἰδαίων ὀρέων ταχέεσσι πόδεσσι
190 καρπαλίμως; τότε δ᾽ οὔ τι μετατροπαλίζεο φεύγων.
ἔνθεν δ᾽ ἐς Λυρνησσὸν ὑπέκφυγες· αὐτὰρ ἐγὼ τὴν
πέρσα μεθορμηθεὶς σὺν Ἀθήνῃ καὶ Διὶ πατρί,
ληϊάδας δὲ γυναῖκας ἐλεύθερον ἦμαρ ἀπούρας
ἦγον· ἀτὰρ σὲ Ζεὺς ἐρρύσατο καὶ θεοὶ ἄλλοι.
195 ἀλλ᾽ οὐ νῦν ἐρύεσθαι ὀίομαι, ὡς ἐνὶ θυμῷ
βάλλεαι· ἀλλά σ᾽ ἔγωγ᾽ ἀναχωρήσαντα κελεύω
ἐς πληθὺν ἰέναι, μηδ᾽ ἀντίος ἵστασ᾽ ἐμεῖο,
πρίν τι κακὸν παθέειν· ῥεχθὲν δέ τε νήπιος ἔγνω."

"Aineias, why have you stood so far forth from the multitude
against me? Does the desire in your heart drive you to combat
180 in hope you will be lord of the Trojans, breakers of horses,
and of Priam's honour. And yet even if you were to kill me
Priam would not because of that rest such honour in your hand.
He has sons, and he himself is sound, not weakened.
Or have the men of Troy promised you a piece of land,
surpassing
185 all others, fine ploughland and orchard for you to administer
if you kill me? But I think that killing will not be easy.
Another time before this, I tell you, you ran from my spear.
Or do you not remember when, apart from your cattle, I caught
you

alone, and chased you in the speed of your feet down the hills of
Ida

190　headlong, and that time as you ran you did not turn to look back.
Then you got away into Lyrnessos, but I went after you
and stormed that place, with the help of Athene and Zeus father,
and took the day of liberty away from their women
and led them as spoil, but Zeus and the other gods saved you.

195　I think they will not save you now, as your expectation
tells you they will. No, but I myself urge you to get back
into the multitude, not stand to face me, before you
take some harm. Once a thing has been done, the fool sees it."

(Lattimore 1951: 409)

This speech can be subdivided into five sections: identification
(178–79), projective analysis (179–86), retrojective narration (187–
94), projection in the negative (195–96), and a projective contract offer (196–98).

The identification consists of a naming ("Αἰνεία") along with a
brief denomination of the action of stepping forth—which signifies
the willingness to engage in contesting—that the addressee has just
performed. Thus, Achilles anchors the flyting dialogics that he is initiating in a specific frame of reference. By simultaneously asking into
Aineias's reason for singling himself out ("Τί;"—"Why?"), Achilles
makes the transition into the section that follows.

In the next eight lines (179–86) Achilles proposes and answers two
questions, both relating to his adversary's hypothetical motives for
daring to face him in battle. This question-and-answer movement
amounts structurally to a kind of dialogue assimilated into a single
speech. In essence Achilles is engaging alternately in second-order
and first-order projective analysis, as he attributes projections to his
adversary and then opposes predictions of his own. The attributed
projections take the logical form of "if X then Y," with the "if X"
clause somewhat suppressed: "if you (Aineias) defeat me in battle,
then you will win honor and lordship"; and "if you kill me, then the
Trojans will give you the land they have promised." Each of these "if
X then Y" projections Achilles confutes with an antithetical projection: "even if you kill me, Priam will not prefer you," and "you are
hardly likely to beat me in any case." Note how natural it is for Achilles, the veteran of many such contests, to impute to his adversary the
eristic motive of desire for honor ("τιμῆς," 181) betokened as lordship or material reward.

In the next eight lines Achilles turns from projection to a self-ag-
grandizing retrojection as he recounts the history of their previous

meeting. Achilles' speech does not *explicitly* attribute to Aineias the qualities of cowardice and martial inferiority; yet the story itself, highly creditable to the Achaian and embarrassing to his foe, obviously serves the ends of comparative evaluation.

The next two lines (195–96) in effect link the central retrojection with the concluding projection through the theme of the intervention of Zeus (divine witness and judge). The sentence contains a projection in the negative—that Zeus will *not* rescue Aineias this time; by implication, then, Achilles is projecting that, if Aineias fights, he will die.

Achilles makes an explicit contractual offer in the last three lines (196–98) as he proposes that Aineias retreat before he is hurt. This warning constitutes the main illocutionary thrust of the speech. Nominally at least, his speech is contractually oriented, paralleling in this regard the first address of the Viking messenger in *Maldon* who similarly proposes two possible contracts—a fight or a capitulation. The speeches of Achilles and the Viking both presume that the addressee does not measure up to the rank of the speaker; thus the contract offer is charged with eristic overtones. In fact, one doubts that Achilles extends the "retreat" option in good faith, since his recent career has hardly been distinguished by compassion and concern for the well-being of his enemies. Rather, one suspects that his "offer" adds up to an insult through its presupposition of extreme mismatch. This fight, Achilles insinuates, would not even be a contest, so great is his own superiority. This implication is not lost on his opponent.

Thus initiated, the precombat Flyting (B^bf) is concluded with Aineias's extended reply (200–58):

> 200 "Πηλεΐδη, μὴ δὴ ἐπέεσσί με νηπύτιον ὣς
> ἔλπεο δειδίξεσθαι, ἐπεὶ σάφα οἶδα καὶ αὐτὸς
> ἠμὲν κερτομίας ἠδ' αἴσυλα μυθήσασθαι.
> ἴδμεν δ' ἀλλήλων γενεήν, ἴδμεν δὲ τοκῆας,
> πρόκλυτ' ἀκούοντες ἔπεα θνητῶν ἀνθρώπων·
> 205 ὄψει δ' οὔτ' ἄρ πω σὺ ἐμοὺς ἴδες οὔτ' ἄρ' ἐγὼ σούς.
> φασὶ σὲ μὲν Πηλῆος ἀμύμονος ἔκγονον εἶναι,
> μητρὸς δ' ἐκ Θέτιδος καλλιπλοκάμου ἁλοσύδνης·
> αὐτὰρ ἐγὼν υἱὸς μεγαλήτορος Ἀγχίσαο
> εὔχομαι ἐκγεγάμεν, μήτηρ δέ μοί ἐστ' Ἀφροδίτη·
> 210 τῶν δὴ νῦν ἕτεροί γε φίλον παῖδα κλαύσονται
> σήμερον· οὐ γάρ φημ' ἐπέεσσί γε νηπυτίοισιν
> ὧδε διακρινθέντε μάχης ἒξ ἀπονέεσθαι.
> εἰ δ' ἐθέλεις καὶ ταῦτα δαήμεναι, ὄφρ' ἐΰ εἰδῇς
> ἡμετέρην γενεήν, πολλοὶ δέ μιν ἄνδρες ἴσασι·

215 Δάρδανον αὖ πρῶτον τέκετο νεφεληγερέτα Ζεύς,
κτίσσε δὲ Δαρδανίην, ἐπεὶ οὔ πω Ἴλιος ἱρὴ
ἐν πεδίῳ πεπόλιστο, πόλις μερόπων ἀνθρώπων,
ἀλλ᾽ ἔθ᾽ ὑπωρείας ᾤκεον πολυπίδακος Ἴδης.
Δάρδανος αὖ τέκεθ᾽ υἱὸν Ἐριχθόνιον βασιλῆα,
220 ὃς δὴ ἀφνειότατος γένετο θνητῶν ἀνθρώπων·
τοῦ τρισχίλιαι ἵπποι ἕλος κάτα βουκολέοντο
θήλειαι, πώλοισιν ἀγαλλόμεναι ἀταλῆσι.
τάων καὶ Βορέης ἠράσσατο βοσκομενάων,
ἵππῳ δ᾽ εἰσάμενος παρελέξατο κυανοχαίτῃ·
225 αἱ δ᾽ ὑποκυσάμεναι ἔτεκον δυοκαίδεκα πώλους.
αἱ δ᾽ ὅτε μὲν σκιρτῷεν ἐπὶ ζείδωρον ἄρουραν,
ἄκρον ἐπ᾽ ἀνθερίκων καρπὸν θέον οὐδὲ κατέκλων·
ἀλλ᾽ ὅτε δὴ σκιρτῷεν ἐπ᾽ εὐρέα νῶτα θαλάσσης,
ἄκρον ἐπὶ ῥηγμῖνος ἁλὸς πολιοῖο θέεσκον.
230 Τρῶα δ᾽ Ἐριχθόνιος τέκετο Τρώεσσιν ἄνακτα·
Τρωὸς δ᾽ αὖ τρεῖς παῖδες ἀμύμονες ἐξεγένοντο,
Ἴλός τ᾽ Ἀσσάρακός τε καὶ ἀντίθεος Γανυμήδης,
ὃς δὴ κάλλιστος γένετο θνητῶν ἀνθρώπων·
τὸν καὶ ἀνηρείψαντο θεοὶ Διὶ οἰνοχοεύειν
235 κάλλεος εἵνεκα οἷο, ἵν᾽ ἀθανάτοισι μετείη.
Ἴλος δ᾽ αὖ τέκεθ᾽ υἱὸν ἀμύμονα Λαομέδοντα·
Λαομέδων δ᾽ ἄρα Τιθωνὸν τέκετο Πρίαμόν τε
Λάμπον τε Κλυτίον θ᾽ Ἱκετάονά τ᾽, ὄζον Ἄρηος·
Ἀσσάρακος δὲ Κάπυν, ὁ δ᾽ ἄρ᾽ Ἀγχίσην τέκε παῖδα·
240 αὐτὰρ ἔμ᾽ Ἀγχίσης, Πρίαμος δὲ τέχ᾽ Ἕκτορα δῖον.
ταύτης τοι γενεῆς τε καὶ αἵματος εὔχομαι εἶναι.
Ζεὺς δ᾽ ἀρετὴν ἄνδρεσσιν ὀφέλλει τε μινύθει τε,
ὅππως κεν ἐθέλῃσιν· ὁ γὰρ κάρτιστος ἁπάντων.
ἀλλ᾽ ἄγε μηκέτι ταῦτα λεγώμεθα νηπύτιοι ὥς,
245 ἑσταότ᾽ ἐν μέσσῃ ὑσμίνῃ δηϊοτῆτος.
ἔστι γὰρ ἀμφοτέροισιν ὀνείδεα μυθήσασθαι
πολλὰ μάλ᾽, οὐδ᾽ ἂν νηῦς ἑκατόζυγος ἄχθος ἄροιτο.
στρεπτὴ δὲ γλῶσσ᾽ ἐστὶ βροτῶν, πολέες δ᾽ ἔνι μῦθοι
παντοῖοι, ἐπέων δὲ πολὺς νομὸς ἔνθα καὶ ἔνθα.
250 ὁπποῖόν κ᾽ εἴπησθα ἔπος, τοῖόν κ᾽ ἐπακούσαις.
ἀλλὰ τίη ἔριδας καὶ νείκεα νῶϊν ἀνάγκη
νεικεῖν ἀλλήλοισιν ἐναντίον, ὥς τε γυναῖκας,
αἵ τε χολωσάμεναι ἔριδος πέρι θυμοβόροιο
νεικεῦσ᾽ ἀλλήλῃσι μέσην ἐς ἄγυιαν ἰοῦσαι,
255 πόλλ᾽ ἐτεά τε καὶ οὐκί· χόλος δέ τε καὶ τὰ κελεύει.
ἀλκῆς δ᾽ οὔ μ᾽ ἐπέεσσιν ἀποτρέψεις μεμαῶτα

πρὶν χαλκῷ μαχέσασθαι ἐναντίον· ἀλλ᾽ ἄγε θᾶσσον
γευσόμεθ᾽ ἀλλήλων χαλκήρεσιν ἐγχείῃσιν."

200 "Son of Peleus, never hope by words to frighten me
as if I were a baby. I myself understand well enough
how to speak in vituperation and how to make insults.
You and I know each other's birth, we both know our parents
since we have heard the lines of their fame from mortal men;
only

205 I have never with my eyes seen your parents, nor have you seen
mine.
For you, they say you are the issue of blameless Peleus
and that your mother was Thetis of the lovely hair, the sea's lady;
I in turn claim I am the son of great-hearted Anchises
but that my mother was Aphrodite; and that of these parents

210 one group or the other will have a dear son to mourn for
this day. Since I believe we will not in mere words, like children,
meet, and separate and go home again out of the fighting.
Even so, if you wish to learn all this and be certain
of my genealogy: there are plenty of men who know it.

215 First of all Zeus who gathers the clouds had a son, Dardanos
who founded Dardania, since there was yet no sacred Ilion
made a city in the plain to be a centre of peoples,
but they lived yet in the underhills of Ida with all her waters.
Dardanos in turn had a son, the king, Erichthonios,

220 who became the richest of mortal men, and in his possession
were three thousand horses who pastured along the low
grasslands,
mares in their pride with their young colts; and with these the
North Wind
fell in love as they pastured there, and took on upon him
the likeness of a dark-maned stallion, and coupled with them,

225 and the mares conceiving of him bore to him twelve young
horses.
Those, when they would play along the grain-giving tilled land
would pass along the tassels of corn and not break the divine
yield,
but again, when they played across the sea's wide ridges
they would run the edge of the wave where it breaks on the grey
salt water.

230 Erichthonios had a son, Tros, who was lord of the Trojans,
and to Tros in turn there were born three sons unfaulted,
Ilos and Assarakos and godlike Ganymedes

who was the loveliest born of the race of mortals, and therefore
the gods caught him away to themselves, to be Zeus' wine-pourer,
235   for the sake of his beauty, so that he might be among the
          immortals.
Ilos in turn was given a son, the blameless Laomedon,
and Laomedon had sons in turn, Tithonos and Priam,
Lampos, Klytios and Hiketaon, scion of Ares;
but Assarakos had Kapys, and Kapys' son was Anchises,
240   and I am Anchises' son, and Priam's is Hektor the brilliant.
Such is the generation and blood I claim to be born from.
Zeus builds up and Zeus diminishes the strength in men,
the way he pleases, since his power is beyond all others'.
But come, let us no longer stand here talking of these things
245   like children, here in the space between the advancing armies.
For there are harsh things enough that could be spoken against
          us
both, a ship of a hundred locks could not carry the burden.
The tongue of man is a twisty thing, there are plenty of words
          there
of every kind, the range of words is wide, and their variance.
250   The sort of thing you say is the thing that will be said to you.
But what have you and I to do with the need for squabbling
and hurling insults at each other, as if we were two wives
who when they have fallen upon a heart-perishing quarrel
go out in the street and say abusive things to each other,
255   much true, and much that is not, and it is their rage that drives
          them.
You will not by talking turn me back from the strain of my
          warcraft,
not till you have fought to my face with the bronze. Come on
          then
and let us try each other's strength with the bronze of our
          spearheads."

(Lattimore 1951: 409–11)

This ostensibly digressive speech makes three major points. Its bulk
is devoted to a lengthy genealogical retrojection, around and through
which is woven Aineias's insistence that he will not be daunted by
mere words. The speech culminates in his injunction to join in battle.

After an opening one-word identification by the patronymic ("son
of Peleus"), Aineias parries the illocutionary thrust of Achilles' speech
in 196–98 by refusing to be intimidated by mere threats unacted
upon (200–202). He repeats and develops this theme twice more, in

lines 211–12 and 244–57. On all three occasions he characterizes as "childish" (200, 211, and 244) the mere exchange of insults unsubstantiated in battle; and in 251–55 he likens such activity to the quarreling of wives. Even women and children can quarrel, but only heroes can fight—a sentiment that reaffirms one of the central tenets of the heroic code. All of these statements amount to a rejection of Achilles' contract offer—that the Trojan should withdraw into the multitude and avoid battle. The fact that Aineias so belabors this point suggests his own awareness of the odds that he is facing.

Several interesting features appear in the first phase (203–11) of the genealogical retrojection. In Achilles' speech, the comparative and evaluative functions figured most visibly in the retrojective narration of the anterior Achilles-Aineias meeting. Aineias responds to this story with a retrojection of his own; yet he modulates from "past deeds" to the other chief retrojective tack, genealogy. The Trojan marks out his position clearly—his ancestry compares with Achilles' as Aphrodite does with Thetis. In short, he is as superior in lineage as Achilles is with respect to their previous battle encounter. This rough balancing implies parity of heroic competence; and so, as he implies in lines 210–11, their relative heroic merits will indeed be tested by a fight whose conclusion is not foregone (since *one set of parents or the other* will mourn this day). By alluding to the outcome of combat, Aineias is indirectly projecting that encounter that Achilles had urged him to avoid. Finally, we should note that this portion of Aineias's speech, and especially 206–09, displays the comparative function more explicitly than does any other portion of the flyting exchange.

In lines 211–12 Aineias responds once more to Achilles' contractual initiation by refusing to settle for mere words in place of heroic action. Because Aineias is willing to submit his claims of comparability to the proof of combat, Achilles might very well be interested in hearing out these genealogical boasts more fully, as the Trojan implies in line 213. At this juncture he embarks on the second phase of his genealogical retrojection, which this time occupies a full twenty-seven lines, only now he switches from his maternal to his paternal pedigree. Scion of an illustrious line, great-great-great-great-great-grandson of Zeus, he can number Priam and Hektor as relatives. Thus, he is a descendant of gods on both sides, fully a match for Achilles on this account. While twice insisting on its veracity (214 and 241), Aineias does not, in this the second phase of his retrojection, explicitly evaluate or compare. Nonetheless, he does characterize himself as boasting ("εὔχομαι," 241; cf. 209); and Achilles' subsequent re-

sponse leaves no doubt that he has construed his enemy's genealogical rehearsal as carrying an eristic intent.

In lines 242–43 Aineias, by commenting on Zeus's ability to increase and to diminish human strength, reaffirms the presence of
that power of judgment that can determine the outcome of battle.
Contests are not private quarrels; supernal witnessing belongs to
their most basic structure. Aineias is further reaffirming the comparability of contestants, contrary to the aspersions that Achilles has
cast. For since the fate of combat depends on the god's pleasure, either Achilles or Aineias is capable of winning. Another beleaguered
flyter, Hektor, calls on the same argument later in this book (20.435–
37).

Now at last Aineias comes to the illocutionary point of his speech
as he negotiates between the possibilities that Achilles has extended
to him and concludes the contractual process. First, he rejects the
possibility of flyting without fighting and expresses contempt for such
exchanges of vituperation (244–55); he even goes so far as to imply
that Achilles' attempt to intimidate him masks a fear of his own
(Aineias's) martial prowess (256–57). Now opening his positive contract projection with the same exhortative phrase, "ἀλλ' ἄγε" ("but
come"), as that with which he opened his negative contract projection
in 244, Aineias invites Achilles to join in a Trial of Arms (257–58).
This offer with its explicit rejection of continued flyting illustrates
how contract negotiation—even for combat—brings an end to verbal
eris. Of the two options that Achilles plotted out, Aineias has accepted
combat; contractual pairings are terminal, and the flyting must now
end. The exhortative tones of Aineias's injunction to battle illustrate
the collaborative underpinnings of this whole flyting venture.

The preliminary verbal duel now concluded, Achilles and Aineias
begin to fight (element C^{bf}). First, Aineias casts his spear, which does
not succeed in penetrating Achilles' shield (259–272); Achilles' own
retaliatory spear throw misses Aineias narrowly (273–83). The two
heroes now prepare for hand-to-hand combat (Achilles' sword
against Aineias's stone) that would have resulted, Homer tells us, in
the Trojan's death (283–90). At this point the gods intervene (291–
339). After discussing the situation with Hera, Poseidon pours a mist
about Achilles' eyes, returns his spear, lifts Aineias out of the fighting,
and in a short speech discourages him from challenging the mighty
Achaian again. This sequence, though intrinsically interesting in
many of its elements, bears only indirect relevance to the flyting and
therefore need concern us no further.

Poseidon now withdraws the mist from Achilles who, surveying the new scene, utters what in this case substitutes for the victory boast (element D1^{bf}, 344–52):

> "ὦ πόποι, ἦ μέγα θαῦμα τόδ' ὀφθαλμοῖσιν ὁρῶμαι·
> 345 ἔγχος μὲν τόδε κεῖται ἐπὶ χθονός, οὐδέ τι φῶτα
> λεύσσω, τῷ ἐφέηκα κατακτάμεναι μενεαίνων.
> ἦ ῥα καὶ Αἰνείας φίλος ἀθανάτοισι θεοῖσιν
> ἦεν· ἀτάρ μιν ἔφην μὰψ αὔτως εὐχετάασθαι.
> ἐρρέτω· οὔ οἱ θυμὸς ἐμεῦ ἔτι πειρηθῆναι
> 350 ἔσσεται, ὃς καὶ νῦν φύγεν ἄσμενος ἐκ θανάτοιο.
> ἀλλ' ἄγε δὴ Δαναοῖσι φιλοπτολέμοισι κελεύσας
> τῶν ἄλλων Τρώων πειρήσομαι ἀντίος ἐλθών."

> "Can this be? Here is a strange thing I see with my own eyes.
> 345 Here is my spear lying on the ground, but I can no longer
> see the man, whom I was charging in fury to kill him.
> Aineias was then one beloved of the immortal
> gods. I thought what he said was ineffectual boasting.
> Let him go. He will not again have daring to try me
> 350 in battle, since even now he was glad to escape my onset.
> Come! I must urge on the Danaans whose delight is in battle
> and go on to face the rest of the Trojans, and see what they can
> do."

> (Lattimore 1951: 413)

Like the vaunt, this speech is fundamentally retrospective in its orientation: Achilles is trying to interpret and evaluate the Trial of Arms that has just taken place. The first three lines (344–46) register his surprise at the sudden disappearance of his enemy. The next two lines (347–48) contain Achilles' response to Aineias's genealogical retrojection in the precombat flyting. Aineias has won his point on that account, Achilles is forced to concede. But in the next two lines (349–50) the Achaian comes to the main issue: Aineias has essentially lost and will not dare face his wrath again. With this boast Achilles concludes the contest and turns to new exploits.

CHAPTER FOUR

The Contest Paradigm in the Structure of Epic and Romance Narrative

INTRODUCTION

In attending to the project of *defining* heroic flyting on different levels and from various viewpoints, I have paid scant attention to the poetic works from which these episodes have been drawn. Nor indeed would delvings into the particular literary problems of particular poems be appropriate here, since my method is ill-suited to such purposes. Until such problems have been addressed, we cannot legitimately construe any particular heroic narrative as transparent to the types of meanings that I have been adumbrating. Nonetheless, I do feel that flyting and contest paradigms participate in the production of literary patternings of many types, and their recognition can bring out dimensions of literary works whose significance might otherwise go unappreciated. Although this point could be illustrated in several ways, in this chapter I concentrate on the role of major flyting exchanges as constitutive strands in the larger narrative structures of epic and romance.

This claim has already been argued in the case of the *Iliad*. As we saw in chapter 2, the main action of that poem flows from a flyting between Achilles and Agamemnon that represents in its essentials a quarrel-and-contract exchange of the guest-host variety. For after flirting momentarily with the notion of direct (battlefield) combat (1.188–222), Achilles chooses an externally directed Trial of Arms: He will prove his superiority to Agamemnon with respect to his ability to defeat Hektor. Thus both movements of his wrath, first against his chieftan and later against his Trojan rival, are implicit in the contractual structure set forth at the poem's opening. In this sense the *Iliad* is the tale of a single contest. It is the recognition of flyting conventions that brings this coherency into view and establishes the cross-cultural generality of the principles on which this coherency rests.

Because *Beowulf* is more episodic in its narrative organization, neither of its flytings participates in such a global movement. Rather, they belong to a chain of commissive interactions through which Beowulf binds himself to his first great exploit of destroying Grendel; after this is accomplished, their force is spent. The first in the sequence, the flyting with the coastguard, modulates into a friendly exchange when the Geat convinces his inquisitor that his intentions are amicable toward the Danish people. The subsequent dialogue with Wulfgar (333–55) refers the question of Beowulf's identity and motivation on to Hrothgar, who welcomes warmly the son of a former guest-friend, Ecgtheow, and accepts his offer of assistance (407–490). The flyting with Unferth intensifies the commitment in Beowulf's previous boasts through the challenge of open human skepticism; further, it brings more plainly into view his standing as a young and relatively untried hero who wants to prove himself. The last in this series, the boast that Beowulf delivers before his retainers in the mead hall just before going to bed (677–87), expresses his unwillingness to fight with a sword when his adversary, Grendel, lacks one. A hero can reap the full sum of glory only if the conditions of combat are equal. All these exchanges are formal, public, and binding. The flytings do not differ from the boasts in their commissive power; yet they do bring out different situational nuances. The flyting with the coastguard, by its movement into the guest-host track, establishes the expectation that combat will be outerdirected (toward monsters) rather than intraspecific and intertribal. The Beowulf-Unferth exchange underscores the point that, by failing in what he has undertaken, Beowulf would lose not only his life but his reputation among men. Thus both the risks and the credit for success are highlighted.

More could be said about flyting in both poems. But now I would like to shift the focus to several new bodies of material from different cultures and eras to illustrate my argument that the flyting and contest paradigms have roots that defy national and cultural boundaries. It is true that the Greek-to-Old English comparison is a happy one, since a warlike mentality is particularly ascendant in much of the narrative poetry from both early civilizations. When the ideological concerns of a narrative work are more diversified, however, agonistic patterns become entangled with other narrative forms in ways that are difficult to unravel. In some poems, the agonistic theme disappears from view altogether, because the universe of human experience provides many topics, of which formal contesting is just one. The primary narrative material in this chapter has been selected with a view to its power in illustrating both the durability of the flyting and contesting themes and their susceptibility to transformation and sublimation under the influence of nonagonistic ideologies. The basic movements toward contract formation and self-glorification persist. Yet they begin to be diverted in new ways and acquire new meanings.

I must preface this chapter with two reservations. First, this inquiry will lead me into fields with which I am less familiar; indeed, in the case of Sanskrit epic, I have been compelled to work entirely with translations. Such indiscretions are unavoidable, however, if one does not wish to see one's topic imprisoned within an artificially constricted orbit. Second, all four narrative works that I will be reviewing exist within settings—for example, sociological, literary, or ideological—that problematize their comparison. Of course, this was true for the Greek-to-Old English comparison as well. Yet in those literary traditions the agonistic theme was dominant enough to justify its own use as a common context. This will be less the case as I trespass further from productions of the "heroic age." Nonetheless, the agonistic thread does persist, and to show this will be my major aim. Within the brief compass allowable for these discussions I will try to indicate how the contest has been reshaped, often in fundamental ways. But the reader will bear in mind that my target is not each literary work as a whole but only one constitutive strand.

The focal material in what follows will include the competition between Arjuna and Karṇa in the *Mahābhārata*; the diplomatic missions exchanged between Arthur and the Roman emperor Lucius in the Middle English *Alliterative Morte Arthure*; the dispute between Roland and Ganelon in *The Song of Roland*; and the beheading contest in *Sir Gawain and the Green Knight*. Representing, like the Homeric epics, a more ancient civilization, the *Mahābhārata* removes us from the European orbit in which the other works are contained. The *Alliterative Morte Arthure* presents us with a late-blooming heroic narrative with strong spiritual ties to its epic ancestors. The *chanson de geste* represents medieval epic in its highly developed continental form, conditioned, like the two Middle English works, by feudal Christianity. Composed in the same century as its Middle English counterpart, *Gawain* moves us from epic to romance, from heroism to chivalry and courtly love. The emergence of recognizably similar structures from such diverse contexts attests to both the malleability and enduring potency of flyting as a dialogic and narrative form.

THE ARJUNA-KARṆA RIVALRY IN THE *MAHĀBHĀRATA*

It is with no small trepidation that I venture into the vast, diffuse landscape of the *Mahābhārata*, whose sheer length (some seventy-five thousand shlokas), encyclopedic inclusiveness, plot complexity, and tangled textual history are hardly to be rivaled in world epic literature.[1] Created and compiled between 400 B.C. and A.D. 400, it is clearly the work of many hands, to be regarded, as van Buitenen says, "not so much as one opus but as a library of opera" (1973: xxv). If we ignore the voluminous digressions, however, we will find a central plot line that is surprisingly coherent. And the flyting-to-fighting sequences, both greater and lesser, contribute materially to its integrity.

With the aims of this study in view, the storyline can be summarized thus. The two wives of the Bhārata king Vicitravīrya have one son each, the blind king Dhṛtarāṣṭra, and Pāṇḍu.[2] Pāṇḍu's wives have five legitimate sons, known as the Pāṇḍavas: the eldest and heir apparent Yudhiṣṭhira, and his younger siblings Bhīma, Arjuna, Nakula, and Sahadeva. Yet unbeknownst to the five brothers, they have been preceded by Karṇa, who is raised by a charioteer and whose true parentage long remains unknown.[3] The Pāṇḍavas' rights of succession to the kingship are generally acknowledged, even though, after Pāṇḍu's early death, Dhṛtarāṣṭra acts as regent while the younger generation grows up. Dhṛtarāṣṭra for his part has one hundred sons, notably the eldest, Duryodhana. This wing of the family is known as the Kauravas, or descendants of Kuru.

From early childhood Duryodhana is jealous of his cousins and makes numerous attempts on their lives. After one of these the Pāṇḍavas, now grown men, escape into the jungle and engage in a series of adventures, one of which culminates in all five of them marrying the princess Draupadī. Reconciled with the Kauravas in due course, the Pāṇḍavas move to Indraprastha where Yudhiṣṭhira becomes universal monarch. Yet now the crafty Duryodhana tries a new plan. Inviting his cousins to his own capital at Hāstinapura, he challenges Yudhiṣṭhira to a game of dice. Yudhiṣṭhira gambles away everything, including himself, his brothers, and their wife. The behavior of Duryodhana, his brother Duḥśāsana, and their confederate Karṇa is particularly outrageous on this occasion, as they undertake (unsuccessfully) to disrobe Draupadī on the spot, before the very eyes of her husbands. Through Dhṛtarāṣṭra's intervention, however, disenfranchisement and slavery become commuted to a thirteen-year term of exile, after which the Pāṇḍavas are entitled to reclaim their patrimony.

Yet when the thirteen years have passed, Duryodhana refuses to keep his end of the bargain. The upshot is the eighteen-day battle at Kurukṣetra, featuring massive armies, supernatural weapons, and dramatic single combats. The greatest warrior of the Pāṇḍavas, Arjuna, meets his long-time rival Karṇa and, with the help of his friend and guru Krishna, kills him; Bhīma likewise kills Duḥśāsana and Duryodhana, as he had earlier sworn to do. These are only several of the many critical battle encounters, extravagantly narrated. In the end, the Pāṇḍavas prevail (despite the annihilation of both armies) and rule in peace until old age.

Thus centering on a conflict that culminates in ruinous battle, this story provides numerous occasions for heroic display of the first order and in this respect bears comparison with its epic counterparts in the Greek and Old English worlds.[4] Yet in Sanskrit epic the heroic ethos is subordinated to the larger concept of *dharma*, an untranslatable term carrying connotations of duty, role, law, and cosmic harmony.[5] The obligation to act in accordance with dharma binds the entire social spectrum; yet dharmas vary according to caste, age, family role, and other factors. What we have called the heroic ethos is incorporated within the dharma of the kshatriya or warrior caste, an instance of what George Dumézil styled the second of his three functions in the constitution of the Indo-European mythological and sociological order.[6] Yet the *Mahābhārata* exhibits an ongoing awareness of the dharmas of the other castes, notably the brahmanical or priestly; and perhaps for this reason its conception of kingship lays more stress on self-control and moderation than the Old English or Homeric traditions do. Thus Yudhiṣṭhira, the very personification of dharma,[7] refrains from flyting as a weakness and an excess. While his brothers and cousins do not always share in his restraint, a general respect for dharma and their elder brother succeeds in containing outbreaks of flyting in large part. Yet precisely because the kshatriya's dharma requires the honoring of one's word, when verbal contesting does make its appearance, its contracts are taken seriously indeed.

All these complexities are represented in that extraordinary contest on which the entire plot of the *Mahābhārata* pivots, the dicing match between Yudhiṣṭhira and Śakuni, acting as Duryodhana's proxy.[8] Although he recognizes that he cannot rival his opponent in skill and trickery, the elder Pāṇḍava nonetheless feels obligated to continue with the game for as long as he is challenged with it; and true to character, he accepts his fortunes with relatively little protest. Bhīma his brother, however, cannot contain himself when he sees their wife Draupadī subjected to sexual abuse, vowing, in the first instance, to tear open the chest and drink the blood of the offending Duḥśāsana (van Buitenen 2: 146), and in the second, to crush the thigh that Duryodhana has bared before her (151). Both boasts Bhīma eventually fulfills in two of the poem's decisive martial encounters. Although these and other verbal sparrings during the dicing match merit detailed study, I cannot undertake the task here because of the complexity of the episode, for all of the flyting is subordinated to the dicing match as the central contestational structure, which in turn ties in with larger epic designs in many ways.[9]

Such a contest—purportedly nonmartial and between kinsmen—ought not to have had such a bloody issue, and thus a violation of ludic conventions is involved.[10] This is reflected in the fact that the flyting breaks out not as an ordered part of the dicing encounter but as a response to its excesses. The quarrels and contracts of this episode, variously honored or broken in subsequent action, become so embroiled that it takes the rest of the epic to untangle them. It is worth noting, however, that the treatment of Draupadī, as much or more than the loss of their kingdom, figures as the Pāṇḍavas' major grievance. As in the *Iliad*, a woman stands close to the point of origination of the dispute.

The Arjuna-Karṇa rivalry, however, is more easily separable as a distinct plot thread. In fact, their relationship underscores one of the key themes of the epic. For in reality they are brothers; yet their bitter enmity leads to a death struggle in which Karṇa is destroyed. As we have seen, Achilles avoids bloodshed within the Achaian army by opting for the guest-host flyting mode. The Pāṇḍavas are not so successful in circumventing internecine fratricidal conflict, despite their own best efforts and those of their adviser Krishna. Transpiring during the boys' adolescence, well before the dicing match and all that flows from it, the Arjuna-Karṇa flyting provides one of the story's early indicators that such a catastrophe is in store.

The quarrel breaks out unexpectedly, at what was intended to be a harmless athletic and military exhibition.[11] Droṇa, a master of the martial arts, has been selected to oversee this aspect of the education of the young princes, both Pāṇḍava and Kaurava, who still live together in relative harmony. When the training of his adolescent pupils has been completed, Droṇa organizes a public tournament at which Arjuna awes onlookers with his dazzling proficiency in archery. So far, this tournament has been conducted, like the athletic games in *Iliad* 23, without verbal dueling and with competition of only a friendly and noninjurious sort.

Choosing this moment to make his dramatic entry, Karṇa, still a stranger to the Bhārata princes, presents himself after the Pāṇḍavas have had a chance to display their skills, boasts that he will match every feat of Arjuna's, and proceeds to do so. Applauded by Duryodhana, Karṇa then challenges Arjuna to a duel. Thus, in the first phase of this unanticipated contest, Karṇa, verbally contracting on athletic exploits and then performing them, has proved that he is at least Arjuna's match; now, through a new flyting challenge, he proposes to demonstrate superiority outright.

In the scene that follows, this martial duel never materializes; yet Karṇa's proposal generates a tension and an expectation that moves inexorably toward its fulfillment on the battlefield seven books later. Although Karṇa has not yet specified what type of duel he has in mind, at this early juncture we might assume that it could still take a nonlethal form. This possibility is soon excluded, however. For now Arjuna, infuriated, initiates a classic flyting exchange. In a brief speech, he begins by questioning his adversary's worthiness to fill the role of a contestant, and then proceeds with his boast: "The worlds that are set aside for uninvited intruders, and for uninvited prattlers, those worlds you shall attain, Karṇa, when I have done killing you!" (van Buitenen 1: 280). Since this tournament is by invitation only, Karṇa does not merit the role of contestant; as a "prattler," moreover, he belongs to the category of those who cannot match their words with deeds. The "glory" that he will win through this contest, accordingly, will consist merely in his admission into that kingdom of the dead reserved for such worthless individuals. Arjuna has thus evaluated his opponent in a most eristic manner and projected a direct, mortal Trial of Arms (C[bf]).

In reply, Karṇa first parries the attack on his heroic qualifications, then amplifies on the "words versus deeds" theme that Arjuna has raised, and finally counter's Arjuna's with a boast of his own: "This stage is open to all, so what of you, Phalguna?[12] Barons[13] are those who are the strongest. Law obeys might. Why abuse, which is the whimpering of the weak? Talk with arrows, Bhārata,[14] until before your teacher's own eyes I carry off your head with mine!" (van Buitenen 1: 280). This exchange seals the contract that Arjuna has proposed. They will fight to the death; indeed, Arjuna's own master of the martial arts will bear witness to the outcome. Although this combat does not eventuate in the course of this scene, the force of the contract endures through more than a decade and many thousands of shlokas to the battle of Kurukṣetra. It is noteworthy, further, that Karṇa explicitly rejects the doctrine of dharma when he asserts that "law obeys might." In their final encounter, Krishna, speaking on Arjuna's behalf, emphatically reminds Karṇa of this adharmic allegiance to power.

Although the essentials of flyting have now been completed, there follows a fascinating interlude in which some of the major flyting concerns that we have discussed in previous chapters come into play. In the foregoing interaction, neither hero saw fit to retroject. Of course, the most recent past accomplishments for both men were the immediately preceding archery displays that had ended in a draw (since it would seem that Karṇa had only matched and not surpassed the feats of Arjuna). Because it had just happened, the contestants evidently felt no need to allude to this competition directly. But now the other major retrojective topic, genealogy, emerges into the foreground. Before an audience that includes the gods Indra and Sūrya,[15] Krpa, acting as master of ceremonies, sets forth Arjuna's lineage and asks Karṇa to identify himself in like fashion. The underlying theme, again, is that contestants ought to be comparable. Having shown his proficiency in the martial domain, Karṇa is now called upon to set forth his genealogical credentials. Thus accosted, Karṇa hangs his head in shame; observing this, Duryodhana seizes the moment to consecrate him as the king of Āṅga, thereby trying to compensate for an ostensible deficiency in lineage through bestowal of royal rank. Yet the matter cannot be set to rest so easily. For now the man that all assume to be Karṇa's father, a lowly *sūta* (or charioteer), makes his entry and embraces his "son." Laughing, Bhīma denies that Karṇa has "the right to die in a fight with a Pārtha" (van Buitenen 1: 281). In reply Duryodhana, Bhīma's old rival, defends his new friend, asserting (in an uncharacteristically democratic spirit) that all kshatriyas have a right to compete. As the day winds down amid a public uproar, the Pāṇḍavas' mother Kuntī, as if to underscore the irony of the entire situation, is overcome with joy as she recognizes Karṇa to be her own child (282)—and thus Arjuna's brother. As we can see, then, this flyting exchange in its totality bears an unmistakable resemblance to verbal duels in Homeric and Old English literature. Aside from its ceremonial character and obvious quarreling and contracting, this flyting particularly features the genealogical retrojection, the identification of the heroes, and the theme that contestants should measure up to certain standards of comparability.

Although a vast stretch of narrative intervenes, Karṇa and Arjuna find the opportunity to fulfill their contract in the eighth book (the *Karṇaparva*) during the seventeenth day of the battle of Kurukṣetra. Like most key events in the *Mahābhārata*, their fortunes of war are spun from the curses and boons of years bygone. Falling victim to one such malediction, in the heat of battle Karṇa suddenly learns that the wheel to his chariot has fallen off. Rendered for the moment helpless, he tries to renew contract negotiation, not to escape battle, but to procure a little time. We have seen this kind of codicillary contracting in the Viking's request of free passage over the ford in *Maldon*. In effect, Karṇa appeals to Arjuna's sense of fair play:

O Pārtha, O Pārtha, wait for a moment, that is, till I lift this sunken wheel! Beholding, O Pārtha, the left wheel of my car swallowed though accident by the Earth, abandon . . . this purpose (of striking and slaying me) that is capable of being harboured by only a coward! Brave warriors that are observant of the practices of the righteous, never shoot their weapons at persons with dishevelled hair, or at those who have turned their faces from battle, or at a Brāhmaṇa, or at him who joins his palms, or at him who yields himself up or beggeth for quarter, or at one who has put up his weapon, or at one whose arrows are exhausted, or at one whose armour is displaced, or at one whose weapon has fallen off or been broken! Thou art the bravest of men in the world. Thou art also of righteous behavior, O son of Pāṇḍu! Thou art well acquainted with the rules of battle. . . . Thou art born in the Kshatriya order! Thou art the perpetuator of a high race! Recollecting the teachings of righteousness, excuse me for a moment, O son of Pāṇḍu![16]

The dharmic notion on which Karṇa insists is that kshatriyas engaged in single combat ought to fight on equal terms. Contests are not merely to be won, but to be won in such fashion that heroic superiority is established. Although expressed in the terms of early Indian ethics and metaphysics, this idea has its roots in the logic of contesting itself and finds expression in many heroic traditions. Beowulf, for example, shows his regard for the same principle when he refuses to bring weapons to his fight with Grendel, on the grounds that this would constitute an unfair advantage over an enemy who does not enjoy the knowledge of such arts.

Arjuna's part in the flyting is now taken up by Krishna, whose retort centers on the theme of dharma and Karṇa's complaint (expressed more fully a few shlokas earlier [Roy 1889: 359]) that he is a just man being treated unjustly:

By good luck it is, O son of Rādhā, that thou rememberest virtue! It is generally seen that they that are mean, when they sink into distress, rail at Providence but never at their own misdeeds. Thyself and Suyodhana [i.e., Duryodhana] . . . had caused Draupadī, clad in a single piece of raiment, to be brought into the midst of the assembly. On that occasion, O Karṇa, this virtue of thine did not manifest itself! When at the assembly Cakuni, an adept at dice, vanquished Kuntī's son Yudhiṣṭhira who was unacquainted with it, whither had this virtue of thine then gone? . . . If this virtue that thou now invokest was nowhere on those occasions, what is the use then of parching thy palate now by uttering that word? Thou art now for the practice of virtue, O Sūta, but thou shalt not escape with thy life! . . . The Pāṇḍavas, who are free from cupidity, will recover their kingdom by the prowess of their arms, aided with all their friends! The Dhārtarāshtras will meet with destruction at the hands of those lions among men [viz., the sons of Pāṇḍu], that are always protected by virtue!

Krishna's response has modulated out of the heroic frame of reference into direct contemplation of the doctrines of dharma and karmic retribution. Karṇa is being punished for his sins. He cannot demand fair treatment because he himself has rejected dharma through his own misdeeds. Interestingly enough, Krishna does not dispute the *truth* of Karṇa's argument[17]—that he is laboring under an unfair disadvantage—but only that Karṇa should have the right to advance it. As on several other occasions, Krishna seems be urging a Pāṇḍava on toward action on a lower plane of morality and by this means breaks another in a series of impasses out of which the Pāṇḍavas would never otherwise have been able to extricate themselves. Following Krishna's advice, Arjuna now takes up his bow and shoots off his enemy's head. His boast has been fulfilled and the contest is ended.

Arthur, Lucius, and Mordred in the *Alliterative Morte Arthure*

Now let us return to narrative poetry of the English alliterative tradition, though from an era postdating the composition of *Beowulf* by some half a millennium. Arguably epic in form, certainly heroic in many of its interests and expressed values, the early fourteenth-century *Alliterative Morte Arthure*[18] casts back to former times both in subject matter and in many of its outlooks. This penchant is well displayed in its flytings, which are numerous and energetic. Possibly descending through the channel of an oral tradition surviving from the Old English period into the efflorescence of the Alliterative Revival, the poem's flytings and contests attest to the durability of these paradigms in the face of vast historical change.[19] At the same time, Christian feudalism has made its impress. Later in this chapter we will see such transformational processes in a more advanced stage in *Sir Gawain and the Green Knight*, a poetic creation of the same general era, and in *The Song of Roland*, composed more than two centuries earlier.[20]

The narrative of the *Alliterative Morte Arthure* features many brief and fairly incidental flytings. I will be concentrating here on two large-scale contests, in one of which flyting plays a significant role.[21] The opening movement of the story, occupying some 2,400 of the poem's 4,346 lines, tells of the exchange of hostile embassies between the Briton's King Arthur and the Roman emperor Lucius, and of the ensuing war, which Arthur wins when he kills Lucius with his own hand. I will pass over the next sections, concerning Arthur's successful siege of Metz and overthrow of the Duke of Lorraine and his subsequent, portentious Dream of the Wheel of Fortune. The concluding phase, however, centering on the conflict between Arthur and his traitorous regent Mordred and conducted with a relative minimum of flyting, offers an interesting foil to the Arthur-Lucius rivalry. The poem ends with Arthur's death and burial at Glastonbury.

The Arthur-Lucius exchange exhibits the classic flyting dialectic of contract negotiation amid competition for glory through formal public disputation. At the same time, there are marked contrasts between this and comparable episodes in the *Iliad* and the Old English; most important, the contesting is conducted less democratically (or only intermittently so) and with greater regard for feudal hierarchies and proprieties. Knights and vassals, for example, do not dedicate themselves so exclusively to the promotion of their own personal glory but have assimilated themselves to a greater degree to the cause and person of their lord. Thus, Gawain initiates a flyting exchange with Sir Priamus with the cry "Arthure!" (2529); and the Briton king himself exclaims this (2245) while launching the charge on Lucius, as though his own name denoted some greater enterprise. Further, feudal rank is more fully taken into account in the selection of adversaries. It is true that Gawain and others often fling themselves indiscriminately into the melee, killing any and all alike; and Arthur himself takes a hand at moments calculated to show that, even by the standard of old-fashioned heroic prowess, he remains supreme. Yet now even the melees are orchestrated with a greater regard for orders of precedence. And for the most part both Arthur and Lucius hold themselves aloof from combat far more than, say, Byrhtnoth does, acting in large part through subordinates and reserving themselves for the greatest of exploits.

This hierarchical restructuring of combat is most evident in the mediated style of the Arthur-Lucius "flyting." For when they finally do meet each other face to face (2242–56), they waste no time on words but come directly to blows. All their verbal dueling has been conducted through an exchange of embassies. Thus, the flyting speeches are divided by long interludes of hundreds of lines and by journeys from one royal court to another. In the process, the scenic unity of flyting has been shattered. Nonetheless, the messages of both kings are delivered at the same *type* of setting. That this environment conduces more to hospitality than warfare does not invalidate it as a venue for hostile diplomacy, since many fields of battle still lie between the two monarchs and will provide their meeting ground. In another momentous change, the written letter has begun visibly to intrude—appropriately enough, since literate communication presupposes the sorts of spatial and temporal gaps that we are witnessing here.[22] If we were to project further along this line of drift, we might eventually find that flyting stands in a historical relationship to the modern diplomatic arts.

In the first flyting speech, addressed on New Year's Day before Arthur and his knights of the Round Table by a Roman senator on behalf of the emperor Lucius,[23] the visitor begins by grounding his address on the authority of the graphic sign, declaring that Lucius salutes Arthur "under his great seal" ("vndyre his sele ryche," 87) and that his injunction is submitted (in written form) to plain view (88–89). Thus the visible *signum* is the enabling radical element by whose virtue this flyting can take place, spanning temporal and spatial distances.

The message that follows exhibits the same "threat-and-intimidation" pattern that we found in the Byrhtnoth-Viking encounter in *Maldon*. Arthur must proceed posthaste to Rome to render accounting (and here the messenger retrojects) for those lands and tributes that the Briton king has withheld in defiance of the emperor's ancestral rights; further, Arthur must answer there to the wrongful killings of Lucius's kinsmen (90–103). These demands assume that Arthur is Lucius's vassal, rebellious no doubt, but hardly in a position to contest on equal terms. If Arthur refuses his overlord's command, Lucius will crush him militarily or capture him if he should try to flee (104–11). The senator closes again by summoning the authority of writing in support of the lord-vassal relationship that he is trying to reimpose: Roman records show that Arthur's father swore fealty in a relationship descending ancestrally from the time of Julius Caesar (112–15). As a whole, the flyting speech extends two contractual options: submission or combat. The retrojection, however, stresses the inferiority of neither Arthur's ancestry nor heroic accomplishment per se, but rather condemns his breach of an ancestrally descending feudal loyalty. Nothing quite like this charge makes its appearance in the Greek or Old English flytings; it reflects the preoccupations of a feudal world.

Arthur's response comes in several parts, and here we see for the first time in this study the narrative dispersal of a single flyting dialogue over several distinct scenes. Arthur's immediate reponse is directed toward the bearers of the message and takes an amusing form. For while he says nothing, he turns upon the Romans such a fiery glance that they collapse at his feet and beg to be excused, since they have acted only as the emissaries of Lucius. Now Arthur abuses the senator verbally, calling him a "crauaunde knyghte" ("craven knight") and a "cowarde" (133); in reply, the senator acknowledges that the sight of Arthur's face has thoroughly daunted him, since the Briton king is the "lordlyeste lede þat euer I one lukyde" ("the lordliest man that ever I looked on," 138)—indeed, a veritable "lyon" (139). This exchange illustrates several themes. The use of "body language" for flyting purposes is paralleled in 1074–1103 (discussed in chapter 2) when the giant of St. Michael's Mount, having been the target of Arthur's vigorous flyting assault, answers by baring his fangs, growling, and giving other nonverbal indications of his animosity. Further, Arthur's willingness to flyt with the messenger in his own person illustrates a recurring conceit in this poem: Although he is a king who can legitimately act through subordinates, Arthur is still the manliest of men and a warrior's warrior, willing to take on anyone anytime. This democratic valorization of merit over blood runs against the grain of the feudalizing tendencies discussed earlier. Now that he has redefined his relationship with the senator in this way— as a man-to-man contest—his adversary immediately capitulates. Thus intimidation has been turned back upon the intimidator. Yet as soon as Arthur's personal superiority has been acknowledged, the king recognizes the distinction between message and messenger to which the senator has appealed. For in truth, the era of simple, unmediated flyting between kings is over; rulers of nations must recognize diplomatic amenities, one of which is that ambassadors cannot be treated like obstreperous knights errant. Despite occasional solo forays against giants and other menaces, Arthur cannot be an Achilles, even though the poet might find it useful to tap into old heroic resonances by pretending the matter to be otherwise.

Now that the issue of direct contesting between himself and the senator has been raised and set to rest, Arthur, acting like a true feudal overlord, declares that he cannot give Lucius reply without first consulting with his vassals (140–51). Redefining his relationship with the senator's party as that between host and guests (152–55), he orders that they be royally entertained; and the poet now amplifies on Arthur's excellence in this new capacity by devoting almost a hundred lines to the description of the feast. Next, in an extended council scene (243–410), the king's knights and princes are unanimous in pledging their support for war. During this conference with his vassals, further, Arthur counterposes to Lucius's earlier retrojective claim the assertion that his own British ancestors used to rule the Roman empire and thus tributes ought to flow from Lucius to Arthur and not the other way around (259–86). At the close of these proceedings, Arthur, in appreciation for their display of loyalty, thanks his men for upholding his "honor" and "manhood" ("My menske and my manhede," 399). As this sequence illustrates, the concepts of honor and selfhood, which it is the project of flyting to uphold, have been enlarged to incorporate both the collective and the personal. For a deliberative exchange has interjected itself explicitly into the flyting process, and boasts and claims proper to flyting have been here introduced, out of the hearing of any adversary. At the same time, the *person* of Arthur remains the standard around which this party to the conflict rallies.

The collectivity of the enterprise now established, Arthur, after a hospitable delay of seven days, gives Lucius his answer, authorizing his message, like Lucius did, through his seal (439). The first half of the speech (419–42) consists largely of boasts, as Arthur sets forth his plans to conquer Lucius's domain. The Briton king explicitly challenges his imperial adversary, if he values—again—his "menske" and "manhede" (433–34), to meet him in battle in the fields of France. Since Arthur has thus publicly ratified the second of Lucius's contract options, going to war, the essentials of flyting have been completed. In the remainder of his speech (443–66), Arthur addresses the matter of the embassy, granting them seven days to leave British soil on pain of death. Thoroughly intimidated as before, the senator craves assurance of safe conduct (467–74), which Arthur grants him (475–78). Once more, the poet wants to have it both ways: Arthur is an honorable king who recognizes dipomatic civilities, yet he is heroically awesome nonetheless.

If this flyting exchange had set the principals in the quarrel against each other face-to-face, it would in itself have given sufficient preparation for a martial encounter. The senator was only a deputy, however; and so the poet introduces a separate sequence depicting the reception of Arthur's message by the senator's master. Setting himself up for a humiliation, Lucius asks whether the senator as the imperial emissary took Arthur's scepter and occupied the higher seat, in token of Roman superiority (511–14). In reply, the senator not only conveys Arthur's defiance but praises him at length as the mightiest and wisest and most honorable of all kings (515–53). That the senator, with his recent experience of the hazards of the go-between, should magnify an enemy thus in the very presence of his liege lord underscores the extent to which the comparison of the two rulers favors Arthur. So great is his glory that the very human medium of exchange has been won over. Lucius, less the man, does not see fit to comment on his deputy's craven performance but merely reaffirms the war contract: The Roman emperor (so he boasts) will send his armies to France to capture Arthur and sieze his lands (554–69). As a flyting interaction, this first extended movement of some five hundred lines has closed to Arthur's advantage on two accounts. His superiority as a hero has been unmistakably registered through the reaction of the senator; and his superiority as an overlord is shown through his solicitation of the counsel and support of his vassals. Lucius, by contrast, acts alone and unadvised, in the manner of a tyrant, and as a hero impresses no one.

The ground has been sufficiently prepared for a military show-down; yet as further buildup, the poet introduces another mediated flyting between the two kings. Perhaps the introduction of this sequence was motivated by a perceived asymmetry in the earlier exchanges. For the former embassy originated with Lucius and carried out its mission for the most part in the court of Arthur. Now the poet balances this through a communication that moves in the opposite direction.

An appeal to Arthur from messengers of the marshall of France, one of Arthur's "subjects", offers the pretext. For Lucius, they complain, has been perpetrating atrocities, burning their cities and murdering their people (1235–62). Outraged, Arthur deputizes Gawain and others to convey to the Roman emperor the charge that he has behaved lawlessly and that now he must either leave his—Arthur's—lands or meet him in battle (1263–78). In its underlying structure, this speech mirrors the senator's opening message closely. Again, the retrojection, which declares the foundation of the quarrel, centers not on heroic performance or genealogy per se but on feudal obligations: Arthur must protect his own people; nor can Lucius claim this function, in view of the way that he has been behaving. And so the Briton king extends two options: flight or battle. Unlike Lucius, however, Arthur openly prefers combat, at which the "Lord of Doomsday" ("Dryghtten at Domesdaye," 1278) can provide a final judgment between their claims.

The Briton king's emissaries make their way to the Roman camp; and at this juncture Sir Gawain comes to the fore. Conveying the essentials of Arthur's message, Gawain gives his speech a highly eristic tone, twice cursing the Roman and his party and characterizing him as a "fals heretyke" (1307), "cukewalde" ("cuckold," 1312), and "the vnlordlyeste lede þat I on lukede euer!" ("the unlordliest man that I ever looked on," 1313). Lucius does not, evidently, carry the same commanding sense of royal presence that Arthur does. Nor does the emperor's reply dampen Gawain's spirits, as we shall see. In fact, Lucius's return message, like Arthur's in lines 419–66, moves in two parts and treats the same two topics, though in the reverse order. In the first part addressed to Gawain the emissary (1327–34), the emperor, for "reuerence of my ryche table" (1331), disdainfully refuses to punish the Briton for his rude words. Turning next to the substance of Arthur's message, Lucius wishes to convey that he will proceed at his own pace, ravaging France and destroying Arthur's castles there (1335–41). In their speeches of response to foreign ambassadors, then, both rulers have addressed themselves in flyting terms both to their royal adversaries and to the message bearers. Overall, the Roman emperor has requited himself well, in that he has chosen the "manlier" contract option even while honoring the principle of diplomatic immunity. At the same time, he has exhibited neither Arthur's spirited willingness to disregard rank in order to engage in man-to-man encounters nor Arthur's ability to cow enemy vassals.

Now the whole affair gets referred down the feudal hierarchy. In a brief retort, Gawain expresses astonishment that such an oaf ("alfyn," 1343) as Lucius would dare to speak thus and expresses the wish that the two of them could meet in single combat (1344–45)—a cutting insult, which functions through its disregard of the hierarchical division that Lucius wants to impose between them and insists rather on the "democratic" criterion of personal martial ability. Now Lucius's uncle, Gayous, enters the fray, labeling the Briton a boy (1351) and braggart (1348). Having found an adversary of more or less his own rank, Gawain takes up the challenge instantly, lopping off the Roman's head and galloping away (1352–55). In sum, this episode, when viewed as a continuation of the flyting between Arthur and Lucius, mirrors the earlier interaction between the senator and Arthur and completes the pattern of mediated flyting between the two monarchs. At the same time Gawain, by engaging in the flyting process personally and consummating his boasts with a martial demonstration, exhibits an initiative that the senator plainly lacked.[24]

The culmination of this vast adversarial pattern arrives at approximately the midway point in the poem (2242–60) as the two principals match off and go at each other head to head. "Flyting" is at this juncture reduced to a minimum: Lucius has already addressed a boastful speech (2223–25) to Gawain, serving perhaps as Arthur's surrogate, while the Briton king contributes merely the cry of "Arthure!" (2245). Naturally Arthur prevails, although the special significance of this encounter may be registered in Lucius's success at least in wounding him on the nose. Arthur draws the pattern to a ritual closure through speech and symbolic action: He returns the bodies of the fallen with treasure to Rome and insists that the Romans now renounce their claims (2290–2351). It is sometimes assumed that this message to the Romans, both as speech and gesture, amounts to an insult.[25] Yet the poet takes pains to depict Arthur treating Lucius's body with considerable honor; indeed, by heroic standards he is exhibiting extraordinary deference and restraint.[26] At the same time, in view of the fact that a major war has just been concluded, one could hardly expect him not to stamp the verbal seal on a victory which is, after all, an accomplished political and military reality.

This pattern, along with virtually all of the other smaller-scale flyt-ings in the poem, occurs prior to Arthur's Dream of the Wheel of Fortune in 3218–3393, universally regarded as the turning point in the poem.[27] In fact, the final thousand-line sequence, though domi-nated by another adversarial pattern in the matching off of Arthur and Mordred, features flyting in only its most reduced and minimal forms. For example, the two principals never engage in an elaborate exchange of embassies such as we saw earlier in the Arthur-Lucius struggle. When Arthur first learns of Mordred's betrayal, though he vows revenge (3559–60), he sends no flyting message to this effect to his rebel vassal; and his subsequent exhortations to his men (3565–90 and 3636–43), though at times echoing some of the invective and abusive style of earlier exchanges, substitute injunctions to battle and retrojective recitations of wrongs suffered in the place of open boasts directed at Mordred.

Two flyting episodes do nonetheless succeed in rekindling some-thing of the old heroic fire. In the first of these Gawain, once again leading an advance party, vilifies Mordred in harsh terms (3776–79):

> "Fals fosterde foode, the Fende haue thy bonys!
> Fy one the, felone, and thy false werkys!
> Thow sall be dede and vndon for thy derfe dedys,
> Or I sall dy this daye, ʒif destanye worthe!"

> "False-bred offspring, the Fiend take your bones!
> Fie on you, felon, and your false works!
> You will be dead and undone for your wicked deeds,
> or I will die this day, if destiny brings this about!"

Here we find most of the elements of classic flyting: Gawain curses and name-calls, condemns Mordred's lineage and actions, and pro-poses battle. Yet the Briton does not project any certitude of victory but only that *one of the two* of them will die in the coming encounter. Gawain's usual boasting style has been much muted.

In the second genuine flyting encounter Arthur himself, when at last he meets Mordred in the poem's climactic duel, has fewer reser-vations on the matter of heroic predictions (4227–29):

> "Turne, traytoure vntrewe—þe tydes no bettyre;
> By gret Gode, thow sall dy with dynt of my handys!
> The schall rescowe no renke, ne reches in erthe."

> "Turn, false traitor, no better [than this] will befall you;
> by great God, you will die by the strength of my hands!
> No man, no riches of the earth will rescue you."

Here the Briton king urges his foe to meet him in battle and definitely foretells his death. Yet both of these flytings are one-sided: In neither case does Mordred reply. Indeed, at no juncture does the unfaithful *leuetenaunte* embroil himself in verbal dueling or invective in any form but confines his remarks to what is in effect a eulogy for Gawain (3875–85). In sum, then, Arthur and his party in this final sequence indulge in flyting and invective comparatively rarely (by the standards of the poem), employ terms of abuse that highlight Mordred's very real and damnable sin of treason, curb hyperbolic tendencies in their boasting, phrase their predictions carefully and in terms that they are able literally to fulfill, and provoke no rebuttal from an enemy who, we gather, privately admits the justice of their claims. In all these ways the flyting spirit has been toned down; and this effect is further reinforced by the dominant elegiac mood generated in the speeches of lamentation, which, through their sheer number and bulk, tend to overshadow such few flytings there are.

How, then, are we to account for the poet's sudden disinclination to depend on the verbal contest theme for the development of his narrative matter, despite the fact that a contest structure—Arthur versus Mordred—still underlies and motivates the narrative movement? The aims of this study do not permit the kind of exhaustive inquiry into the specificities of the *Alliterative Morte Arthure* as an individual literary work that a full answer to this question would demand. In brief, however, I think we can reasonably assert that the resonances of the contest theme do not fit in with the poet's designs at this stage in his "tragedy." Flytings foreground the themes of glory and heroic identity. Yet for Arthur and his men these aims have already been achieved to a considerable degree through his overthrow of the Roman empire. Moreover, the Dream of Fortune's Wheel was intended precisely to relativize achievements of this kind, to point out that high attainment inevitably leads to a downfall.[28] By continuing to build his narrative around flyting and the flyting contract, by continuing to tap into the archaic associations of this theme, the poet would simply have been reinforcing the very standard of measure whose limitations it is now his purpose to expose. This does not necessarily mean that either the poet or Arthur has rejected the heroic *ethos*; to the contrary, Arthur and Gawain continue to flyt in a limited way, and their very restraint in doing so seems to be a mechanism by which the poet keeps them from discrediting themselves. At the same time, the action of the poem clearly shows that eventual failure and death are endemic to the human condition. And to this problem, the path of heroic endeavor can ultimately provide no answer.

In overview, then, the *Alliterative Morte Arthure* exhibits two large-

scale contest movements conditioned, in the first case, by the mediation of vassal go-betweens, and in the second, by medieval concepts
of fortune, mutability, and tragedy. In the next two sections I examine poems in which contesting is even more profoundly transformed
through the activity of specifically Christian ideological constructs.

ROLAND AND GANELON IN *THE SONG OF ROLAND*

The foregoing discussions of the *Mahābhārata* and the *Alliterative
Morte Arthure* have argued for the presence of classic contest structures, transformed but recognizable. In this section, however, I study
the uses of a contest that never happens. The focal episode is that
conflict between Roland and his stepfather Ganelon upon which the
major action of the late eleventh- or early twelfth-century Old French
masterpiece, *The Song of Roland*, is predicated. Though plainly a
quarrel, the Roland-Ganelon exchange cannot qualify as a heroic flyting. Yet Ganelon's very failure to set forth his grievances on the
ground of an open, public test—until he is compelled to do so in the
poem's final section—is integral to his offense. Indeed, his condemnation in the vision of the poem links heroic nonperformance with
Christian sin.[29]

The heroic contest by nature lends dignity to both its contestants,
since the greatness of the one adversary is measured by the other.
Medieval Christianity found it difficult, however, to conceive of Islam
as a genuine rival, for the slightest implication of comparability of
faiths would relativize that which for an entire civilization had to remain absolute.[30] Logically, or theologically, the validity of Christian
revelation cannot be measured by its fortunes in war. The distinction
between worldly power and spiritual truth is nowhere more emphatically displayed than in the life of Christ himself. Yet a culture that
still prized military achievement—and the violent history of the early
Middle Ages, and particularly the spirit of forcible Christian prose-
lytization embodied in the first Crusade, conduced to such an outlook—would be attracted to story forms that fuse spiritual and martial values. Because Christians were believed to be superior to Muslims
in every way, the ritual contest, still honored as the public measure of
manly worth and superiority, ought to bear these feelings out.[31]

Yet no Christian in the European Middle Ages could overlook the
fact that, in military terms, the inferior religion seemed often to prevail. Many rationalizations could, of course, be devised; indeed, almost a millennium earlier, St. Augustine had addressed the same
kind of problem in *City of God*. Yet *Roland* represents a different response, at least at the level of belief and consciousness depicted in its

contesting. Virtuous Christians like Roland can be overcome by wicked Saracens through the same means as those by which Jesus fell to the connivings of his enemies: treachery. In open testing, the Saracens always lose. But just as Jesus was, for a time, overcome not simply by the opposition of enemies but by betrayal of one in his own immediate circle, so the Franks suffer a tragic though temporary reversal because of the shameless defection of one of their own tribe.[32]

Any representation of Ganelon as a heroic adversary who flyts and fights would have ruined this conception. Yet because the contest paradigm is a natural expression of the militarized, heroic narrative mode that Turoldus has adopted, he uses it as one of the narratorial sticks with which the traitor is beaten. If Ganelon wanted to quarrel and could not reconcile himself to the humiliation he had endured, he ought to have offered challenge in open, heroic terms. In doing so he would no doubt have exposed himself to the charge of rebellion and disobedience; but at least he would have redeemed his reputation as a man. But to his shame, not only does he fail to flyt, but he lets others do his fighting for him. On all these accounts his behavior contrasts starkly with that of his valiant if hotheaded stepson.

The quarrel between Roland and Ganelon, like that between Arthur and Lucius's envoys, opens in the context of a diplomatic interaction between kings, though in this case the flyting principals are not representatives of the opposing forces but members of the same nation. Thoroughly cowed by the display of French might that he has witnessed over the past seven years, the Saracen ruler Marsile sends Blancandrin to Charlemagne, offering both tribute and a conversion to Christianity if the French monarch will lift the siege of Saragossa and go home. When Charlemagne solicits the opinions of his barons, Roland speaks forcibly against acceptance of the offer, pointing out previous instances of Saracen treachery (196–213).[33] But Ganelon advocates the opposite course, personalizing his attack on Roland through comments like "Ja mar crerez bricun" ("Indeed, believe a fool to your own misfortune," 220), and "Laissun les fols, as sages nus tenuns" ("Let us leave off with fools and hold with wise men," 229). While Ganelon does not specify who these fools might be, contextually his meaning is plain, and thus his speech serves to raise the level of animosities. At the same time, the council setting cannot very well accommodate heroic flyting—with all its martial entailments—among its very members, particularly when relations with an external enemy are precisely the matter under review. The hazards of such outbreaks are, indeed, all too vividly dramatized in the *Iliad*. Further, the familial bond between Roland and Ganelon (although, significantly, the tie is by marriage and not by blood) ought to discourage mortal engagements.

Until this point, Roland and Ganelon have merely performed their duties as advisers. Choosing the more conciliatory policy with respect to their Saracen enemies, Charlemagne now asks for a volunteer delegate to Marsile's court. Naimes, Roland, and Turpin offer themselves but are peremptorily rejected by Charlemagne, who insists that none of the Twelve will be selected (262). Roland now nominates Ganelon, and this suggestion wins the general approval of the Franks (277–79). Yet Ganelon's response to this assignment contrasts markedly with that of his stepson. For he accuses Roland of maliciously violating the familial bond between them; further, he threatens (290–91):

> "Jo t'en muvra un si grant contraire
> Ki durerat a trestut tun edage."

> "I will set in motion such a great opposition
> as will last throughout your entire life."

This statement, together with a similarly ambiguous threat in 300–301, is Ganelon's closest approximation to a flyting contract projection. Yet as such it is thoroughly defective. For while he has promised to act against Roland in some way, and although, in retrospect, one can draw the inference that Roland's "life" (or *edage*) is not going to be a long one, by no means has he specified a martial test by which their differences will be resolved. Indeed, the nature of his threat is thoroughly obscured under vague language and double entendre. The same applies to his subsequent comment (300–301):

> "Einz i frai un poi de legerie,
> Que jo n'esclair ceste meie grant ire."

> "First in this matter I'll do something a bit reckless
> before I clear away this my great anger."

The word *legerie*—connoting lack of weight and even frivolity—in no way communicates, in a publicly intelligible fashion, Ganelon's real, private intentions.[34]

Roland's responses aggravate the quarrel; but since no flyting contract has been proffered, none can be ratified. He acknowledges that a threat of some kind has been made in his assertion that threats don't bother him ("Ço set hom ben, n'ai cure de menace," 293). Thus dismissing his stepfather's wrath, Roland now offers to deliver Charlemagne's message in his place (294–95). This brief speech leaves it to Ganelon to specify the contents of his threat more explicitly and thus to define the interaction as a flyting, if he wants to do so. At the same time, Roland's offer, which ostensibly removes the grievance and reaffirms goodwill, actually highlights the discrepancy in bravery between the two men. Ganelon's subsequent veiled threat (300–301) only provokes Roland to laughter (302), a response further accentuating his refusal to take his stepfather seriously as a heroic adversary. Although their motives differ, neither Ganelon nor Roland has been willing explicitly to adopt an adversarial stance. By contrast, Agamemnon and Achilles retroject, project, compare, and evaluate; and Achilles binds himself to martial demonstration in an explicit flyting contract that, in the course of the story, he fulfills to the letter.

Ganelon's eventual acceptance of Charlemagne's embassy is accomplished in the same spirit that he displayed in his dialogue with Roland. On the one hand, he repeatedly proves himself the coward: He complains that he will die in Saragossa and never see his son again (310–16), blames Roland for his misfortunes (322), seems to approve the view of his sympathizers that one of such noble ancestry ought to be spared such a mission (350–56), and generally exhibits a lamentable dearth of heroic enterprise. Yet the veiled threats continue: He declares that he has no love for Roland (306), defies the twelve peers (326), and most significant of all, drops the gauntlet that the emperor offers him (331–35). When the French take this as a bad omen, Ganelon reaffirms that "vos en orrez noveles!" ("You will hear more news about this!" 336). Although we as readers have been alerted to the possibility of what is to follow, his compatriots fail to appreciate the severity of his disaffection. Yet the blame must lie with Ganelon, for he will neither contest nor serve in the right spirit; at the same time, he will not renounce his anger. For unmanliness of this kind only the traitor's path remains.

This opening eristic exchange is curiously mirrored some five hundred lines later when Ganelon, now formally committed to treachery, has delivered Marsile's message back to Charlemagne. Making preparations for his march back to France, the emperor asks nominations for a leader of the rearguard force (740–42). Ganelon names Roland (743–44), just as Roland had named him earlier.[35] Hearing this, Roland expresses contradictory reactions. First, he thanks his stepfather and swears to perform his office bravely (753–59); then, he curses him (764–65):

> "Quias le guant me caïst en la place,
> Cume fist a tei le bastun devant Carle?"

> "Did you expect me to cast down the gauntlet in this place,
> just as you did with the rod before Charles?"

Roland reiterates this comparison when he assures the emperor (766–70) that, unlike Ganelon, he will not drop the bow that Charlemagne is giving him as the current *signum* of imperial authority. Bédier rationalizes Roland's reversal of position in his two speeches to Ganelon on the grounds that, while he cannot evade the responsibility that has been conferred upon him, he wishes to convey that he recognizes Ganelon's real intentions.[36] The hero's part requires an enthusiastic acceptance of hazards; by exhibiting this, Roland saves his own face even while heaping further shame on his stepfather. At the same time, he cannot be so naive as to overlook the parallels between this and the earlier exchange and, in consequence, the hostility that Ganelon has shown. Once again, stepfather and stepson have quarreled; further, the evaluative, comparative, and retrojective functions have come more and more visibly into play. Yet still, no contract has been made, either explicitly or tacitly. For neither man has proposed a martial format for the adjudication of the quarrel. Any projected sequel at this stage has its place only in the mind and machinations of Ganelon the defector and his new Saracen friends.

The battle scenes that follow require no close examination here. Obviously the fact that it is Roland who finds himself thus beleaguered is a consequence of the Ganelon-Roland quarrel; yet while Roland displays his valor and prowess on a grand scale, Ganelon takes no part in the fighting at all. Thus he cannot in *heroic* terms claim the credit for Roland's death. Roland's adversaries in war are the Saracens; and his personal heroic victory in this contest is signaled when he strikes off Marsile's hand, kills Marsile's son Jurfaleu, and puts most of their force to flight (1902–12). As so often happens, combat has culminated in the personal matching off of principals. At the same time, the Saracens must bear the ignominy of having used the advantages of surprise as well as superior numbers. Indeed, an interesting attestation to the heroic imperative to challenge enemies openly occurs late in the battle of Roncevaux when Oliver, blinded and near death, strikes his companion on the head. Identifying himself, Roland gently chastizes his friend with the comment, "Par nule guise ne m'aviez desfiet!" ("In no manner have you challenged me!" 2002). The same charge could be turned against the Saracens: They too attacked without formal warning—indeed, in violation of a treaty. In overview, if we measure the progression from the Roland-Ganelon quarrel to the battle of Roncevaux against the standard of the flyting-to-fighting pattern, we will find it grossly defective. For neither the flyting nor the fighting has been conducted in honorable fashion; more significant, the contractual link between them has been missing altogether. For this Ganelon and the Saracens reap the shame (*honte*), and Roland the credit for having requited himself so forcefully in such trying circumstances.[37]

Before we turn to the ordeal and judgment of Ganelon in the poem's final movement, I would like briefly to consider one legitimate flyting-to-fighting sequence that does spring up between Christians and Saracens. This exchange, which occurs, significantly enough, at the climax of the military encounters between these two forces, incorporates an important transformation in the structure of the flyting, brought about by the distinctively Christian ideological imperatives at work in this poem. Whereas the battle at Roncevaux had pitted a count against a Spanish king, in the subsequent French revenge sequence the conflict has been referred up the hierarchy, so that now the main adveraries are the emir Baligant and the emperor Charlemagne himself. Inevitably, and in the decisive encounter, these two men meet, exchange cries ("Preciuse" and "Munjoie," 3564–65), and go to blows.[38]

After almost two laisses of indecisive fighting, however, they relax these efforts in order to embark on a contractually oriented flyting exchange. Baligant opens with a retrojection: Charles has offended, first, by killing the emir's son, and second, by challenging his sovereignty in Spain; on both accounts an apology is due (3589–94). Now the emir extends the contract projection: The French emperor should become his vassal and accept Spain as a fief. Structurally this resembles threats of the *Maldon* variety. At the same time, Baligant does not specify the alternative—that, should Charles fail to accept, the emir will kill him; further, the terms he has proposed are highly favorable to the French. The toning down of the eristic element in this offer no doubt suggests the esteem in which the emir holds his adversary.

Charlemagne opens his reply by rejecting this proposal as shameful, for he will not negotiate with pagans (3595–96). Now he extends his own offer: If the emir will convert to Christianity, the emperor will protect him (3597–99). Both speeches have turned in part on the concept of vassalage; acceptance of this role would constitute an admission of defeat and thus would provide grounds for the termination of combat. This lord-vassal relationship occupies the same place in the feudal flyting exchange that abject surrender did in the *Iliad*. Yet Charlemagne has insisted on a new condition: acceptance of the true religion. Vassalage centers on a *personal* commitment; yet conversion hinges on a personal identification with a *transpersonal* ideological system. Thus the *matter* of argument, the flyting content, has been depersonalized, at least so far as religion can be judged the real issue here. This transformation is indeed of the greatest significance, for it signals a displacement of the macho ethic of heroic narrative and a movement toward the grounding of "heroic" claims in a new level of abstraction. *Roland* differs from the *Alliterative Morte Arthure* in this respect. For while Arthur too barters with the token of feudal precedence, he never disputes underlying ideological principles. In this, he and Lucius are in accord. Nor indeed should we press the claim too far in Charlemagne's case. For after Baligant has disdainfully rejected his offer as "evil lecturing" ("Malvais sermun," 3600), Charles proceeds to cleave his head open. And the fact that he can do so at an age of more than two hundred years (539 and 552)—which plainly deprives Ganelon of any excuses on that account—must be taken as a strong statement of his manly and heroic superiority. The overall contest frame, in short, remains man-centered. Yet within this shell a new abstracting and universalizing process is afoot.

Even though Ganelon has avoided direct martial encounter with Roland, Turoldus refuses in the end to exempt him from the form of judgment that a proper flyting ought to have entailed. Thus the final section of *Roland* devotes itself to Ganelon's trial, which is accomplished by means of a formal combat as a judicial proceeding. The judicial duel is a complex subject in its own right, with its own history and rituals.[39] It does, nonetheless, seem to be related to the flyting-to-fighting contest process, particularly in its recognition of deeds as the test of words and in its perception of the divine Witness as Judge; to argue this relationship in full, however, would require a lengthy study. In any case, Ganelon is on trial for treason; he is not engaged in fulfilling a contract he has made with Roland. Yet an underlying and dimly articulated connection with the unfulfilled heroic contesting paradigm in the poem may help to motivate this episode all the same. For in the wake of their quarrel, Roland has vindicated his heroism in battle. It now remains for Ganelon to do so, even if "treason" constitutes the issue at hand.

And in fact Ganelon chooses once again to fight through a surrogate. He appeals to his kinsman Pinabel to uphold his case; and after Pinabel has agreed to this, Ganelon himself recedes from the foreground of action until laisse 289, when, in the aftermath of the judicial combat, he is drawn and quartered. In the meantime, attention has centered on Pinabel and his opponent Thierry who, in the moments immediately before their mortal encounter, engage in a brief, contractually oriented flyting. In a remarkable opening speech, Pinabel offers to become Thierry's vassal in exchange for the latter's concession of defeat (3892–95). Since vassalage has hitherto betokened martial capitulation, Pinabel is, in effect, offering his opponent the spoils of victory if he will merely allow him to win his case—a rather

duplicitous proceeding that one might expect from someone upholding Ganelon's part. Thierry peremptorily rejects this contract proposal (3896–98) and proceeds to dispatch his enemy. The evasions of
the duties of heroism have been brought to an end. Roland's death
has been avenged through a contestational process, and the story has
run its full circle.

SIR GAWAIN AND THE GREEN KNIGHT

Our final example, drawn from the fourteenth-century alliterative
romance *Sir Gawain and the Green Knight*, departs from the heroic
model more profoundly than have our previous cases. Surprisingly,
however, in terms of the *external* narrative, the contest between the
poem's protagonist and his mysterious adversary turns out to have
followed the typical four-step sequence (Engagement, Flyting, Trial
of Arms, and Resolution) rather closely. The flyting, too, is a relatively conventional heroic specimen from the structural standpoint (if
not in its "special effects"), providing scope for eristic expression even
as it contracts on a martial encounter. Nonetheless, the *Gawain* poet's
approach differs from standard heroic treatments of the contest
theme in that he has given it a new kind of inwardness. The establishment of heroic identity through feats of arms is not his interest.
Rather, the "test" he poses (and in the end *Gawain* is about a "test"
and not a "contest") points to a concept of the human individual in
which heroic-agonistic values no longer play the dominant part. The
flyting-to-fighting sequence is just a shell, the residual memory from
a heroic past in which a new kind of "game" (*gomen*) is now being
played.[40]

The pattern in its broader outlines can be quickly delineated. During the New Year's celebration of Arthur and his knights, a mysterious Green Knight makes his appearance and proposes a rather bi-
zarre contest, which will take the form of an exchange of blows.
Gawain takes up the challenge (and thus the Engagement is complete), and a contractually oriented Flyting ensues. In the first phase
of the Trial of Arms Gawain decapitates his adversary who, quite un-
perturbed, picks up his head and rides off. After a year, as per their
agreement, Gawain sets out to find his adversary so that he may duly
submit to decapitation and thus complete the contractually designated combat. He meets him at the Green Chapel and suffers the
blow, which only nicks him. At this juncture, the Green Knight dis-
closes crucial information, including his own true name and ties of
kinship that bind him to Gawain. Both men agree that further combat is unnecessary, and the interaction modulates into a process of

friendly bonding, not unlike that between Glaukos and Diomedes. With this ritual Resolution (which retrospectively formalizes the "gift giving" of the green girdle), the interaction comes to an end.

This brief summary should show two things. First, the contest pattern is absolutely crucial to the development of the story. Second, when we conceive of *Gawain* in terms of this pattern alone (even ignoring its inability to account for the temptation sequence in the poem's second and third parts), we reduce the romance to utter superficiality and externality. The contest is but the sleight of hand by which the *Gawain* poet conceals his real intentions until they are ripe. But how is this deception accomplished?[41]

Comprising the chief action in the first of the poem's four sections, the flyting arises out of what ought to be a guest-host setting, although its ambivalence with respect to the hospitable (guest-host) and hostile (battlefield) contest options plagues this duel throughout. Yet the festive occasion plainly conduces to ingroup joviality and hospitality and friendly sporting with outsiders. We are specifically told, in fact, that Arthur is reluctant to join in the feasting until he has heard some strange tale or entertained a knightly challenge (90–99).[42] And so, after the Green Knight has made his appearance (to which the *Gawain* poet devotes almost four stanzas) and has asked to speak with the leader of the proceedings (224–27), Arthur welcomes this exotic visitor warmly, identifies himself by name and position ("Þe hede of þis ostel"), and invites the stranger to declare his purpose (252–55). If Arthur's welcome is accepted, guest-host relations should follow. Even a contestational exchange—which, as we have seen, Arthur would be quite happy to countenance—has every prospect of following a guest-host pathway. Ultimately we learn that this is exactly what has happened, though for most of the poem the appearance is otherwise.

The Green Knight responds with what proves to be an initiatory flyting speech. He rejects Arthur's offer to join in the festivities as incompatible with his "ernde" ("errand," 257). Turning instead to the attributive-evaluative function, he declares that it is the reputation of Arthur's knights as the world's worthiest in deeds of arms as well as in courtesy that has brought him there (258–64). Pointedly he does not represent this as his own view, leaving open the implication that he means to try their merits against his own. Yet he confirms that his intentions are not warlike, in token of which he bears a branch and wears no armor (265–71). Nonetheless, in the conclusion of his speech he projects what is beginning to sound like a heroic flyting contract offer: If Arthur is as bold as men say, he will grant him the *gomen* ("game") that he asks for (272–73). As a whole, this speech gives rather mixed signals. On the one hand, it seems to be exhibiting several of the characteristic flyting movements: It rejects simple hospitality; without retrojecting explicitly, it alludes to the credit of past deeds of Arthur's men; it refers to attributive-evaluative acts (that is, the praise commonly bestowed on Arthur's court) in a way that implies an intention to undercut it (probably through eristic comparison between Arthur's men and the Green Knight himself); and it offers to inaugurate contract making. On the other hand, the Green Knight has failed to identify himself, has characterized his aims as peaceable, has avoided overt insults, and has left the precise content of his contract proposal unspecified. Most of these matters he will clear up shortly, and all in due course. Yet the confusing initial impression accurately registers the movement of an untraditional motive within this relatively traditional speech form.

In a brief reply Arthur, choosing to construct the Green Knight's offer according to its most enterprising possibility and thus to prove himself unintimidated, declares that his "chivalrous" ("cortays") visitor will not lack for battle if he seeks it (276–78). Of course, the Green Knight has already denied such an aim; but as Arthur recognizes, the rhetoric of his speech has suggested otherwise.

Now the Green Knight brings the eristic nature of his mission more plainly into view. In an insulting comparison, he declares that he does not wish to fight because Arthur's knights are "beardless children" who could not match him in arms (279–82). In the absence of a worthy opponent, he offers a "game" or "play," if any are so bold as to accept it.[43] His "Christmas game" ("Crystemas gomen," 283) entails an exchange of blows, the first to be delivered by one of Arthur's party immediately, the second in return by the Green Knight twelve months hence (285–300). At this point no one could mistake his speech for anything other than flyting. Yet which variety is it, the more or the less lethal? The Green Knight certainly proposes no conventional battle;[44] in this sense it is true that he does not come to fight. Yet an unhindered blow by one of Arthur's henchmen ought surely to prove fatal to its recipient. What could be the sense of speaking of a return blow in twelve months? But the fact that the Green Knight not only mentions this second phase to the combat but emphatically builds it into his contract offer seems to imply that his "game" is not to be a deadly one after all, an implication squarely at odds with the kind of match that he is proposing. Arthur's courtiers, like all readers of the poem, could hardly be unaware of these peculiarities. Indeed, the eccentricity of the contract is so obvious that critics seldom feel called upon to explicate it; and the absence of commentary by the poet and his characters likewise seems to register their sense of the futility of discussing what is thoroughly unintelli-

gible and absurd. At the same the flyting has been problematized. For
the distinction between life-threatening and merely ludic contests is a
fundamental one that flyters cannot afford to leave undetermined
(since one likes to know whether one is apt to get killed or not). Yet
on this most crucial point the Green Knight's offer is thoroughly ambiguous.

It is therefore perplexity, not fear, that underlies the astonished
silence (301–2) with which Arthur's men greet this remarkable
speech. Yet now the Green Knight forces their hand. For he shames
them with the recollection of their great fame and accomplishments,
which have all been, as he puts it, "ouerwalt" ("overthrown," 314) by
the mere words of a single knight; "For al dares for drede withoute
dynt schewed!" ("For all cower for dread without a blow offered!"
315). Now Arthur's party has no choice but to act, and as a prereq-
uisite to action it must construe the Green Knight's overture reduc-
tively and according to its most obvious sense. Apparently he is asking to be killed or, if he should miraculously survive the assault, to
kill in return. From now until the poem's climax none of Arthur's
party—including, of course, Gawain—ever seem to question the cor-
rectness of this interpretation and the horizon of prospects that it
brings with it. Yet the interpretation is wrong nonetheless. The contest is really of the nonlethal, guest-host type.

Confronted, however, with immediate, open, public shame, Arthur
takes the initiative.[45] He grants the visitor's demand, foolish ("nys,"
323) though it is, denies that any of his men have been daunted, and
takes up the ax with the intention of dealing a blow. Yet now the
principle of feudal proprieties intrudes. Gawain enters the Engagement process, asking for the privilege of taking on this duel himself
and noting the uncivility of kingly embroilment in such an affair
(348–51):

> For me þink hit not semly, as hit is soþ knawen,
> Þer such an askyng is heuened so hyʒe in your sale,
> Þaʒ ʒe ʒourself be talenttyf, to take hit to yourseluen,
> Whil mony so bolde yow aboute vpon bench sytten . . .

> For it does not seem to me fitting, as it is truly known,
>   that such a request is raised so high [i.e., is directed to such a highly
>   ranking person] in your hall,
>   even though you yourself be desirous to take it upon yourself,
>   while so many [men] so bold sit about you on the bench.

Here as elsewhere Gawain displays extreme tact and courtesy, in this
case toward his own lord: By setting Arthur's desire to engage in the

contest against the unseemliness of his doing so, he implicitly characterizes his master's delegation of the contest as a sacrifice and thus frees him from possible imputations of cowardice. Continuing in this vein, Gawain now argues that, as the weakest and least intelligent knight present, whose general worthlessness is redeemed only by his kinship to the king his uncle, his own death would be a small loss (354–57). Although it is addressed to Arthur, Gawain's speech nonetheless participates in the flyting, since it secures for himself the role as Green Knight's adversary. Its eristic character appears in the belittlement to which it subjects the visitor's strange challenge. Further, Gawain has indirectly retrojected, in the sense that his allusion to the uncle-nephew relationship dignifies his own lineage. At the same time, the profession of personal inadequacy represents the influence of an ideal quite foreign to the older heroic ethos. Open bragging—however it may befit the rude and unsocialized Green Knight—would violate the standards of courtesy Gawain feels compelled to uphold. Yet flyting is impossible if one party makes no attempt to defend its honor at all. Gawain has resolved this problem by valorizing himself not through evocation of his own personal merit but by designating himself a representative of Arthur and his court[46] whose high honor ought not, through a worthier exponent, be more directly engaged in such a ridiculous affair.

Now that the adversaries have been designated, the Green Knight reinitiates a new phase of the flyting that is concentrated on what prove to be key themes. In a brief yet significant three-line speech (378–80) the visitor makes two requests, first, that Gawain rehearse the terms of their contract, and second, that he identify himself. The dialogue over the next thirty-odd lines revolves around these two topics: Gawain answers his adversary's demands (381-85); the Green Knight expresses satisfaction with this response but insists that Gawain agree specifically to *seek him out* in twelve months (387–97); Gawain asks accordingly for the Green Knight's name and address (398–403); and the Green Knight agrees to provide these after Gawain has dealt his blow, which he should do at once (404–14). Throughout this interchange the Green Knight has abandoned insult and concentrated exclusively on the identitive and projective-contractual aspects of flyting. Although Gawain responds in good faith on both accounts, his adversary, without actually falsifying, withholds information that would show that he does not conceive the contest in the same way that Gawain does. He avoids naming himself, so that Gawain has to fight with an unknown. Indeed, if at this juncture he had betrayed his name and ties with Morgan la Fay, the contest could not have proceeded as it did. And although he does himself observe the terms of the contract that he so carefully reviews with Gawain, the Green Knight is not interested in the exchange of blows for its own sake. Rather, he wishes to see whether Gawain will honor his pledged word ("trawþe", 394) and bring his action into conformity with his speech, despite the apparent prospect of sure death. Of course, the traditional heroic code likewise insists on the bonding between words and deeds, as we have seen repeatedly. Yet in heroic epos the bond does not exist merely for its own sake; the very purpose of the flyting contract is to provide a setting in which actual martial prowess can be displayed and assessed. Although the *willingness* to fight is a precondition, no epic hero worth the name could uphold his reputation by exhibiting mere willingness without the corresponding deed. Conscious of these heroic resonances in the dialogic genre in which he has participated, Gawain cannot help but attach primary importance to the actual exchange of blows. And in this he is misled. For neither the Green Knight nor the *Gawain* poet is so much concerned with martial externalizations of heroism as with the *interior reality* of those corresponding human qualities. The contest openly contracted on is not the real test. It is merely a facade, a cover for a deeper probing into the interiorities of Gawain's mind and soul.

Now that the contract has been established and repeatedly confirmed—far more so than flyting heroes normally find to be necessary—the action can take over. In a brilliant stanza the *Gawain* poet describes the decapitation of the Green Knight, whose head subsequently delivers the final speech of this flyting exchange (448–56).[47] Here again he recurs to the same two themes of *contract* and *identity*: Gawain must fulfill his promise or be declared a "recreaunt" (456); he himself is known as the Knight of the Green Chapel. Obviously this self-identification is far from complete. The poem's first section concludes in an apostrophe in which the poetic narrator himself warns Gawain against being frightened away from completing his promised venture (487–90); ostensibly this intrusion by the narrator serves to reinforce the heroic standard of measure, whereby words must be matched by deeds. Nonetheless, it has by this stage become patently obvious that the encounter with the Green Knight involves far more than a mere exchange of blows in the usual heroic manner. Yet the intruder's secret remains altogether undisclosed. And in the meantime Gawain is duty-bound to acquiesce to the flyting-to-fighting pathway that the heroic code prescribes for him.

The large, central portion of the romance, parts 2 and 3, appears at first reading to be a digression, and it is precisely the system of expectations arising out of the heroic contest pattern that creates this false impression. For flytings project open, definite tests; the hero will not be measured by some standard of which he is unaware. Thus Gawain has no reason to associate either the "game" in which he engages with his Yuletide host or the host's wife's seduction attempts with his primary contract with the Green Knight. Yet his host is in fact the Green Knight in disguise. Gawain's failure to link these episodes—his failure to recognize that he is being examined on facets of his humanity that fall outside the spotlight of interest of the warrior's code—renders him susceptible to the lady's offer of the green girdle and thus occasions his "fall."

And so the martial combat element (C) in the contest pattern—comprising in this instance the return blows that the Green Knight delivers to Gawain at the Green Chapel in the poem's fourth section—does not, in the usual heroic manner, provide the setting in which the hero prevails or falls, but merely brings into view a failure that had occurred previously. True, Gawain exhibits a slight weakness during the martial exchange when he flinches away from the Green Knight's first, terrible stroke. And his adversary converts this, through comparative retrojection, into material for some first-rate flyting abuse: Such a coward, he says, could not be the Gawain of high repute; since he (the Green Knight) took his blow a year earlier in Arthur's court without cavil or quiver, he deserves to be acclaimed the better knight (2270–79). This speech reinforces the competitive, heroic criterion that has governed the contest in its outer structure. Gawain obliquely counters this charge by observing that he, unlike the Green Knight, cannot restore his head once it has been cut off (2280–83); the contest, in other words, is unequal since it pits heroism against magic. Yet here and throughout this complex interaction, Gawain reaffirms his resolve to fulfill his end of the contract. And the Green Knight, who, despite appearances, concentrates his abuse into particular, calculated moments, more than once praises him for doing so.

The climax of the poem arrives when the Green Knight reveals the true motive behind the game; and if one has not sufficiently appreciated the power of traditional meaning inhering in the contest form, the shock of this revelation will not fully register. His three swings—two of which were feints while the third delivered a mere surface wound—correspond to Gawain's earlier dealings with the Green Knight in his former capacity as host, during a phase of the story that seemed to have nothing to do with the beheading contest at all. For during the first two days of his game with the Green Knight disguised as lord of the castle, Gawain, in keeping with their agreement, returned his winnings, specifically the kisses given him by the lady, while on the third day, motivated by desire to save his own life, he failed to offer up the green girdle. Thus the flyting *contract*, which the Green Knight conspicuously foregrounded in the poem's opening scene, has been linked with a later contract. In each case Gawain has been measured strictly by his success in fulfilling his pledges; and his minor lapse in each instance arises from the same weakness, fear of death. The two contracts are related (and herein lies the poem's central deception) by the fact that the host and the Green Knight are the same man. For this reason the Green Knight concludes the dialogue by identifying himself, as previously he had refused properly to do: His name is Bertilak de Hautdesert, and he has been put up to this scheme by Morgan la Fay, Arthur's half-sister. Bertilak elaborates on the affiliations of kinship between Arthur and Morgan (2463–66), thus pointing out, in effect, that the contest has all been "within the family." And so the event has borne out the veracity of the Green Knight's initial claim that he did not come to fight (265–71, 279). The contest was indeed of the guest-host sort, nonlethal, ludic. Further, Bertilak has himself honored the terms of all his contracts, and this fact needs to be taken into account by those who would claim that the poem actually *rejects* the heroic code. Yet the outer shell of heroic action has been radically transformed as to its inner significance, converted, in effect, into an allegory of Gawain's soul. Not merely the martial virtues of strength and bravery but all aspects of a much-enlarged concept of "honor," which encompasses the fulfillment of promises, courtesy, humility, sexual continence, and religious devotion (symbolized in the pentangle), have been bound together into an integral totality, mirroring ideals that are Christian through and through.

Thus *Gawain*, while heavily dependent on the traditional contest pattern for its narrative structure, has sublimated those imperatives that generated this form in the first place. The *Mahābhārata*, the *Alliterative Morte Arthure*, and *Roland* are similarly concerned with integrating the heroic paradigm with nonmartial religious and social ideologies. Yet although those three epics illustrate the contest's increasing interiorization of "foreign" (nonagonistic) ideals, the root heroic drives for success and glory remain in all three cases vital. *Gawain*, however, represents the last degree in the opening of the contest to new intensities of introspection and the conversion of heroic motives into quite another kind. After this radical reorientation, the usefulness of the heroic paradigm in the "high" literary tradition has been spent. I do not mean to say that it vanished immediately, since obviously it did not,[48] or that *Gawain* specifically was the efficient cause behind this change. The poem stands rather as an indicator of a larger cultural turning away from the celebration of warfare as a principal theme of narrative literature. Of course, many poems, plays, and novels since the Middle Ages have treated martial subject matter. Yet seldom have they done so from a purely heroic stand-point; even when the heroic strain is present, it has usually been tem-pered by other influences to a greater degree than *Beowulf* and the *Iliad* were. And during the last century or two, writers aspiring for literary "greatness" have been as anxious to escape association with the heroic ethos—at least in any "crude," "simplistic," "bloodthirsty" form—as, in the ages of Homer and Virgil, they were incited to seek it out. Glory mongering is no longer a motive of which prestige writ-ers can approve. The celebration of this theme, together with the he-roic contest paradigm that gives it its superlative expression, has fallen down the hierarchy of institutionally endorsed artistic aims to find its home in television, movies such as the *Rocky* films, cartoons, and other vehicles of popular culture.[49]

CHAPTER FIVE

Genre and the Verbal Duel

GENERIC DIVERSITIES

The study of several heroic flytings within their larger narrative settings in the preceding chapter has shown that these verbal duels contributed materially to the development of plot. Now I would like to situate the heroic flyting in another kind of context—that of the larger world of verbal dueling itself. Formal disputation could, in a rough sense, be described as a dialogic genre; and this recognition might provide us with powerful tools in the study of cultural forms. Yet not all agonistic dialogues are of a type. A heroic flyting, a courtroom trial, and a presidential debate, for example, share general resemblances that might alert us to important, submerged premises in each of these interactions. Yet it would be foolish to overlook the equally significant differences between them. Criteria need to be developed that can both distinguish and interrelate various modalities of verbal contesting.

The value of a typology of adversarial dialogic forms becomes more apparent when one reflects on the role that contesting has assumed in cultural history. Again, the classic inquiry in this field is Ong 1981 (esp. 119–209), which studies *agōnia* in the academy, sports, politics, religion, and other facets of contemporary life. Particularly noteworthy is the connection between contesting and that tradition of discourse in which you and I, the reader and author of this book, are at this moment participating. Ong casts brilliant searchlights into the disputative heritage of the academy, rooted in the "agonistic noetic" of oral tradition, culminating in the debate-oriented, masculinized, Latinate intellectual efflorescence of the Middle Ages, and yielding in recent centuries to a less combative educational system in which women participate. Thus the very forms of thought in intellectual study were, in part, hammered out through a history of increasingly sublimated warfare. The academy is merely one such arena, for contesting suffuses cultural expression on many levels, overt and covert. Heroic flyting stands as one of the major historical and literary antecedents to the more "civilized" contests of the modern world. A more principled understanding of its interrelations with other agonistic forms and the kinds of "game rules" by which the violence lurking in the background of these interactions has been controlled might give insight into what we are and where we have come from.

The world of verbal contesting is vast—to survey all of its possibilities would require a major scholarly work in its own right. What I propose to undertake here is an analytic taxonomy based on a select sampling. The three varieties of verbal disputation that I will focus on are heroic flyting, "playing the dozens," and academic debate. My aim will be to discover those logical variables inherent in the contest situations by which the interrelations between these dialogic genres can be schematized. In order to juxtapose such divergent dialogic types, I will be compelled to tear instances of them from their native literary or sociological settings. Yet this dislocation and recontexting will enable us to articulate the stratum of largely unconscious generic choices by which, in each case, they come to be what they are.

THREE SAMPLE GENRES

Heroic flyting—the public exchange of personal insults and boasts between warriors contracting on a martial test—needs little in the way of definition. Yet for convenience of reference I summarize below two flyting-to-fighting episodes, the first between Beowulf and Unferth (centering on *Beo.* 499–606), and the second between Achilles and Aineias in *Il.*20.158–352. The reader will recall that these represent heroic flyting in its battlefield and guest-host forms, respectively:

> Traveling to Denmark with his band of Geats, Beowulf presents himself before the Danish king Hrothgar and offers to rid the kingdom of Grendel, who has been raiding the Danish hall, Heorot, at night (194–498). Unferth, one of Hrothgar's henchmen, relates a derogatory version of a youthful swimming match between Beowulf and Breca and predicts that the Geatish hero will fare poorly against Grendel if, indeed, he dares the venture (499–528). Beowulf responds with his own account of the swimming contest, returns charges against Unferth, and predicts that he will prevail against the monster (529–606). That night Beowulf outwrestles Grendel, who escapes with a mortal wound (710–836). Later, Unferth offers Beowulf a precious sword, Hrunting, which the Geat accepts graciously (1455–91).

> Aineias and Achilles meet on the plains before Troy. Achilles reminds his adversary of their former encounter in which he, Aineias, came out the loser and warns him that if he does not withdraw he will now meet his death (*Il.* 20.178–98). Aineias responds with a long narrative account of his

own genealogy and urges Achilles to give over the haggling and to fight (200–58). They exchange spear throws; and just as Achilles is about to kill Aineias with his sword, Poseidon, after discussing the matter with Hera, lifts the Trojan out of the battle (259–339). Achilles, realizing that Aineias's ancestral boasts must have had some substance, nonetheless declares his victory and moves on to other encounters (344–52).

Unlike these instances of heroic flyting that appear in literary texts, the following "sounding" sequence was recorded by William Labov (1972) in the course of his field research with inner-city black adolescents.[1] "Sounding," also referred to as "playing the dozens," "signifying," "woofing," "cutting," and by other names, is a ritualized exchange in which each contestant finds new and extravagant ways of insulting his opponent's mother or some other person with whom he is closely identified. By the unstated rules governing this activity, which Labov describes in considerable detail, the contestants must not take insults personally; this mechanism presumably helps to prevent physical brawls. The following sequence (1972: 311) is typical of many in Labov's study:

Your mother got on sneakers!
Your mother wear high-heeled sneakers to church!
Your mother wear a jock strap!
Your mother got polka-dot drawers!
Your mother wear the seat of her drawers on the top of her head!

Although many of the particular rules and constraints that Labov articulates are clearly unique to the sounding genre, generally related varieties of insult genres occur in other cultures. The verbal dueling among Turkish adolescents, studied by Dundes, Leach, and Özkök (1972), and "truly frivolous talk" of Mayan boys, studied by Gossen (1974: 97–106), provide good examples.[2] The poetical flytings of the Scottish *makars*, represented in "Polwart and Montgomerie Flyting" and "The Flyting of Dunbar and Kennedie," fit into the same general mold.[3] Analogues could easily be found from other parts of the world.[4] The celebrated seventeenth-century Japanese writer Saikuku Ihara, for instance, describes the festivities on New Year's day when the company divides into two groups; with the lights dimmed and faces unrecognizable, members of each side take turns in heaping abuse upon each other (1965: 89–90). One could draw further parallels with verbal dueling in the *Canterbury Tales*, as between the Miller and Reeve or the Friar and Summoner.[5] Flytings of these types, which I will call "ludic," must be differentiated from heroic flyting, with its serious claims and martial entailments. The criteria underlying these determinations will be set forth shortly. In any case, both these ludic and heroic varieties can still bear the name of "flyting," if we restrict this term to verbal contesting with an ad hominem orientation.

By designating "debate" as my third genre, I intend something narrower than the full range of activities to which this word in its broadest sense can refer; in some contexts, this label might even be attached to flyting or sounding exchanges. The phenomenon I mean to single out might be better called "intellectual debate"—that is, debate conducted in a nonmartial environment that centers on some issue with intellectual content apart from the personalities of the contestants, and that does so with (purportedly) no further end in mind than to arrive at the truth concerning this issue. Since early times the academy has been a particularly enthusiastic sponsor of this mode of discourse, although, needless to say, it can flower in other environments as well. The example that I have chosen, from Lorenzo Valla's *Dialogue on Free Will*, was written as a contribution to a continuing dialogue in the Christian Latin tradition since the time of Augustine and before. Represented as the record of a conversation between Lorenzo and a friend of his, Antonio Glarea, the *Dialogue* opens with an attack by Antonio on Boethius's famous account in the *Consolation of Philosophy* of how human free will and God's prescience can coexist. Antonio has just held forth on the position that, since God foresees the future, he has thereby deprived humans of their free will, since they are bound to act in accordance with his foreknowledge. The following excerpt illustrates a typical debate exchange:

Lor. You say God foresaw that Judas would be a traitor, but did He on that account induce him to betrayal? I do not see that, for, although God may foreknow some future act to be done by man, this act is not done by necessity because he may do it willingly. Moreover, what is voluntary cannot be necessary. . . .

Ant. You say Judas acted voluntarily and on that account not by necessity. Indeed, it would be most shameless to deny that he did it voluntarily. What do I say to that? Certainly this act of will was necessary since God foreknew it; moreover, since it was foreknown by Him, it was necessary for Judas to will and do it lest he should make the foreknowledge in any way false.

Lor. Still I do not see why the necessity for our volitions and actions should derive from God's foreknowledge. For, if foreknowing something *will be* makes it come about, surely knowing something *is* just as easily makes the same thing *be*. Certainly, if I know your genius, you would not say that something *is* because you *know* it is (Valla 1948: 163).

Even though Lorenzo and Antonio insist that they fight for the sake of truth and not for the sake of argument (Valla 1948: 166), nonetheless, at several points, they use explicitly martial metaphors in reference to their debating: "Do not expect me to give in to you easily or to flee without sweat and blood"; or "Let us contend closely in hand-to-hand and foot-to-foot conflict. Let the decision be by sword, not spear" (Valla 1948: 163; see also 166 and 169 for similar figures). This illustrates the dual nature of the academic debate tradition as, on the one hand, an impersonal quest for truth, and on the other hand, a highly personal contest.

VARIABLES OF GENERIC DIFFERENTIATION

As I have indicated in the cases of flyting and debate, the examples I have chosen represent merely one kind of dialogic activity that, in scholarly parlance, often goes under these names; examples of other types of "flyting" and "debate" would not conform to the same patterns. This practice might seem to leave me open to the charge of circularity, for I have selected these episodes of verbal contesting by their ability to meet certain criteria. Can I legitimately use these same examples as a means of validating these same principles?

This criticism presupposes that it is my aim merely to enunciate a more exacting account for distinctions and nomenclatures that are already well recognized, whether within the cultures and historical periods from which the examples are drawn, or within the context of current scholarship. Yet such is not the case. Instead, I am trying to identify principles that, whether or not consciously conceived as such, are *real*, that represent fundamental alternatives in the actualization of verbal contests, and that can be used to distinguish legitimate classes of these, even if they were not acknowledged in the explicit critical consciousness of the societies that produced them. For example, the body of material that the term flyting has been used to designate in fact subdivides into two types, one of which (heroic flyting) brings with it martial entailments, whereas the other (ludic flyting) does not. I submit that a verbal contest that incorporates the possibility that the contestants will kill each other afterward is a significantly different activity than a verbal contest that does not arouse this generic expectation; and even though both of these might now go under the label of "flyting," this distinction would have been at least *functionally* recognized by societies that countenanced both kinds. This is an example of what I call a "real" distinction—that is, real to people living human lives in the world.

The kinds of flyting, sounding, and debate exemplified are particularly serviceable because they dramatize several major contrasts in verbal contesting. How shall we bring these out, that is, what will be our principle of comparison? I have already rejected traditional generic distinctions within the cultural environments that produced my examples. Although such study has its own interest and importance, it cannot provide a sound basis for cross-cultural comparison. The same problem would confound a purely formalist analysis that tried to identify patterns or structures strictly internal to the dialogue *as text or discourse*. For the forms of discourse tend to derive, in one sense or another, from the literary tradition or language or cultural context in which that discourse occurs. Formal comparisons across the lines of culture and tradition are liable to run up against every kind of difficulty, since often a superficial formal likeness belies an underlying dissimilarity of origin and function. Perhaps, if undertaken with due perspicuity and sophistication, such an approach might bear fruit. Yet for our present purposes a much more productive line offers itself.

The basis for my analysis will in fact be pragmatic, centering on the relationship between the discourse and the context of its production.[6] At least four areas or variables in this world-to-dialogue relationship seem to be involved in differentiating heroic flyting, sounding, and debate as dialogic genres. These are the choice of subject matter, the referential mode, the locus of resolution, and the social context. I will define the possibilities in each of these areas in terms of poles or binary oppositions; yet it should be kept in mind that a given contest or contest genre might locate itself somewhere between the poles, adopting thus a "mixed" approach to that particular facet of the world-to-dialogue relationship. Recognizing, then, the existence of degrees of variation, the framework of possibilities in these four areas can be schematized as follows:

A. Subject matter: contestant-oriented or other-oriented
B. Referential mode: serious or ludic
C. Locus of resolution: external or internal
D. Context: intergroup or ingroup

A. Subject Matter: Contestant-Oriented or Other-Oriented

Since contests arise out of the need to assert and prove selfhood, in a sense the true subject of any verbal contest is the contestants themselves; that this presupposition is embedded in the basic structures of contests is borne out by the range of defensive or belligerent stances frequently adopted by debaters even when they are purportedly engaged in a "purely" intellectual inquiry. And yet, though personal victory or personal defeat remains the point of contests, personal issues can be to varying degrees expressed or repressed in the explicit matter of debate: The repression of personalized content constitutes a means of ritualization, whereas the expression of the personal element brings the eristic or disputatious aspect of the contest more to the surface and thus de-ritualizes it in this respect. Contestant orientation predominates in heroic epic. In intellectual-debate traditions in the Western world, personal attack comes to be seen as a violation of the rigor of argument, as is indicated in the notion of the "ad hominem fallacy." In between the two extremes of the totally personal and the totally nonpersonal falls a wide range of material. The Middle English poems, *The Owl and the Nightingale* or *Wynnere and Wastour*, for example, indulge in ad hominem attack along with debate on abstract issues.[7] The same could be said for much of the debate poetry of the medieval Latin period.[8]

B. *Referential Mode: Serious or Ludic*

In many verbal contests the contenders are engaged in making assertions that they intend as true statements and that are interpreted and responded to as such. These assertions belong to what I am calling the "serious" mode of reference, in that they are understood as referring to the individuals that they designate in a literal or "serious" way. In other contest genres, by contrast, insulting is engaged in purely for its own sake, as an exhibition of the speaker's proficiency in this verbal skill, and no one participating in the speech event in any capacity imagines that the insults are true or intended as such. This speech activity is ludic or, if one prefers, fictionalized, in the sense that the normal connections between statements and the world of reference have been severed.[9] Mode of reference is entirely independent of subject; it concerns not the *matter* of assertions but how they are meant to be interpreted. (Obviously, "serious" and "ludic" are not intended as evaluative labels. A "ludic" exchange can have serious dimensions or overtones as, for example, when the contestants become angry, or when it comprises a crucial episode in a "serious" work of art, or in various other ways. My distinction concerns exclusively the applicability of statements in their expressed form to their designated referents.)

John Searle has proposed a theory of the differences between fictional and nonfictional discourse that may be of service here. According to Searle, assertions normally conform to "certain quite specific semantic and pragmatic rules. These are:

1. The essential rule: the maker of an assertion commits himself to the truth of the expressed proposition.
2. The preparatory rules: the speaker must be in a position to provide evidence or reasons for the truth of the expressed proposition.
3. The expressed proposition must not be obviously true to both the speaker and the hearer in the context of utterance.
4. The sincerity rule: the speaker commits himself to a belief in the truth of the expressed proposition."[10]

In general, nonfictional discourse conforms to these rules whereas fictional discourse does not. The essential function of these rules is to "establish connections between language and reality." Fictional discourse, however, entails its own set of "extralinguistic, nonsemantic conventions that break the connection between words and the world" (Searle 1979: 66). Thus, fictional and nonfictional discourse bring with them different presuppositions about the way in which they refer discourse to external reality.[11]

This fundamental distinction between fictionalized ("ludic") and nonfictionalized ("serious") discourse creates an important division within the world of the verbal contest, as will become clearer when I turn to a closer examination of my examples. The fictionalization of contests provides an avenue of ritualization, in that it distances the contestants as persons from the words spoken; nonfictionalization, however, promotes a more open expression of the eristic or querulous. As I noted in my discussion of subject matter, a range of possibilities extends between the poles of the "personal" and "nonpersonal." It was my former view (Parks 1986b: 447) that, in mode of reference, a contestational statement had to be either fictionalized or nonfictionalized, and that no middle ground was possible. I admitted at the time that contestants could always lapse into interpreting nonpersonal statements personally or vice versa, but held that this would constitute a breakdown or modulation of the original activity. It now appears to me, however, that the line can be blurred on more accounts than I had originally allowed. Poems like the Eddic *Hárbarð sljóð* may be generically "mixed" on this point, proposing some of its claims "seriously" and some "ludically." In such instances there would be oscillation between one statement (or group of statements) and the next. Yet a statement might be ambiguous in its mode of reference. Labov has shown how ambiguous "sounds" can lead to trouble and "spoil the game"; this would suggest that sounding groups have only a limited tolerance for ambivalently ludic insults. The possibility has to be entertained all the same. Nonetheless, I continue to feel that the notion of "play" constitutes something of a prime in human consciousness. Although I can envision a contestant moving in and out of a play mode or voicing polyvalent utterances that articulate several possibilities, some ludic and some not, people in the world need to know how much and in what respects a statement should be taken as a "joke." Scholars love to undermine these distinctions, but many might respond in a different spirit if the dean or chancellor were to issue a serious?/playful?/serious-and-playful? memorandum recommending a 50% reduction in faculty salaries. I suspect, indeed, that cases of "waffling" on the serious-ludic distinction would appear more frequently in artificial and "literary" dialogues, and especially in scholarly interpretations of them. In "natural" verbal duels, of the kind that spring up in real-life settings, greater clarity would usually be demanded. Most people care about their reputations and want to know if and how these are being attacked. These speculations seem to be borne out by the evidence in the work of Labov (1972), Dundes, Leach, and Özkök (1972), and Gossen (1974).

The serious or ludic character of verbal contests has an important structural consequence. When the contest statement—particularly an insult—is intended in the serious or nonfictional mode, the adversary or butt frequently feels obligated to defend himself by denying it; when the statement is intended fictionally or ludically, however, denial is superfluous and even, in the case of sounding, a rule violation. Thus, the serious contest genres tend to progress from one contestant's attack (A insults B) to his opponent's self-defense (B denies A's insult) before proceeding to that opponent's counterattack (B insults A). Contests of the ludic variety, however, more often move directly from attack (A insults B) to attack (B insults A). I must emphasize, however, that this association between mode of reference and structure describes a tendency and not an invariable law.

C. Locus of Resolution: External or Internal

This variable concerns where that contest activity occurs on the basis of which victory or defeat is determined. If the contestant wins or loses primarily on the basis of his performance within the verbal contest, the locus of resolution is, by my terminology, "internal." If he wins or loses primarily on the basis of some subsequent contest performance of his outside the verbal contest, the locus of resolution is "external." To restate the issue in slightly different terms, this factor concerns the extent to which the verbal contest is self-contained and self-fulfilling. Sounding, for example, resolves internally, in the sense that sounders win or lose purely on the strength of their performance as sounders; in this respect the sounding session is discrete and self-contained. Heroic flyting, however, resolves externally, in that the flyters tacitly or explicitly agree on some subsequent test that is martial rather than verbal. As these two examples suggest, the pathway of internal resolution tends to restrict the scope of aggression whereas external resolution permits contestation to expand outward into some further, nonverbal domain.

To avoid confusion, I need to differentiate the locus of resolution from the locus of judgment. Contests regularly occur before viewers, who act as witnesses. In some contest modes an external party or parties involve themselves more actively in the contesting process, as occurs in a courtroom when a jury passes judgment as to who has won.[12] In such cases the process of judgment is usually separated temporally as well as spatially from the actual verbal contest, and from this point of view the contest has been "resolved" externally. Yet, according to the distinction I am trying to make, this would really exemplify internal resolution, since judgment is based on the contestant's performance within the verbal contest rather than on some contest performance of his that occurred subsequently. The jury's verdict, while obviously a crucial part of the contesting process, is not a contestational act in itself, but rather a judgment concerning a verbal contest that *occurred* (past tense) prior to the decision. Other "external" factors can in a similar way enter into the contestation without themselves being contestational in their own nature; the actual winning or losing, though involved with these factors, does not occur *in* them but *in relation to* them. For example, the defendant on trial for the murder of X wins or loses his case on the basis of the courtroom proceedings as verbal contest; his having killed or not having killed X, though obviously of crucial relevance, was not in itself a contestation act. One "wins" the trial, not the murder. By contrast, in the Beowulf-Unferth episode, the fight against Grendel—an event external to the verbal contest—is clearly part of the actual contesting process.

Although the distinction between internal and external resolution is fairly clear-cut in the examples I am considering, many cases are more ambiguous. In a political debate such as those between Lincoln and Douglas or Kennedy and Nixon, for example, the outcome is ostensibly determined on the basis of considerations internal to the debate; that is, the electorate on election day gives its verdict as to who "won" (past tense) the debate, to the extent, at least, that the election can be seen as a direct verdict on this matter. The candidate's subsequent performance in office is a separate and noncontestation fulfillment of duties, according to this (more or less) "official" view. In reality, however, elected public servants often orient much of their performance in office toward fulfilling their campaign boasts and toward an upcoming election, and thus the tenure of office becomes, in effect, another aspect of the political contest. On balance I would argue that campaign debates are internally resolving, since the contestational motive explicitly and overtly governs the campaign process, whereas performance in office is overtly governed by other considerations. Yet the case is an ambiguous one and could be argued the other way.

D. Context: Intergroup or Ingroup

Because the contest as a symbolic and ritualized event implicates the community, the communal affiliations of the contestants have a major bearing on the form of contestation and the amount of hostility that can be expressed. If the two contestants belong to the same community, obviously they must confine the expression of adversativeness to some degree; otherwise they might unleash forces that could ultimately tear the community apart. When the contestants represent different communities, this consideration is irrelevant, and so, in general, the eristic impulse is granted greater freedom of expression. This correlation between intergroup contexts and high eristic intensity is complicated, however, when the two social groups themselves are engaged in some kind of bond-producing interaction; such environments seem to restrict the scope of contestation more than other kinds of intergroup situations do. Further complexities can be generated when the boundaries of the community or communities are uncertain or changing. In short, the relationship between contests and their social environments is an involved topic in its own right. Nonetheless, the distinction between the single- and multiple-community contest remains the most basic factor in this relationship and one that reveals much about the structure of contestational motives and the avenues available for their expression.

In each of these four areas, as I have tried to indicate, one option tends to promote the expression of the adversarial or eristic motive while the other tends to promote ritualizing or distancing.[13] Of course, the intensity of adversativeness or competitiveness in a contest is really a function of the quality and intensity of motives in the minds of the participants. The structure of a contest or contest genre regulates not the degree of emotional involvement so much as the channels through which it expresses itself. The division of each of the binary oppositions into an "eristic" and "ritualizing" alternative allows for the hypothesis that, in general, the eristic motive will express itself more freely in those areas where the rules of the contest select an eristic alternative and less freely where they select the ritualizing one. Of course this distinction is crude, since often a range of possibilities extends between the eristic and ritualizing poles, as I have tried to suggest. Nonetheless, for clarity I summarize these distinctions in Table 1.

APPLICATION

Let us now analyze our examples against the framework in Table 1. Although the scope of this discussion will be confined to the particular instances cited previously, these are typical and may be used as a basis for generalization about the classes of contests that they represent.

1A. Flyting: Subject Matter—Contestant-Oriented

In their predictions as well as their narrations, Unferth, Beowulf, Achilles, and Aineias all focus explicitly on incidents relating to their own personal worthiness or their foes' lack of it. Future-oriented personal reference concentrates on upcoming tests (the Beowulf-Grendel and Aineias-Achilles fights); retrospective personal reference deals with past heroic exploits (the Beowulf-Breca or previous Aineias-Achilles encounters) or genealogy. It is worth noting that the five speech functions detailed in chapter 3—identification, retrojection, projection, evaluation-attribution, and comparison—all lend themselves to personal attack. Clearly this group of topoi is designed for contestant-oriented verbal contest genres.

1B. Flyting: Referential Mode—Serious

All four contestants speak seriously, in the sense that they intend the claims that they make to be taken as true. Thus Beowulf feels obligated to correct Unferth's distorted version of the swimming match (Beo.530–81), whereas Achilles in his concluding speech notes that,

TABLE 1
Variable Features of Verbal Dueling

	Eristic	*Ritualizing*
A. Subject matter	Contestant-oriented	Other-oriented
B. Referential mode	Serious	Ludic
C. Locus of resolution	External	Internal
D. Context	Intergroup	Ingroup

contrary to what he himself had at the time supposed, Aineias's genealogical boast must have had a foundation in fact (20.344–52). Since truth claims are taken seriously, the structure of debate usually incorporates a movement from attack to defense to counterattack.[14] Thus Beowulf denies Unferth's charges as a preliminary to his own countercharges and boast; similarly, Aineias defends his own self-worth through the genealogical narration as a preliminary to his own invocation to battle.

I should note in passing that "ludic" differs from "heroic" flyting with respect to the referential mode. It can be assumed, for example, that Montgomerie does not expect anyone literally to believe him when he accuses Polwart of "peeping" like a mouse (Cranstoun 1887: "Polwart and Montgomerie's Flyting," lines 1–4); nor does Polwart in his reply think himself obliged to refute this charge. These contestants, then, are progressing from insult to insult, omitting the defense.[15]

1C. Flyting: Locus of Resolution—External

In both of the examples, flyting eventually gives way to a martial test. Thus, the Beowulf-Unferth exchange serves as a preliminary to Beowulf's fight with Grendel, whereas the Achilles-Aineias quarrel culminates in a fight. In both cases the martial combat—itself a contestation activity—provides the means of resolving the issues raised in the flyting. Both Achilles and Unferth have implied that their adversaries lack true heroic stature. Disputes of this kind cannot finally be resolved in the sphere of words but only in the sphere of heroic action. The relationship and movement between these spheres is negotiated through the flyting contract. All this has been discussed in detail in chapter 2.

Once again, ludic flyting contrasts with its heroic counterpart regarding locus of resolution, for there is no reason to doubt that the flytings of the Scottish *makars* resolve internally, without recourse to arms. At the end of "Dunbar and Kennedie," for example, the poet asks us, "Juge ʒe now heir quha gat the war" ("Judge ye now here who got the worse," 554). The reader, in other words, is being asked to pass judgment on the basis of the verbal exchange he has just witnessed (read); the implication is that the contest has been completed but for the judgment process.

1D. Flyting: Context—Intergroup

All four heroes represent different tribes or nations; as discussed in chapter 2, heroic flyting typically presupposes a plurality of social groups. There are exceptions, such as the Achilles-Agamemnon quarrel, but they are comparatively rare. It is indeed doubtful whether the types of societies depicted in *Beowulf* and the Homeric epics could endure very much of this kind of interaction, with its violent and militaristic overtones, without being torn apart by internal vendettas. Only between separate groups, who are liable to fight with each other anyway, can this mode of interaction be sustained on an ongoing basis. Ludic flyting, by contrast, seems to occur between members of a single social group.

The social context of heroic flyting seems to influence the heroic interaction in another way. As noted in chapter 2, flytings in guest-host environments lead to indirect and nonlethal martial tests, whereas flytings in battlefield environments are apt to culminate in direct combat. Once more the personal duel betrays itself as a highly public activity, responsive to larger community needs and conditions.

2A. Sounding: Subject Matter—Contestant-Oriented

As Labov shows, sounds are regularly targeted at the sounding adversary, or more often, at the adversary's mother, a relative, or some other closely associated person.[16] In its manner of attack, we might describe sounding as insult through metonymy: Through his links, especially of the familial sort, with the specified target, the contestant adversary presumably partakes of this same abuse. Flyters in heroic epic similarly feel that their own honor is at stake when the honor of their ancestors and kinfolk has been impugned.

2B. Sounding: Referential Mode—Ludic

Although sounding can indeed become a fiercely competitive activity with considerable consequences in terms of an individual's prestige within his social group, it nonetheless remains ludic, in that no one believes that the insults are literally true or that they were intended as such. Indeed, as Labov shows through some fine examples, when sounding begins to be interpreted as carrying personal reference— that is, when insults contain propositions that might actually be true—the ritualized exchange deteriorates (1972: 330–34). Because sounds, though personal in their subject matter, are not interpreted personally, denials are inappropriate—indeed, as Labov argues, they constitute a violation of the rules of sounding, for to deny is to imply that the sound might have been intended as a true statement. Thus, the ludic character of sounding produces, as a structural consequence, a movement from insult to insult, with self-defense prohibited.

2C. Sounding: Locus of Resolution—Internal

As a matter of practical reality, a sounding exchange might dissolve into a brawl. Yet according to the unspoken rules of sounding (and our subject is, after all, generic conventions) victory is produced by the contestant's performance within the verbal medium. Labov proposes various criteria for "excellence" in sounding (see esp. 1972: 344–48), and stresses the role of the group in the evaluation of sounds (1972: 325–27). And as his entire analysis makes evident, sounding is a test of one's proficiency in a verbal skill. It does not point to some further test outside its own boundaries.

2D. Sounding: Context—Ingroup

"Generally speaking," Labov notes, "extended ritual sounding is an in-group process, and when sounding occurs across group lines, it is often intended to provoke a fight" (1972: 341). Most of the recorded sounding material was produced between members of a single social group; still, Labov cites an example where intergroup sounding culminated in a murder (1972:341–42). These observations support the position that intergroup contexts are more conducive to the expression of hostility than ingroup contexts are.[17]

3A. Debate: Subject Matter—Other-Oriented

The explicit topic of Lorenzo and Antonio's debate is divine prescience and human free will, not their own personal worthiness. Yet, as I have noted, the personal and contestational underlay is alluded to several times when the two friends jokingly refer to their exchange in military terms. According to the conventions that govern this type of contest, the matter of discussion should be radically separated from the personal qualities of the disputants, and truth rather than any personal consideration should provide the criterion of judgment. Overt personal attack indeed betrays a weakness in that it amounts to an open admission that one is acting on the contestational motive rather than in the spirit of pure, disinterested intellectual inquiry.[18] Reference to this personal dimension of the debate activity can be made in jest only. Yet whether it is openly acknowledged or not, the contestational motive continues to operate, as those participating in debates know full well. The purging of personal content from the matter of discussion provides one means of distancing and ritualizing the aggressive display.

3B. Debate: Referential Mode—Serious

In academic debate, truth claims are of the utmost importance. Lorenzo and Antonio each responds on the assumption that his debating adversary has been representing the point of view he proposes as the true one. Accordingly, each of them takes pains to acknowledge and refute the points made by his rival. Antonio, in the quoted passage, goes so far as to repeat what is in his view the substance of Lorenzo's argument before asking the question "What do I say to that?" as a preface to his own reply. His practice differs in this respect from that of the sounder, who disregards his rival's insult and proceeds directly to one of his own.

3C. Debate: Locus of Resolution—Internal

Contestation in this kind of intellectual debate confines itself to the verbal medium, and victory is determined on the basis of one's performance within that medium. In the case of the *Dialogue*, Antonio more or less capitulates—overwhelmed by the rightness of Lorenzo's position—about halfway through, and the second half of the exchange is principally exposition on Lorenzo's part. There are, of course, debate forms—such as parlaying between nations on the brink of war—that contain the possibility of an external resolution (armed attack) if the peace talks fail; yet this very possibility distinguishes such negotiations generically from academic debate.

4D. Debate: Context—Ingroup

Lorenzo and Antonio are, by their own profession, close friends and therefore belong to the same community according to any definition that could possibly bear on this dialogue. This bond clearly motivates the many conciliatory and tension-reducing comments that recur throughout the exchange. The joking references to hand-to-hand combat, for example, provide a mechanism for recognizing the adversarial relationship that they have for the time being adopted while in the same stroke relativizing and distancing it through metaphoric exaggeration. Similarly, the exchange opens and closes in a friendly manner, and the "contestants" drop an assortment of compliments at strategic points. All of these countercontesting remarks are unmistakably motivated by concerns deriving from their coparticipation in larger modes of interaction. Contestants cannot forget that their contests must be nested in human community.

As we have observed throughout this study, contests usually occur before witnesses, and in this respect the Lorenzo-Antonio encounter would appear to be anomalous. This anomaly in fact attests to the peculiar and fascinating status of this particular document on the margins of both oral and literate discourse. On the one hand, the *Dialogue* purports to be the record of a conversation; yet it was composed in writing and undoubtedly entailed, in its textual form, vast revisions of the original oral exchange, if there ever really was one. And as a literate reworking of an oral type of encounter, the *Dialogue* incorporates a reference to witnessing and judgment of a distinctly literate variety. For at the end of their conversation (Valla 1948: 182), Antonio urges Lorenzo to write out an account of this exchange so that others can benefit from it; Lorenzo agrees to do so, explicitly noting that others will become the "judges in this matter." The "public setting" for this debate, in other words, is the written document itself, through which the public can witness a type of encounter that is, in its natural form, oral.

The conclusions from the foregoing discussion on the world-to-dialogue relationships presupposed in flyting, sounding, and debate respectively are summarized in Table 2. In overview, note that heroic flyting selects the eristic alternative in all four areas, whereas sounding and debate follow the ritualizing path in three areas out of four. It *cannot* be assumed therefore that flyting lacks ritualization, for rituality is not confined to the four areas of difference that we have been examining. Yet it should not surprise us that flyting is characteristically far more violent in its issue than either of the other two dialogic modes.

EXTENSIONS

The genres that have been studied here do not exhaust all possibilities in the realization of verbal contests. A mock debate, for example,

TABLE 2
Feature Analysis of Three Verbal Dueling Genres

	Subject Matter	Referential Mode	Locus of Resolution	Context
Flyting	Contestant-oriented	Serious	External	Intergroup
Sounding	Contestant-oriented	Ludic	Internal	Ingroup
Debate	Other-oriented	Serious	Internal	Ingroup

could combine nonpersonal subject matter with a ludic referential mode; however, the *Njáls saga*, like many other narratives, contains episodes in which insults intended and interpreted ludically nonetheless bring about mortal encounters. The field is a wide one; and if particular cultures should choose—as they well may—to countenance only a limited selection and to define these in eccentric ways, I see nothing within the logic of the verbal contest itself that either prohibits this or causes it to be so.

My aim has been to develop a framework by which heroic flyting can be interrelated with other, radically different contest forms. One of the merits of this attempt is that it runs against the grain of a certain elitism that resists recognizing the kinship between high philosophical discourse, on the one hand, and lower-class street banter, on the other. Yet the behavioral paradigms involved are not unique to philosophers or epic heroes or any other stratum of humanity, fictional or otherwise. Recognizing the agonistic interaction itself as a significant context makes possible the unmasking of many hidden determinants within or behind culturally formative discursive modes, past or present. To what extent has this very study, for example, been shaped by contestational demands? Are you as reader and I as author adversaries? Not entirely, I would suspect, in most cases. Scholarly inquiry permits and even fosters a spirit of common enterprise. At the same time, as quickly becomes evident at scholarly symposiums, the role of adversary is institutionally sanctioned and available to anyone who wishes to adopt it, within the many, unstated limits that scholarly convention imposes. Thus, the theme of contest is far from irrelevant to contemporary concerns. To the contrary, it may have helped create many of those basic noetic constructs by which we express and know.

By viewing dialogue in its relation to the "real world," I have tried in this chapter to break the solipsism of discourse and to recognize its continuity with a wide field of cultural experience. The four variables of subject matter, referential mode, locus of resolution, and social context index distinct and important aspects in the pragmatics of verbal contests. At the same time their mutual independence (since no one is strictly determined by another) enables us to define and distinguish different types of adversarial dialogic exchange in terms of constellations of features. Such a conceptual apparatus should assist in any attempt further to relate heroic flyting to other dialogic forms in a history of verbal contesting. And it may be of more general assistance in articulating the forms of conflict in human life, and perhaps even in discovering pathways to their resolution.

CONCLUSION

Contest and Culture

MAN, whatever else he might be, is a rhetorical creature. And, in many of his moods, a belligerent one as well. Rhetoric and belligerence meet in the verbal contest. Since they meet so often, verbal contesting has exerted a vast impact on human culture. But since man is many things besides rhetorical and belligerent, the verbal contest has to adapt itself to many settings. Thus much of its history has been a history of multiforms and disguises. In consequence the contestational character of many of our institutions and ways of life has been insufficiently appreciated.

I say "man" and "he" advisedly because, to the limits of my familiarity with the topic, men have historically exerted an overwhelming dominance in this speech and dialogic activity. Sheer numerical preponderances should not be overlooked here. The fact that males, both human and animal, engage in high-display threat interactions with much greater frequency than females do suggests perhaps that they like it more. Of course, women too disagree and express such disagreements verbally. Sometimes these disputes become formal and agonistic in the manner of a true verbal duel. Moreover, even within the limited setting of the intermale contest, I have no doubt that the image of femininity in the female-male sexual axis provides a key motivational determinant. For in these macho exchanges, sexual identity is very much to the point. All of these questions, though inherently of immense importance, would demand a sounding of the unconscious depths underlying visible expressions of contestation; and for such a project, the methodology that I have chosen for this study is poorly adapted. Nonetheless, I would defend my approach and choice of starting point. For just as a work of in-depth literary hermeneutics must begin with a full comprehension of the particular language employed (its syntax, vocabulary, etc.), similarly a study of contests must begin with what is present and consciously articulated. For what is unseen can be approached only through what is seen. In heroic narrative generally, men seem to have tried to exclude women from the category of potential "heroic adversaries," and I intend this phrase to carry all the connotations of projected physical assault, posited comparability in mode of combat and admissible measures of heroic self-worth, and so forth, that I have explicated in the first three chapters of this book. Within this relatively closed system, in service of its own self-stipulated aims, the intermale contest has created its own distinctive patterns. Whether women have *through direct participation* contributed materially to the the development of heroic verbal contesting as a genre, or how they will do so in the future, remains to be seen.

Yet before we hasten to discover ways in which this might be so, we should pause to consider whether verbal dueling is a desirable cultural function in the first place. Commonly, as I have noticed, scholars who have devoted great time and energy to a subject end up implying that the object of their study is in itself inherently "good." This is probably one of the affective concomitants of the labor of love that any thoughtful work of scholarship must be. I am fully convinced, moreover, that unless one can open oneself to a point of view sympathetic to the phenomenon one wishes to investigate, one will never understand that phenomenon in its inwardness; all one's accrued learning will remain essentially barren and superficial. For this reason I have tried to enter imaginatively into the vision and sensibility of flyting heroes; and in the process I have found superlative expression given to a vital and poignant dimension of human experience. Nonetheless, my considered response is an ambivalent one. For while life may often demand agonistic aggression, *agōnia* can in turn prove life-denying. At this crucial turn in its history, humankind will need to summon all its wisdom to this problem if we are to succeed in negotiating the difficult passes ahead.

If it shows nothing else, the evidence of heroic flyting should prove that contests exert an ineluctable appeal on the psyche (or the male psyche at least—the feminine perspective on this problem remains, for the most part, unarticulated within heroic texts). For the ego-self seems spontaneously to perceive contests as the arena in which it can prove its worth, in its own eyes and in the eyes of community. This theme of "proving yourself" is obviously a recurrent one in human societies; and while we should perhaps hesitate to impute similar mental states to animals, we can certainly observe that the correlating human behavioral patterns in such contests have infrahuman analogues. Having pitted as stakes nothing less than their sense of self, contestants experience great euphoria on winning. So it is that the quest for glory generates tremendous motive power, most evident in the self-abandonment of warriors in battle or in the unquenchable ambitions of such conquerors as Alexander the Great, yet intelligible on a gut level to masses of the population who consistently respond to such figures. At the same time, contests produce not just winners but losers; and herein lies their tragedy. The greatness in Homer's representation of battle lies not in his having adopted some antiheroic stance that brings him into convenient accord with many late twentieth-century academicians disenchanted with the war in Vietnam or the presidency of Ronald Reagan. His greatness as a war poet is that he depicted the contest completely, in both its aspects.[1] War, to Homer, is fascinating, awesome, unavoidable; its call stirs to the depths of one's being, and winning brings with it a gratification hardly to be rivaled in human experience. Yet Homer never forgets that such glory is secured at the price of death and humiliation. For every exulting Achilles there is a Hektor dragged in the dust. Agony and annihilation underlie the heroic self-fulfillment. I can think of no better emblem for this dynamic in the "play" of human consciousness than the Homeric image of the victorious hero boasting over a fallen and dying enemy. While we may mask this figure or soften its contours, I do not believe we will ever succeed in eradicating it from human life.

Nor would it be in all respects desirable to do so; for contesting behavior serves many valid uses. Perhaps paramount among these is its ability to bring about controlled destruction. Destruction is the precondition of any affirmation: What is or should be requires a space for its being. A community that wants to live at peace, for example, may have to resist aggression from the outside. And though we may not usually think of intellectual life in these terms, many scholarly and artistic achievements have an extraordinarily destructive aspect. The progress of Socrates through one of his dialogues, in which he reduces to rubble the conventional wisdom of the Athens of his age, is not unlike the advance of a tank brigade through a modern city. Even today in the academy, destructiveness is often required, in the need to upend previous thinking on a subject before one's work will be accepted for publication. In this domain of destruction, agonistic behavior has the virtue that it insists on situating conflict in the context of public human meaning. As we have seen, heroic flyters are incurable interpreters. They do not kill as predators do,[2] pragmatically, by any effective strategem, although warriors who have forsaken agonistically styled contesting may behave in this way. But as contestants and as flyters, they cannot find satisfaction without valorizing their performances in terms of publicly recognized codes. And the needs of their communities, which are built into these codes, condition and restrict combat in various ways. Thus, heroic contesting, unlike the "mindless violence" with which it is sometimes equated, makes it possible to target aggression meaningfully and to spare the rest.

Such are the merits of contest culture. And yet, when one looks back over humankind's troubled history of warfare, not least of all our own century with its worldwide conflicts and genocidal pogroms, one cannot but mark the incalculable suffering that intertribal and international contesting has caused. In our own time we live within horizons encircled by nuclear warheads, products of an armaments "race" that a global contest mentality continues to fuel. Plainly the time has come for humanity to turn away from violence and destructiveness, if, indeed, it wishes to survive. Nor can we blame this problem on international politics alone. Academic life represents another arena suffused with competitiveness institutionally upheld through habits and practices descending from the academic past.[3] Undoubtedly combativeness has in the past sponsored great intellectual achievement. Yet in my view it is beginning to lead us into a condition of creative sterility. For example, the criterion of "originality" forces one to treat a certain proportion one's colleagues and intellectual ancestors as adversaries. Much has been gained by this. Yet it produces much pettiness and triviality as well, especially as the growing body of published scholarship makes it more and more difficult to articulate insights that are genuinely new—new, that is, if one tries to read the work of one's predecessors fairly and without "misprision." These—the political and the academic—are just two instances of a competitive tendency that has proliferated to excess in the contemporary world. The future-well being of humanity demands an antidote. Mere reaction will not suffice; condemnation will never get rid of contesting but only drive it underground. The needed reorientation will entail an understanding that does not reject but, to the contrary, embraces the depths of our humanity with all that we find there.

It is in this context that the turning away from agonistic patterns in the prestige literature of recent centuries, along with a corresponding feeling on other layers of contemporary culture that relations between people and nations ought not to be conducted in a warlike frame of mind, takes on a special significance. This large-scale reorientation in the consciousness of humanity has not yet succeeded in displacing the dominant competitiveness in many and perhaps most life arenas. On the other hand, overt contesting in many public settings finds fewer sanctions than it once did. Ong (1981) has documented the movement away from an agonistic style in the academy, a movement that began to gather visible momentum at the same time that women were gaining admission into the educational system. The persistence of the habit of competitiveness side by side with the attack on agonistic patterns in the surfaces of cultural expression may be responsible for a certain confusion that reigns at the present time. We are supposed to be sensitive, humane, compassionate, builders of a kinder and gentler world; at the same time, television and other media continually urge us to be aggressive and to look out for number one. We are caught in a limbo, lacking the clear-cut contestational forms through which we could channel and regulate aggressiveness in many spheres, and without having yet found another way to conduct our social interactions.

In this context the recent emergence of articulate female perspectives on matters of governance and social relations is fraught with significance. It is true that feminism, like the Afro-American and other minority and third-world movements, has, whether of choice or necessity, often framed its platforms agonistically. Indeed, in the context of contemporary culture, one doubts whether any movement that eschewed *agōnia* in its many manifestations, gross and subtle, could have achieved a position of prominence. The conflictual spirit attending many aspects of the current renegotiation of gender relations will probably have to continue for some time. Nonetheless, to me one of the most noteworthy trends often evident within or in association with women's movements has been the critique of combative styles and institutions. In this I see a continuity with the past; for in heroic literature only the highly exceptional woman plays the role of combatant in contests. Of course, these "exceptions" themselves participate in patterns with vital bearing on our theme. Yet we must not succumb to the view that those women in epic who at first blush seem noncombative, even "passive," are therefore the mere helpless victims that the male-dominated heroic traditions out of which these epics arise would have them be. By accepting this judgment we would be acceding to the very standard of measure (i.e., that human worth equates with fighting ability) that most needs to be called into question. If women had told them, the stories would have run differently. The agonistic strain in literature sees value principally in terms of warfare, although great heroic poets can often see beyond these limitations. Yet no society thrives by war alone; and in the keeping of peace heroic narrative seems implicitly to grant to women a special role. In Anglo-Saxon literature women are sometimes called the peace weavers (*freoðuwebban*); the warrior and hero Odysseus longs to escape from trials and warfare to a life at harmony with his environment with his wife Penelope. Even the reluctance of male fighters to engage females as heroic adversaries carries a hopeful possibility that we should not too quickly toss aside. Ordinarily this reticence is construed as a male unwillingness to treat with women as equals. And this interpretation is undoubtedly correct, so far as it goes. Yet this very ostensible contempt for women as warriors—a pancultural theme in heroic flyting—may at the same time contain the tacit acknowledgment that women perform functions that the men of heroic literature, with their belligerent ways, should not interfere with. I am convinced that heroic literature is predicated on such an understanding. The power and focus of agonistic narrative is achieved by excluding from its purview most of life. And in the process it covers over those mechanisms of balance by which cultural stability and continuity were, in real fact, maintained.

The time is now long past when men can expect or even should want to maintain the kind of dominance in contemporary life that is represented in the prevailing outlook in heroic narrative. The perpetuation of these old patterns would today be in no one's real interests. Nonetheless, heroic flyting should not be treated as merely another vicious anachronism. As Ong (1981) in particular has argued, contemporary culture is everywhere suffused with the agonistic heritage of centuries and millennia past. What are we to do with this vast residue of old habits? Our legal system, for example, centers on a traditionally hallowed adversarial relationship between prosecution and defense. Does sublimated combat of this kind necessarily provide us with the best method of securing justice? And if not, with what should we replace it? The current imperative for world peace demands a thorough-going reassessment of institutions and cultural practices of exactly this kind. And in such a reassessment, heroic flyting has the special virtue that it depicts the agonistic mentality in an especially distilled and what we might even call naive form. We ourselves would be naive if we were to suppose that agonistic behavior can be done away with simply by labeling it "stupid" and "macho." Like sexuality, its roots run too deep. Yet if its sources, aims, and structures are adequately understood, its expression might prove susceptible to intelligent guidance. Indeed, as I hope this book has shown, epic heroes themselves, when they have shifted out of the modality of free-lance violence into that of agonistically styled contesting, are acting in conformity with a variety of codes—a codified concept of heroic selfhood, a socialized notion of honor with its various entailments such as the matching of deeds to words, and so forth. If we understand how these principles work and what their multiforms in diverse settings might be, we can proceed to try to defuse the conflictual tendencies running rampant in the current world scene without in that very process waging another futile war with what resides in our own nature.

Far from a mere oddity of antiquated literary forms, heroic flyting is one of the most universal of all speech genres. An extraordinary range of human conflicts are preceded by rhetorical volleys of essentially this kind; even animal combat frequently arises out of a semiotic exchange whose root significations seem to fall into the flyting pattern. Although its role in particular institutions and activities (such as prestige literature) varies from age to age, one doubts whether any society has ever lacked it altogether. By bringing it into the orbit of intelligent recognition within those circles that most devote themselves to the study of cultural forms, we stand a better chance of comprehending adequately what we as community are and how we should conduct our affairs.

Notes

Introduction

1. For an examination of courtroom interaction from the standpoint of discourse analysis, see Drew 1985.

2. The recent turn toward dialogics, spearheaded by the Anglo-American discovery of the works of Mikhail Bakhtin, promises to open new inroads into this topic. Bakhtin's obvious preference for the novel vitiates, in my view, his appreciation for epic and other forms less developed, as he would have it, toward the ripeness of heteroglossia (see Bakhtin 1981: 3–40; for a critique, see Parks [forthcoming]). The general brilliance of his work nonetheless ensures that it will exert an enduring influence in this line of study.

3. For an introduction to Scottish flyting, see Kinsley 1979: 282–86 and Bawcutt 1983.

4. I find in Bessinger 1978 six instances of the verb: *flitan* in *Solomon and Saturn* 1.179; *flite* in *Beowulf* 507; *flitende* in *Beowulf* 916; *fliteð* in *Andreas* 1199 and *The Riming Poem* 62; and *oferflat* in *Beowulf* 517. Related nouns, adjectives, and adverbs cited in Bosworth and Toller 1898 and Toller 1921 include *(ge-)flit* ("contention"), *(ge-)flita* ("fighter"), *flitend* ("wrangler"), *flitere* ("brawler"), *(ge-)flitful* ("contentious"), *(ge-)flitlice* ("contentiously"), *geflitfulness* ("contentiously"), *unflitme* ("without dispute"), and such compounds as *flitcræft* ("the art of disputing"), *flitcræftlic* ("belonging to disputation"), *flitgara* ("site of a contest"), *(ge-)flitgeorn* ("contentious"), *(ge-)flitmælum* ("by strife; contentiously"), *fyrngeflit* ("ancient strife"), *fyrngeflita* ("ancient adversary"), and *geflitgliw* ("mockery").

5. All references to Homer will be based on the Oxford texts (*Homeri Opera*, vols. 1–4). In citations I will use the abbreviations *Il.* and *Od.* for the *Iliad* and *Odyssey*.

6. Nonetheless, Hesiod's account of the mischief of Eris and the genesis of the quarrel that culminates in the Trojan War does constitute a relevant mythological background for the Homeric epos; for more on the theme of *eris* (strife) in Hesiod's *Works and Days*, see Peabody's fine discussion (1975: 236–47 and the relevant notes, esp. 471–77; see also 268–72).

7. Henceforth I will refer to *The Battle of Maldon* as *Maldon*; I will use the abbreviation *Beo.* to designate *Beowulf* in line references.

8. See *Elene*, esp. 417–826, *Andreas* 1168–1388, *Juliana*, esp. 242–530, and *Solomon and Saturn*, which appear respectively in vol. 2: 77–89, 35–41, vol. 3: 120–28, and vol. 6: 31–48, of the *Anglo Saxon Poetic Records* (1931–1953). Despite the fact that the poetic narrator uses the infinitive *flitan* to characterize the dialogue of Solomon and Saturn, in reality this is less a flyting than a catechism, through which Saturn is instructed in Christian doctrine. The same holds for the *Prose Solomon and Saturn*. The disputes in *Elene*, *Andreas*,

and *Juliana*, though plainly contestational, are doctrinal in their subject matter and do not bring with them the same kind of martial entailments that we will find in *Beowulf* and the *Iliad*.

9. The topic of a heroic age and heroic literature has long interested literary historians, as in the classics of Ker (1897), H. Chadwick (1912), H. Chadwick and N. Chadwick (1932–1940), and Bowra (1952). Though the Chadwicks in their extraordinary comparative survey treat several quite distinct literary traditions, genres, and modes, the "heroic" is a recurrent concern throughout; particularly pertinent to the Greek-Teutonic comparison is vol. 1: 13–95. For more recent studies in this kind of subject area, see Whitman 1965, Luce 1975, Swanton 1977, and Niles 1983.

10. For summary discussions of these and other secular heroic Old English poems with introductions to major interpretive issues and leads into scholarship, see Greenfield and Calder 1986: 134–57.

11. For introductions and reviews of scholarship relating to oral-formulaic theory in Homeric and Anglo-Saxon studies, see J. Foley 1981b: 27–122, 1985: 3–76, and 1988; Edwards 1986 and 1988; and Olsen 1986 and 1988. The possibility of oral-derived or residually oral "literary" works is now admitted by most oralists; see, for example, Niles 1983. On the slow breakdown of the oral noetic and its transformation through the technologies of writing, print, and the electronic media, see Ong 1982; J. Foley (1983) studies the interaction of oral and literate assumptions in sample literary texts.

12. For several "classic" treatments on these topics, see Arend 1933 and Parry 1971: 404–7; Lord 1938: 440, 1965b: 68–98; and Fry 1968. For more recent studies, see the citations in the previous note.

13. Clover 1980; see also Clover 1974.

14. See, for example, Pritchett 1985, and van Wees 1988.

15. For a classic treatment, originally published in 1910, see Gardiner 1970; see also H. A. Harris 1966 and Olivová 1985, an introductory account pictorially supplemented and with a good bibliography.

16. For a valuable treatment of the Greek "contest system," see Gouldner 1965: 41–77. Of relevance to verbal contesting in the *Iliad* are Fenik 1968 and Kirk 1978. Fenik 1986 attempts a cross-cultural comparison (between Homer and the *Nibelungenlied*) not unlike the present study.

17. For several early studies, see Knobloch 1886, Selbach 1886, Jeanroy 1925: 45–60, Walther 1920, and Heusler 1943: 105–8.

18. See, for example, Wagner 1936 and Bø 1969. Other citations can be found in Alford and Seniff 1984.

19. For an extended inquiry into the interrelations of gender and contesting, see Ong 1981. Brandes (1980), working in the field of Andalusian folklore, provides relevant case material.

20. Women in medieval literature are the subject of a fast-growing scholarship; on the Old English period, see Chance 1986.

21. On these flytings, see Warnke 1986.

22. Nonetheless, *De Amore* seems often to represent a successful seduction as a kind of ceremonialized "victory" on the part of the male wooer, as is

implied in the capitulum prefacing these debates, which reads "How love is won, and in how many ways" (1.6.1). At the same time, the lady cannot exactly be called the loser, since the affair can proceed only by her sanction; and in Andreas's cases for the courts of love, queens play the judge. The relationship between much amatory flyting and "contesting" is obviously rather complicated and would take some unraveling. In any event, the termination of amatory flyting in marriage or seduction need not imply victory for either male or female. Both Benedick and Beatrice, for example, must suffer a certain loss of face in acknowledging their love for each other.

23. For this reason I could not call these formal verbal duels, which is not at all to deny the effectiveness of the taunts. Yet they do not occur in the context of a single set of rules binding equally for both parties. The men, for example, can be shamed for their failure to take action in the martial sense, whereas the women cannot. On the other hand, the women lack the access that the men enjoy to the legal institutions (such as the Althing) where these quarrels could be negotiated. The "contestants," in other words, are never established on the same footing.

For an excellent expression of this theme in the work of Chaucer, an author relatively free from the macho heroic ethic and willing to accord to his female characters considerable scope of expression, see Herry Bailly's criticisms of his wife and her belligerent promptings in the prologue to the *Monk's Tale* (*The Canterbury Tales* VII.3081–3111).

Chapter I

1. The literature on aggression and animal behavior is, of course, vast and beset with its own controversies: indeed, Crabtree and Moyer's *Bibliography of Aggressive Behavior*, which represents the contributions of many disciplines and approaches, lists 3,856 items in its first volume (1977, covering research through July of 1975) and 3,636 more in the second volume (1981) covering just the next four years. Pioneers in ethological study were Niko Tinbergen and Konrad Lorenz (for two well-known studies, see Tinbergen 1961 and Lorenz 1966). The turn from ethology as the study of animal behavior to sociobiology, which views behavior in the light of its adaptive value, gained momentum after the release of Edward O. Wilson's epoch-making and controversial volume, *Sociobiology* (1975); especially pertinent is his chapter on aggression (242–55). Since the publication of Wilson's book, research has proliferated along many lines; scholarship today seems to be characterized by nothing so much as its rampant heterodoxy. I have found particularly helpful the surveys in Moyer 1976, Baron 1977, and especially Barash 1982, Alcock 1984, and Trivers 1985. Ong (1981) has built important bridges between these fields and humanistic and cultural study; see particularly his chapter "Contest and Sexual Identity" (51–96), which reviews much of this ethological and sociobiological ground in the course of an argument situating human agonistic and contesting activity in its cultural and "noobiological" setting.

2. This observation has been made eloquently by Huizinga in one of the

truly great and enduring scholarly studies in this subject area (1955: esp. 89–104).

3. On this topic, see Axelrod 1984: 73–87. See also Trivers's discussion of this example (1985: 362).

4. See, for example, Goodall's discussion of the barks and screams that chimpanzees sometimes employ in conjunction with body threat display (1986: 314–15).

5. Dramatically absent from Moyer's list is territorial aggression, which, he argues, is reducible to other more fundamental patterns (see 1976: 209–26). He also proposes, though he does not elaborate upon, "instrumental" aggression (see esp. 14–15 and 120–23).

6. Klopfer 1985; see also Adler 1979.

7. Competition for resources does not always take the form of contesting; "scrambling," in which "each participant attempts to accumulate and utilize as much of the critical resource as it can, without regard to any particular social interaction with its competitors" (Barash 1982: 340) is the other main pattern. For more on this distinction, see Barash 1982: 339–43.

8. The problem of the genetic determination of behavior is a complex one; see Barash 1982: 29–31 for discussion and examples. As his cases illustrate, some behaviors seem to be directly the product of genetic encoding. Toward others, however, the member of a species may be innately predisposed, but a behavior will not come into expression without learning or environmental cues. Heroic contesting would seem to belong to the latter category.

9. For a full discussion of game theory, see Maynard Smith 1982; for an introduction, see Barash 1982: 165–83. Evolutionary game theory suggests interesting connections with Huizinga's study of play, which, as he points out, precedes culture. For every dog in its neighborhood rollicking knows the rule that "you shall not bite, or not bite hard, your brother's ear" (Huizinga 1955: 1). That is, dogs recognize the imperatives of a certain gamesmanship that both authorizes and restrains aggressive displays. Plainly canines did not learn the idea of play from humans; it results from a long evolutionary process. Yet the dog himself neither knows nor cares about such ultimate sources. From his standpoint, as Huizinga points out, this kind of cavorting is simply a great deal of "fun." This sense of "fun" is no doubt the subjective state attending such evolutionarily beneficial behavior.

10. Much of what follows draws on commonplaces of ethological and sociobiological scholarship as represented, for example, in chapter and section headings. Invoking several of these distinctions and arguing in general for the comparability of human and animal behavior (as against critics of Lorenz and other ethologists) is Eibl-Eibesfeldt 1979. My discussion of "rituality" presupposes that it functions to contain violence; for a landmark exploration into questions of this kind, see Girard 1977 (particularly relevant to the contest dyad is his chapter "From Mimetic Desire to the Monstrous Double," 143–68). I cannot agree with Girard that rites of all kinds are related to the problem of violence, though this is much the case for contests.

11. Vermeule (1979) provides a fine discussion of animal and predatorial

imagery in Homer in her chapter on "The Happy Hero." In some of her remarks, however, I do not feel that she takes the distinction between predatorial, interspecific violence and contestational, intraspecific aggression sufficiently into account.

12. The pioneer in this subject was William Hamilton, whose article on "The Evolution of Social Behavior" (1964) Trivers calls "the most important advance in evolutionary theory since the work of Charles Darwin and Gregor Mendel" (1985: 47). For an introduction to kinship theory, see Trivers 1985: 44–47, 109–44.

13. Note how the intrusion of this theme redirects the course of the flyting-fighting exchange between Menelaos and Euphorbos in *Il.*17.19–42.

14. See, in illustration of this point, the description of Hrethel's dilemma (*Beo.*2428–71) or the accusation of brother-slaying that Beowulf levels at Unferth (*Beo.*587–88). Agamemnon found himself in a dilemma not unlike Hrethel's when, for the sake of his army, he must kill his own daughter Iphigeneia; and in Aeschylus's version of the story it is for this crime that he must forfeit his life.

15. With reference to *Beowulf* this theme was eloquently dilated upon by Niles in a fine study of that poem (1983: 213–23); see also his discussion of community as the poem's ruling theme (224–34).

16. Wilson 1975: 248. See, for example, Goodall's discussion of xenophobia among chimpanzees (1986: 331–32). The idea of "group selection" has been rejected by most evolutionary ecologists, although it still finds occasional advocates; see, for example, V. C. Wynne-Edwards 1986. In any event, to argue for the adaptiveness of reciprocity in ingroup situations is not to argue for group selection.

17. The Achilles-Agamemnon quarrel almost becomes that; yet, significantly, each man's grievance centers precisely on the other's alleged failure to honor the reciprocal commitments that their respective roles require: Achilles is not respecting Agamemnon's authority, whereas Agamemnon is not divvying up battle booty fairly.

18. E. O. Wilson was much criticized by those who believed that his sociobiological explanations implied endorsement for unethical social policies. Yet to submit that a state of affairs exists and has causes is not to approve it; indeed, reformers above all others should study these causes, if they want their reforms to work. For a brief introduction to the sociobiological controversy, see Alcock 1984: 505–6.

19. For full narrative accounts and analysis of dominance struggles among chimpanzees, see de Waal 1982: esp.85–139; on sex differences, see 194–99.

20. A dramatic example is provided by the verbal contesting among Turkish adolescents (Dundes, Leach, and Özkök 1972) in which each dueler tries verbally to represent himself and his adversary as playing, respectively, the male and female roles in an aggressive homosexual assault.

21. As pivotal a concern as it has been in many societies, honor (and its converse, shame) has been the subject of an enormous scholarly literature. Nagy 1979, for example, has provided detailed semantic and contexting

studies of a range of Homeric terms. Bauman's (1986) excellent treatment of honor (*drengskapr*) in thirteenth-century Iceland centers on the interdependence of honor and performance, a matter to be considered shortly. While they do not pertain to the particular epochs and literary traditions under review here, the studies collected in Peristiany 1966 explore some of the comparative implications of the subject.

22. Ong 1981: 64–76; see also Neumann's discussion of individuation and the "terrible Mother" (1954: 63–88).

23. The same idea finds pointed expression in *Beo.*1468–72, when the poet tells us that Unferth's failure to undertake the adventure against Grendel's mother resulted in a loss of honor (*dom* and *ellenmærðu*) in favor of the Geat.

24. On the relationship between honor and ritual defilement in the *Iliad*, see Friedrich 1973.

25. See Havelock 1963: 197–214 and passim; also pertaining to this discussion is Havelock 1978.

26. *Nicomachean Ethics* 1.5.4–5. In the same spirit see Boethius's *Philosophiae Consolationis* 2.6–7 and 3.4–6, in which Lady Philosophy exposes, from the standpoint of a rational critique, the essential vacuity of honor, power, fame, and other gifts of fortune that most people indiscriminately accept as goods.

27. Many Homerists would take issue with this view of Achilles. For an ongoing debate on matters of this kind, see A. Parry 1956, Claus 1975, and Nimis 1986; see also Dodds 1951: 28–63 and Arieti 1985 on related problems of shame and guilt. Arieti 1986 and Schein 1984: esp. 89–127 have provided sensitive recent treatments of Achilles' alienation; King 1987: 1–49 offers a generally favorable assessment of Homer's Achilles as the prototype in a long classical and medieval tradition. In view of the diversity of opinion, I should stress that my argument here does not depend fundamentally on my reading of Achilles as a character in the *Iliad*. It centers rather on the norms of that heroic ethos that underlies and informs the heroic contest. The *Iliad* draws on these; and whether or not it reworks them in the light of an emerging nonheroic ideology is not of primary concern to me. Most Homerists would in any event agree that, even if Achilles is undertaking to question the heroic order, his critique is an incipient one when compared, for example, with that of Plato. One would be hard put to recover an accurate idea of the heroic contest from the Platonic dialogues. In Homer, however, such contests parade across the narrative foreground; nor can an alleged Homeric critique of the heroic ethos account for the shape that these contests assume.

28. For a discussion of Odysseus's alienation from and eventual reunion with his proper generic "office," see Parks 1981 and 1983.

29. For a classic study of this ubiquitous Old English figure, see Greenfield 1955.

30. In this and the next paragraph I have made heavy use of Liddell and Scott 1925–1940 and Chantraine 1968–1980 for the Greek, Bosworth and Toller 1898 and 1921, Holthausen 1963, and Barney 1985 (an excellent discursive introduction to word groups) for the Old English. For an interesting

study of the vocabulary of *The Song of Roland* in the light of cognate themes, see Jones 1963.

31. For fuller discussions of *kleos* in Greek epic and lyric poetry, see Nagy 1979 and 1986. Finkelberg 1986, denying that the Homeric phrase "κλέος ἄφθιτον" ("immortal fame") is indeed formulaic or traditional, gives a good introduction to related formulary problems. King 1987: 28–49 provides a recent treatment of the interrelation between *timē* and *kleos*.

32. For an important diachronic and linguistic treatment of several of these and other terms for honor, particularly as they relate to the Germanic institution of the *comitatus*, see Lindow 1976: esp. chap. 5, 126–43. Lindow identifies, notably in the later Scandinavian vocabulary, a gradual displacement of heroic, martial conceptions in favor of an "honor of social utility" requiring "peaceful social interaction among individuals" (Lindow 1976: 142).

33. Nagy 1979: 222. On the theme of praise and blame, see also Dumézil 1943. For a discussion of "shame" versus "guilt" culture as the distinction pertains specifically to the *satirical* verse of several early Indo-European societies, see Ward 1973.

34. Such episodes and accusations abound in Old English heroic verse, as is represented, for example, in the charge of fratricide that Beowulf hurls at Unferth (*Beo.* 587–88), or the implied treachery of Hrothulf, or in the contrast between the bravery of Wiglaf and the cowardice of Beowulf's faithless retainers, or in the desertion of Odda's sons in *Maldon* 185–201. The conflict in *The Fight at Finnsburg* and the Finnsburg digression in *Beowulf* begins with an act of treachery in violation of a marriage compact.

35. For a valuable treatment of this and other problems we have been discussing, see Gouldner 1965: esp. 41–77.

36. See especially Huizinga 1955: 46–75; ceremonial "slanging"—that is, flyting—matches, Chinese, Roman, Arabic, Greek, and Germanic, are treated on pp. 65–71.

37. On this episode, see Butler 1969: 99–100.

38. See Tinbergen 1961: 44–96, and Clutton-Brock, Guinness, and Albon 1982: 104–42.

39. See Chatman 1978: 19, 96–145. Story, to Chatman, designates the progress of action in the fictional world; discourse refers to the representation of that action through the linguistic (or cinematic) medium.

40. Homerists have long debated the relative importance of single and massed fighting; for a recent review of this and related problems, see Pritchett 1985: 7–33. In a revisionary treatment Van Wees (1988) challenges what he characterizes as the traditional, tripartite distinction between single, massed hand-to-hand, and massed missile combat. Whatever might be said for or against van Wees characterization of the actual battle tactics that Homer presumably represents (and can we indeed assume that Homer's conception of battle was, from a military standpoint, a coherent one?), Van Wees's account does not give adequate recognition to the narrative and rhetorical foregrounding that the man-on-man matchup receives in the *Iliad*.

41. See Mueller's discussion of the chain of retribution in Homer (1984:

98–101). Though not so clearly articulated as in the *Iliad*, the *Alliterative Morte Arthure* shows patterns such as these in incipient form; see, for example, ll.1767–1871 and 2755–2810. Gaier, in a detailed study of ceremonialized single combat in the fifteenth century, gives evidence for variations away from the closed one-on-one encounter: Sometimes combats feature a succession of duels between different adversaries, or between one contestant and a string of opponents; in other cases several sets of contestants fight simultaneously (1985 and 1986: 430–31). And of course many tournaments (and battles) are collective melees. Yet the single combat was a well-recognized and prevalent pattern in its own right, as his review makes clear.

42. See Trivers 1985: 368–75, de Waal 1982: 144–49 and passim, Goodall 1986: 318–19.

43. Mueller, like many other Homerists, notes the special Homeric interest in the "single encounter" (1984: 80–95); but this is by no means unique to the *Iliad*. Jones discusses this problem and provides a range of medieval citations illustrating disdain for victories secured through two-on-one attack, unequal weaponry, and so forth (1963: 16–17). Gaier (1985 and 1986) reviews in depth fifteenth-century versions of the single combat. In sum, the single combat is so widespread in literature and other forms of cultural expression that it needs to be recognized as a meaningful phenomenon in its own right.

44. In a famous article enunciating an assortment of "epic laws," Olrik (1965) proposed the "law of two to a scene" of which the passages we have been discussing would be instances. See Rosenberg's (1975: 107–8) invocation of this principle as it relates to the Beowulf-Unferth exchange. Whatever might finally be the status of this "law" in epic encounters generally, a dyadic tendency is indeed evident in epic *contests*.

45. Nora Chadwick 1927. In fact, this exchange is similar to the *Lokasenna* in the *Poetic Edda*, in which Loki humiliates each of his fellow gods and goddesses in turn.

46. See *The Fight at Finnsburg*, esp. ll.18–27, in *Beowulf and the Fight at Finnsburg* 1950: 246.

47. Mueller calls this "the most serious violation of fairness" in the *Iliad* (1984: 79); note that the "violation" consists precisely in the denial of the one-on-one principle.

48. The notion of comparability is related to the principle of "doubling," which Kroll (1986) finds in many of Beowulf's struggles. This does not, in Kroll's view, include the Beowulf-Unferth exchange, however, since Unferth does not measure up to the standard of Grendel or the dragon. Feldman (1979) and Brennan (1985) assess Unferth's contribution more positively.

49. For a fuller treatment of Iliadic instances of the formal duel, see Kirk 1978. For a fascinating discussion of such rivalries, see Girard 1977: 143–68.

50. See Barash's comments on the general efficacy and adaptive value of the inhibitory mechanisms usually triggered by an adversary's capitulation in animal contests (1982: 354–57).

51. Ong 1981: 45. The same Latin word *testis* in its plural form (*testes*)

means "testicles," which, as Ong points out (1981:98), further suggests the need that the male ego experiences to prove its masculinity through "external" witnesses.

52. An interesting intermediary situation presents itself in Chaucer's *Knight's Tale*, in which Palamon and Arcite—rivals for the love of Emelye—first fight privately in a forest glade. This contest, however, is broken off by Emelye's guardian, the duke Theseus, who on further reflection reschedules the combat in the form of a tournament to be held in a year's time. Thus, a private conflict in the courtly romance mode has been made public again.

53. For a superb discussion of Zeus as the "All-Knowing Watcher" (198), see Griffin 1980: 179–204.

54. For a fine treatment of this theme in *Beowulf* with a careful review of the relevant passages, see Smithers 1970.

55. See Ong's discussion of the masculinized, agonistic heritage of Roman Catholicism and the peculiar roles of Jesus and Mary in this milieu (1981: esp. 167–83).

56. The association between the heroic contest and the court of law merits exploration; for a treatment of the latter topic from the standpoint of discourse analysis, see Drew 1985.

57. For a treatment of the movement from mnemonic to written record in English society from the Norman invasion through the early fourteenth century, see Clanchy 1979.

58. For a classic treatment of the subject, see Renoir 1963; see also Reinhard 1932, J. Foley 1978a (esp. 234–40), Nolan and Bloomfield 1980, Conquergood 1981, Torrini-Roblin 1984, and Murphy 1985. See also Lumiansky 1952 for a treatment of what I am calling peer witnessing in that poem.

59. An interesting though atypically explicit indication of a contestant's awareness of the witness occurs in *Il.*20.423–27 when Achilles, noting Hektor's approach, addresses a boast ("εὐχόμενος ἔπος ηὔδα," "boasting he spoke a word") to some unspecified hearer(s) exclusive of his Trojan enemy who is referred to in the third person.

60. See Chatman 1978 and Genette 1980 for more detailed discussions of this and related narratological problems.

61. See particularly the discussion of *kleos* in Nagy 1979 and Nagy 1986, as well as Opland 1980: 1–27, 257–66. See also Dumézil 1943, which treats related themes from an Indo-European perspective. Also pertinent (in the connection between honor and performance) is Bauman 1986.

62. For a detailed treatment of these Old English expressions, see Parks 1987b; see also Parks 1989.

63. See Pizarro 1976: esp. 15–130. On "early epic scenery" generally, see Andersson 1976.

64. Clover 1980: 447; her reference is to Phillpotts 1920: 158. See also Pizarro 1976: esp. 75–102. Pizarro discusses the sea setting with reference to the Danish coastguard scene in *Beowulf* on 75–78 and with reference to *Maldon* on 89–101.

65. Diodorus 5.28.5; I quote from vol. 3, p. 171 in the Loeb edition.

66. Diodorus 5.29.2–3 (vol. 3, p. 173).

67. See Earl 1983, which outlines the peculiar psychological symbolism of the hall in the context of the transformation of the Anglo-Saxons from a pagan, tribal society to a paternalistic, Christian one. Since this process depended on a peculiar historical and sociological situation, one could hardly expect the hall to figure so largely in the Greek world. There are, of course, halls in Homer, but hospitality is not so inextricably tied to them. Indeed, the Greek love of athletics would require that large-scale festivities be held outdoors.

68. See Paul the Deacon 1974: 44–45.

69. For the definitive treatment, see Byock 1982.

70. For more on this embassy, see chapter 4.

CHAPTER II

1. McDowell 1985, a review of verbal dueling, deals with exchanges of the ludic type. On flyting in *Örvar-Odds saga*, see Lönnroth 1979. Bax and Padmos (1983) give detailed attention to the contestational structure of *Hárbarð-sljóð*, upholding the traditional distinction between the *senna* and the *mann-jafnaðr*.

2. Although he does not deal with the contesting aspect specifically, Drew (1985) has provided a valuable recent study of the uses of language in courtroom interactions. This is a rich subject since, in contemporary society, trials are the most important institutionalized form of verbal contest.

3. For seminal studies on oral themes and type scenes, see, in addition to Arend 1933, M. Parry 1971: 404–07; Lord 1965b: 68–98; Fry 1968; Peabody 1975: 168–215. For further bibliography, see J. Foley 1981b: 79–91, and 1985: 11–77 and passim.

4. Clover (1980: 445) notes that the attempt to differentiate between "exchanges of insults and threats" (the *senna*) and exchanges of boasts (the *mann-jafnaðr*) fails because "neither category has a pure representative. One searches the corpus in vain for an unambiguous example." Bax and Padmos (1983) try nonetheless to uphold the validity of this generic distinction in the *Hárbarðsljóð* (contrary to Clover 1979), although, as they acknowledge, both modes come into play in this Eddic poem. See also Pizarro's discussion of these terms (1976: 1–14). Holtsmark (1966 and 1970) provides definitions of the *mannjevning* and *senna*. Flyting (and I follow Clover in accepting this more inclusive term) is actually a mélange of speech acts and motifs, resulting in part from the opposition of the eristic and contractual motives. "Eristic" derives from the Greek work *eris*, which means "quarrel, strife, rivalry." For a fascinating discussion of the theme of *eris* and *neikos* (a near synonym) as it pertains to Hesiod, see Peabody 1975: 243–47. Nagy discusses these words in the context of praise and blame poetry (1979: 223–24 and elsewhere).

5. This definition paraphrases the one in Parks 1986a: 296.

6. See Searle 1979: 1–29 for a discussion of "commissives" as a speech act type.

7. For earlier treatments that range to other literatures, see Reinhard 1932,

which reviews numerous instances and traces the development of the form of speech designated by the Old Norse and French word *gab* (Norse *gabb*); and Einarsson 1934, which compares Old English boasting, particularly in association with drinking, with the Icelandic *heitstrenging*. For *gomen* and *gab* as modes of play, see Torrini-Roblin 1984.

8. "... μύθων τε ῥητῆρ’ ἔμεναι πρηκτῆρά τε ἔργον," spoken by Phoinix to Achilles in *Il.*9.443. On this passage, see Notopoulos 1952.

9. In this respect "heroic" differs from "ludic" flytings, typified by "The Flyting of Dunbar and Kennedie" (Kinsley 1979), which feature verbal virtuosity without martial entailments. For more on this point, see chapter 5.

10. Beo.593–94. A few lines earlier, Beowulf points out that, on an account of fratricide, Unferth will suffer punishment in hell, "þeah þin wit duge," "though your intelligence is strong" (i.e., "though your are able to provide a good account for yourself in words").

11. In his fine commentary and study of *The Song of Roland*, Cook, though he emphatically rejects the traditional view of a Roland succumbing to Christian *superbia*, stresses the poem's endorsement of the view that one should honor one's spoken commitments: "Roland sacrifices himself and his men to the ideal of the given word. . . . Structurally the thing that matters most is that his promise is finally accepted and that he carries it out despite the suffering, while his enemies cannot carry out theirs" (1987: 193–94). For more on this poem, see chapter 4.

12. From Wolfram's famous "apology" at the end of book 2 (Wolfram 1980: 68).

13. For a fine discussion of this interdependency between honor and poetic performance, see Bauman 1986.

14. Cf. Bloomfield 1969 for a discussion of the *iudicium dei* with reference to *Beowulf* and *Maldon*.

15. Murphy 1985: 105–6. For an important study of *beot* and *gylp*, Old English words for boasting, see Nolan and Bloomfield 1980.

16. In Parks 1988 I discuss this type of framing structure, which often occurs in association with the "X killed Y" motif in the *Iliad*; on this matter see also Beye 1964: esp. 346–48, and Fenik 1968: 17. Other notable discussions on ring structure include Whitman 1965: 87–101, and Niles 1983: 152–62; on the device in literary traditions other than the Greek and Anglo-Saxon, see Lord 1986: esp. 53–64, and Fenik 1986.

17. See, for example, Hektor's speech to Achilles, *Il.*22.278–88.

18. See the rescues of Alexandros (*Il.*3.373–82), Idaios (5.22–24), Aineias (5.311–51, 432–53, and 20.288–339), Hektor (20.438–54), and Agenor (21.596–601). Zeus contemplates doing the same for Sarpedon and, again, Hektor, but is discouraged by Hera and Athena (16.426–61 and 22.177–85).

19. See, for example, the encounters between Agamemnon and Peisandros and Hippolochos (*Il.*11.122–48); Idomeneus and Othryoneus (13.361–84); and Akamas and Promachos (14.476–86).

20. Edwards (1980) finds that Homer elaborates on a range of type scenes to varying degrees and in various ways, in accordance with his artistic de-

signs. In fact, most recent research in oral theory has stressed the plasticity of traditional structure. For a fascinating discussion of formula and formularity with far-reaching implications, see Nagler 1974: 1–26 and passim. On other recent directions in oral-formulaic scholarship, see J. Foley 1988: 94–111.

21. J. Foley 1986b: 17. For other discussions of the problem, see J. Foley 1986c and 1987b.

22. This subject of verbal and corporeal abuse inflicted by victors on their victims is superbly treated in Segal 1971. The absence of armor-stripping episodes in the Old English flyting-fighting episodes should not be attributed to the lack of interest on the Anglo-Saxons' part. Booty is one of the rewards of battle, and the Beasts of Battle were not the only ones sensible to the potential gains in a field full of corpses. In fact, *Maldon* 159–61 narrates a Viking attempt to strip the armor from a wounded Byrhtnoth. Even more explicit is the despoiling of Ongentheow by the Geats after their victory at Hrefnesholt (*Beo.* 2985–88), in what sounds very much like the Iliadic practice. These do not grow directly out of a flyting exchange and so do not immediately pertain to my argument. Waldere's reference to his corselet (*Waldere* 2.16–17) in his flyting speech to Guthhere, however, seems to attest to the pertinence of arms stripping to the Old English contesting process (for more on this episode, see later discussion). I suspect that a greater quantity of Old English battle narrative would reveal the same association between formal contesting as such and the victor's carrying off the victim's war gear and other personal effects as a sign of victory.

23. For other instances in the *Iliad*, see the Agenor-Achilles contest (21.544–611 and 22.7–20), and Ares' scuffle with Athena (21.391–415).

24. Hermes, for example, bitterly urges Leto to go ahead and brag about her victory before the other deities. See Nestor's and Diomedes' discussion on this problem of the shame of intimidation (8.139–66). Diomedes, in fact, "redeems" himself in 11.343–67.

25. In other instances, of course, outmatched warriors make their getaway before the contest can start. For an analysis of the formulaic structure of supplication scenes, see Edwards 1980: 5–8, 25–26. For a discussion of four parallel instances, see Fenik 1978b.

26. As Mueller points out, the author of the *Iliad* takes special interest in death and the moment of death in battle (1984: esp. 82–89). See also Griffin 1980: esp. 81–102.

27. *Il.*21.34–135. This episode was foreshadowed in 20.463–72, in which Tros managed to clasp Achilles knees but was cut down evidently before he had time to make his petition. This killing is narrated without direct discourse of any kind.

28. See 4.473–89; 4.494–504; 5.43–48; 5.49–58; 5.59–68; 5.69–75; 5.76–83; 5.148–51; 5.152–58; 5.533–40; 5.541–60; 5.610–26; 6.12–19; 6.21–28; 7.8–10; 8.300–308; 11.101–21; 11.221–47; 11.328–34; 12.378–86; 13.170–82; 13.363–84; 13.660–72; 14.442–48; 15.429–35; 15.638–52; 16.284–92; 16.570–80; 16.593–602; 16.603–7; 17.304–11; 17.346–51; 17.574–81;

17.608–23; 20.381–92; 20.407–18; and 20.484–87. I cannot vouch for the completeness of this list, but it should suffice to illustrate the typicality of the motif. For two contests in which this ring structure device culminates in a vaunt (element D1), see 14.486–506 and 20.381–95; similar ring structure devices serve to introduce the adversary-victims as part of the Engagement element (A) in 21.34–48 and 21.139–44. For more on this topic, see Parks 1988. The number of martial encounters between particular warriors in the *Iliad* totals about 140 (Mueller 1984: 80).

29. See especially Fenik 1968 and 1986.

30. *Il*.20.344–52 and 449–54. This latter speech was addressed in the same form, word for word, much earlier—again to Hektor—by another Achaian, Diomedes (11.362–67). Diomedes' warlike intentions had similarly fallen short of the the mark; in that case Apollo was only indirectly responsible, having bestowed on Hektor the helmet that turned back Diomedes' spear. Nonetheless, like Achilles, Diomedes has clearly fared better in the course of fighting. His vaunting might be interpreted as a response to the taunts Hektor had addressed to him three books earlier (8.161–66).

31. On the generality of monomachy in ancient Greece and other Mediterranean cultures, see Pritchett 1985: 15–21.

32. For more on this poem, see chapter 4.

33. On the theme of the *cohortatio*, in Homer and later Greek literature, see Keitel 1987.

34. For a detailed analysis of the rather elaborate patterns surrounding the Hektor-Aias encounters in the central battle books, see Whitman and Scodel 1981.

35. In another instance of one contest mirroring another, Teukros, in the passage immediately following the one we have just discussed, tries to shoot Hektor but is thwarted by Zeus, who breaks his string. In place of vaunting, Teukros comments to his brother on this evidence of divine opposition (467–70); Aias in reply urges him to give up archery and attack with his spear (472–77).

36. On backgrounds to the poem, see the introduction to Zettersten's edition (*Waldere* 1979: 1–12) and Greenfield and Calder 1986: 145–46. Both include references.

37. Much critical debate centers on the assessment of Byrhtnoth's judgment and motives in acceding to this Viking request. See, for example, Tolkien 1953 and Bessinger 1962. See also Scragg's survey and interpretation of the problem in the introduction to his edition (1981: 36–41). On the *Maldon* "flyting," see E. Anderson 1970.

38. Hektor similarly tried to add to the base flyting contract of combat a further agreement of nonmutilation in his final encounter with Achilles (22.250–58); however, in that instance his enemy chose to reject all compacts categorically (261–72).

39. Lines 198–201. For more on the boasting theme, see Conquergood 1981.

40. Chap. 27; for a discussion see Lönnroth 1979.

41. In fact, Germanic literature much concerned itself with this theme of bravery in the face of death and defeat; one is reminded, for example, of Hogni's contemptuous laughter as Atli's men cut his heart out in the *Atlak-viða*. *Maldon* presents us with more pious and less recalcitrantly pagan versions of the same response.

42. I set forth this view more fully in Parks 1981. See also Edwards 1975, Powell 1977, and Murnaghan 1987: 56–117 and passim.

43. The parallels between these episodes have often been noted; see particularly Lord 1965a, which draws out many of the resemblances that I will be discussing. Another valuable treatment is Irving 1968: 66–76.

44. I have argued this point in more detail in Parks 1981.

45. For several of the many important treatments pertinent to Unferth and the office of *thyle*, see Rosier 1962, Eliason 1963, Ogilvy 1964, Rosenberg 1969, Baird 1970, Hollowell 1976, Feldman 1979, Clover 1980, and Brennan 1985.

46. I am not for the present treating the Breca episode, with which a major part of the speeches of Unferth and Beowulf are concerned; see the discussion of "retrojection" in chapter 3.

47. See *Beo*.426–32, 480–88, and 655–61. See also Brennan's interpretation of this problem (1985: 8–10).

48. For excellent treatments of these episodes individually, see Gaisser 1969 and Irving 1968: 50–56.

49. Athena makes an exception of Aphrodite (5.131–32): War falling outside the domain of the love-goddess's expertise, Diomedes can attack her with impunity, and in fact does so (5.311–54).

50. In fact, the poetic narrator undercuts this resolution, pointing out Glaukos's foolishness in exchanging golden armor for bronze (234–36). My aim in this study, however, is to articulate narrowly those traditional processes by which flyting and contesting episodes have been generated; and that perspective cannot, as I see it, explain this ironic touch on Homer's part. Interpretations would have to concentrate on the way in which the contest pattern has here been *used*.

51. Both the episode and fragment can be found in Klaeber's edition of *Beowulf* (1950). For an overview, see Greenfield and Calder 1986: 143–45. For expositions of critical positions and bibliography of earlier scholarship, see Fry 1969 and 1974.

52. Klaeber provides a useful review in his introduction to *The Fight at Finnsburg* (1950: 231–38). For a fuller study of backgrounds, see Tolkien 1982.

53. Unless one construes something of the sort from the *Beowulf* poet's ironic comment (1071–72): "Ne huru Hildeburh herian þorfte / Eotena treowe . . ." ("nor did Hildeburh need to praise the good faith of the Jutes. . . .").

54. Klaeber reviews many of these problems in his notes to the digression (1950: 170–76), and again in his introduction to *The Fight at Finnsburg* (1950: 231–38).

55. Lines 24–27. Klaeber glosses "swæþer" as "'which one of two things,' i.e. victory or death" (1950: 252, note to line 27). We find here another superb expression of the theme of destiny (through the agency of the supernal witness?), which has taken the place of a boast. Cf. *Il*.20.435–37.

56. For other discussions of Odysseus's island and home adventures in the context of hospitality conventions, see Edwards 1975, Powell 1977, Parks 1981, and Murnaghan 1987. On the significance of hospitality and guest-friendship generally, see Finley 1978: 99–103. More distantly pertinent is Hansen 1972.

57. See Lord's important cross-cultural explorations in this oral genre (1965b: 158–85 and 242–59, and 1969); see also Zhirmunsky 1966, J. Foley 1978b and 1980, Coote 1981, and Parks 1983. Murnaghan 1987, while focused on Homer only and not attending to the return song as such, explores in depth and from multiple perspectives problems of disguise and recognition, hospitality, interactions between the hero and his wife, and other pertinent matters.

58. See Frame 1978 for an important study of the origins and theme of *nostos*.

59. A useful translation of relevant portions of the saga appears in Garmonsway and Simpson 1980: 93–107. Panzer (1910) found a common Bear's Song tale in *Beowulf*, *Hrólfs saga kraka*, and some two hundred other Germanic folk tales. Working explicitly from Panzer's formulations, Carpenter (1946: 136–56) found vestiges of the same pattern in the *Odyssey*. These possible connections may provide some further grounding for my comparison at this turn.

60. It is true that Odysseus and the suitors are natives of the same region. Yet as I have tried to argue, until the massacre, their relationship is defined through reference to the guest-host paradigm, presupposing that the guest is a foreigner. Odysseus sustains this falsehood by means of his disguise, on which see Murnaghan 1987.

61. For a brilliant exploration in this subject area, see Ong 1981: 119–209.

62. Wealtheow uses her speech of thanks to Beowulf as an occasion to remind Hrothulf of his debt to herself and her husband Hrothgar and his consequent duty to support her children (who are Hrothulf's cousins) if Hrothgar should die before he does. Her speech indicates a distrust in her husband's nephew that his behavior in the analogues would amply warrant. Not all are agreed on Hrothulf's culpability, however; for a dissenting view, see Morgan 1972.

63. In this Eddic poem the god Loki, forcing his company upon the Æsir who are drinking beer in the hall of Ægir, defeats each of his fellow gods and goddesses one at a time in a series of vituperative exchanges. Formally the *Lokasenna* is not unlike the string of verbal contests in which Cet mac Matach puts down the men of Ulster in *Scél Mucci Mic Dathó* (see N. Chadwick 1927).

64. Byock finds that feuds in Icelandic saga are developed through combinations of three narrative elements or *feudemes*: conflict, advocacy, and resolution. The working out of Icelandic feuds is conditioned by the complex

Icelandic legal structure, which orients itself around exactly this kind of interaction. I feel, nonetheless, that Icelandic saga features many flyting exchanges of the heroic sort, and that the contractual force binding boast to heroic exploit is operative in these cases. Nonetheless, because of its implication in a larger system of law, the unfolding of the flyting-to-fighting bond is far less straightforward. On the theme of feuding (*fæhð*) in *Beowulf*, which has both familial and intertribal associations, see Kahrl 1972.

65. For studies in a variety of ingroup flyting genres of the "ludic" variety, see Dundes, Leach, and Özkök 1972; Labov 1972: 297–353; Gossen 1974: esp. 97–111; Bawcutt 1983; McDowell 1985; and my comments in chapter 5.

66. Thersites' lack of heroic qualifications is not so much a function of battlefield nonproficiency (for we never see him in this setting) as of *class*: unlike Achilles, Agamemnon, and Odysseus, he is nonaristocratic. Nagy (1979: 259–64) characterizes this the "worst" of the Achaians (*Il.*2.16, "αἴσχιστος," "most base,") as the paradigmatic exponent of blame poetry, in contrast with which epos defines itself. Rose (1988), in a Marxist reading, interprets the episode as an incipient class struggle. Feldman (1979) treats Thersites from a comparative standpoint. For a review of Thersites the "railer" within a monumental study of satire in its associations with invective, magic, misanthropy, and other global themes, see Elliott 1960: 130–40. Ward 1973 studies such invective and social lampooning from an Indo-European viewpoint.

67. Achilles' about-face on the matter of ingroup conflicts has parallels in the dominance struggles of baboons. As Trivers (1985: 379–80) observes, the alpha male is far more likely to play the peacemaker and support the prospective loser *after* he has attained the alpha position than *before*. On dominance, coalition formation, alpha status, and related problems among Gombe chimpanzees, see Goodall 1986: 409–42. Achilles, while not actually displacing Agamemnon as *anaks*, has, in a manner of speaking, won their dominance struggle, and he is plainly the presiding figure on this occasion. My point is not to compare Achilles to a baboon but to suggest that his behavior may have roots in determinants common to many life forms.

68. As Edwards (1980) shows in detail, the first book of the *Iliad* makes use of many type scenes that appear elsewhere in various forms in the Homeric canon. Some of these typical scenes or elements (such as the "Pondering Scene," "Divine Visitation," and "Mediation Scene") occur in the course of what I am calling the Achilles-Agamemnon flyting. Edwards's footnotes contain detailed references to pertinent scholarship.

69. In setting forth this construction of the plot of the *Iliad*, I do not mean to imply that other global organizing principles should be rejected. To the contrary, in a work the size and complexity of the *Iliad*, numerous patterns could have been—indeed, plainly were—at work simultaneously. For two important global interpretations of the epic's design, see Whitman 1965: 249–84, 367–70, on "geometric" or ring structure (cf. Niles 1983: 152–62), and Nagler 1974: 131–66, on the withdrawal-devastation-return pattern.

70. *Il.*1.254–84. See Edwards 1980: 15 on mediation as a type scene.

71. Patroklos interrupts Meriones in his flyting with Aineias (16.617–31)

because, as we noted earlier in this chapter, Meriones is letting words substitute for deeds. Achilles, for his part, is anxious to abort potential flytings during the athletic competition in book 23 for reasons that were discussed earlier.

72. An interesting parallel occurs at the end of Chaucer's *Pardoner's Tale* (*Canterbury Tales* VII.941–68). Here the Host, the presiding figure and peacemaker in earlier quarrels, himself gets involved in a flyting with the Pardoner, at which juncture the Knight—the leading aristocrat among the pilgrims—steps in and restores the peace.

73. *Il.*1.233, 239, "ὅρκον," "ὅρκος," "oath," or in other contexts, "witness to an oath," or "the power of that by which one swears." This term foregrounds both the contractual character of this flyting and the presence of the divine witness (cf. Griffin 1980: 179–204).

74. For an excellent discussion of this and cognate passages in Homer, see Scully 1984. For a briefer review and other references, see Edwards 1980: 12–13.

75. For a fine treatment of this topic and episode, see Nagler 1974: 167–98.

CHAPTER III

1. For bibliographic citations and annotations, as well as an introduction to relevant topics and problems, see J. Foley 1985 and 1988. For state-of-the-art bibliographic essays on oral studies, see, for the ancient Greek, Edwards 1986 and 1988, and for Old English, Olsen 1986 and 1988: on "themes and type scenes," 1986: 577–88. See also J. Foley 1981b: 79–91.

2. This dimension of narrative structure, comprising the linear sequencing of linguistic or discursive materials, corresponds to what Jakobson calls the axis of *combination*, the domain of *metonymic* thought (1973; 1960). However, the correspondence between this line of structuralism and oral-formulaic studies breaks down with Jakobson's second mode or axis, that of *selection*, which is not, in fact, situational or scenic.

3. See particularly Propp's discussion of *functions* and *moves* (1968: 25–65, 92–117); of course, Propp attends to other problems apart from narrative sequencing, such as the nature and sphere of the dramatis personae. Although few studies can rival Propp's in its complexity and comprehensiveness, many scholars have succeeded in identifying common narrative cores in multiple episodes; for two fine examples among many, see Baugh 1959 and Edwards 1980.

4. Fry (1968) nonetheless exhibits an awareness of the absence or presence of linear (temporal) ordering in his distinction between oral themes and type scenes: The former are not tied to the narration of an event, whereas the latter are. Thus, to Fry, type scenes are defined by their *narrativity*.

5. For an excellent introduction to theory and research in these areas, see J. Anderson 1985: esp. 73–102. Many cognitive psychologists deny the association with the visual modality specifically, insisting that visual information is merely one source of perceptual input into an aspect of memory that is es-

sentially spatial and abstract. For a discussion of "episodic memory," see Martindale 1981: 209–37.

6. These two duels, of course, include fighting as well as speech. Generally pertinent as well is Fenik 1968, although he does not attend to verbal dueling as such.

7. Clover 1974. See Byock 1982: 55–56 for a critique of this scheme. Byock himself is concerned with a feuding process far more involved than anything characterizable as "flyting." For a comparative analysis of the speeches of Beowulf and Unferth, see Clark 1981, who finds a common sequence of formal address, insult, story, assessment of story, and "conclusion for the present."

8. The most thorough study of physical settings in early epic is Andersson 1976. Andersson finds scene (i.e., description of physical environment) to be "impressionistic and formalized" (36) in the *Iliad*; but *Beowulf*, registering in his view a Virgilian influence, scene is vividly and intensely visualized. For his discussions of these two poems, see 15–37 (37–52 for the *Odyssey*) and 145–59.

9. Their article is, in part, a response to Clover's characterization of the *Hárbarðsljóð* as a generic farce (1979). Bax and Padmos raise the point of truth claims, arguing that this condition of speech is suspended in verbal duels. As I will try to show in chapter 5, the pertinence or suspension of truth claims—that is, whether statements are intended "seriously" or "ludically"—is one of the crucial distinctions on the basis of which generic distinctions among verbal contests can be made. Also on these Nordic genres, see Holtsmark 1966 and 1970.

10. This is not always the case in flytings in the Germanic world; see Clover's discussion of the "content" of flyting matches (1980: 453–59). Sexual innuendos figure prominently into many verbal dueling modes; see, for example, the *Lokasenna*, or even more dramatically, the dueling practices described in Dundes, Leach, and Özkök 1972.

11. In intraspecific agonistic encounters in the animal world threat displays often substitute for actual combat; and winners seldom continue the fight when the opponent has surrendered (see Barash 1982: 54–57). In their analysis of the *Hárbarðsljóð*, Bax and Padmos (1983) allow for the possibility of unilateral withdrawal.

12. On the supplication type scene in Homer, see Edwards 1980: 5–8.

13. In a similar spirit Beowulf explicitly renounces weaponry in his fight with Grendel, since his adversary has none (677–87). See Bloomfield's discussion of this problem in the judicial duel (1969: 551). For other scholarship in this problem, see citations in Alford and Seniff 1984.

14. On *topoi* cf. Curtius 1973: 79–105.

15. J. Harris (1979: 66) finds likewise that the *senna* opens with what he calls a "Preliminary, comprising an Identification and Characterization."

16. In this respect flyting differs from, say, academic debate, which purports to be objective, dispassionate, and therefore nonpersonal. The insistence on referring abstractions to the sphere of the human life-world is char-

acteristic of oral-based thought, as Ong points out (1982: 42–43). The practice of naming at the outset of speeches cannot be explained (in Homer at least) on grounds that the poet needed to clarify speaker and addressee to his audience: For quite frequently the speaker, addressee, or both are named in the speech introductions, before direct discourse has begun. For a study of these speech introductions, see Edwards 1970.

17. Thus, in pursuance of his contestational aims, he is drawing on aspects of his adversary's identity and reputation as a traditional *metonym*; on this topic, see Foley 1987b.

18. Similar to these episodes in the initial questioning and genealogical response, though lacking the final reconciliation, is the Achilles-Asteropaios encounter in *Il.*21.139–204. On the theme of inquiring as to a stranger's identity in Middle English romance literature, see Baugh 1959: 425–26. Another important treatment with bearing on this subject is Bax 1981, which deals with the ritualization of hostile encounters between medieval knights. On deixis, see Levinson 1983: 54–96; naming and other forms of flyting identification might be conceived as a kind of deixis by which flyting as a generic activity is tied to a specific instance.

19. See Ong's comments on homeostasis and the priority of the present in oral cultures (1982: 46–49).

20. As Clover points out (1980: 458–59), Unferth and Beowulf are disagreeing over *interpretations* rather than the facts of the episode. Specifically, Unferth wishes to characterize the adventure as a contest, whereas Beowulf does not.

21. Although his interests lie more with medieval grammar and sign theory, Bloch 1983 (esp. 64–127) is of potential relevance here. Bearing on the problem of genealogy in romance epic is Duggan 1986: 741–45 and Jones 1963: 58.

22. This distinction between illocutionary and propositional contents of an utterance is explicated more fully in Searle 1969: 29–33. For a systematic treatment of the varieties of speech acts, see Searle 1979: 1–19.

23. I am indebted throughout this section to Labov's masterful study of the sounding among inner-city American blacks (1972: 297–396); see especially his comments on the evaluation of narrative (366–75).

24. This exchange is not, strictly speaking, a flyting, since Sarpedon and Hektor are not directly contesting with each other in the agonistic style. Nonetheless, the same process of attribution and evaluation is at work. Needless to say, this charge of "cowardice" is standard flyting fare; see, for example, the taunt that Hektor directs at Diomedes in *Il.*8.161–66 and the perturbation in Diomedes that this causes (167–71). For further discussion of the "rebuke pattern," see Fenik 1968: 49–55, 159–89. Generally pertinent as well is Keitel's discussion of the *cohortatio* (1987), though this form of oration is from a leader to his troops and not the other way around.

25. Labov 1972: 336–37; see also his "law of interpretation," 338–39.

26. Interestingly enough, however, sounders seem in their own fashion to

concern themselves with "genealogy," in that, in most cases, the insult targets are one of the addressee's parents.

27. J. Harris (1979: 69–71) and Clover (1980: 457–58), while acknowledging certain affinities, likewise point out areas of difference between the two activities.

28. Possibly the distinction between *senna* and *mannjafnaðr*—if in fact this distinction can be upheld at all (for conflicting views, see Clover 1980 and Bax and Padmos 1983)—consists in the degree of foregrounding of the comparative function. I see no reason why the foregrounding of this function could not constitute a defining convention in a particular verbal contest genre in some cultural tradition.

29. Labov 1972: 343–44. In fact, on this point Labov is following Erving Goffman, who proposes three other such properties: that a "third-party role is necessary," that the third party can become a participant, and that "considerable symbolic distance is maintained and serves to insulate the event from other kinds of verbal interaction" (Labov 1972: 344). The "third-party" role here seems to correspond to what I discussed earlier as "witnessing" (see chapter 2).

30. Bax and Padmos (1983) use this principle in their analysis of the Eddic *Hárbarðsljóð*; see also Bax 1981.

31. These two categories correspond roughly to proposition (reference and predication) and illocution. See Searle's discussion of these subjects (1969: 22–23, 54–127, and passim).

32. Although he is critical of speech act approaches, Levinson discusses this kind of conversational interactivity under the rubric of "adjacency pairs" (1983: 303–8).

33. In their analysis of the *Hárbarðsljóð* Bax and Padmos (1983) analyze pragmatic alternatives of this sort.

34. On such difficulties, see Levinson's critique of discourse analysis (1983: 286–94).

35. All these problems have been studied more fully by scholars working in pragmatics, conversational and discourse analysis, and related areas. Since flyting is a species of "conversation" in the most general sense, this scholarship could shed much light on flyting as dialogic interaction. Such an inquiry would take us too far afield, however, and would not highlight those elements of interaction most characteristic of flyting and verbal contesting as such. Several pertinent studies include Austin 1975; Grice 1975; Pratt 1977; Sacks, Schegloff, and Jefferson 1978 (and other essays in this volume); Levinson 1983; and various of the essays collected in van Dijk 1985.

Chapter IV

1. For brief introductions to the two great Sanskrit epics (the *Mahābhārata* and the *Rāmāyana*), see van Buitenen and Dimock 1974 and van Nooten 1978; van Nooten 1971 offers a useful book-length review of the *Mahābhārata* alone. In the introduction to the first volume of his translation, van Buitenen (1973: xiii–xliv) surveys the epic's plot and complexities, textual and

other. For a superb abridged translation, see Narasimhan 1965. For the transliteration of names I have followed Narasimhan's practice as summarized in his extremely helpful glossary (1965: 219–34), although I have used, in preference to Kṛṣṇa, the more familiar form Krishna. Van Buitenen's translation is based on the Poona critical edition, the standard source. In references to the *Mahābhārata* in this section I will introduce major sections by citing book and chapter, but in the following, more detailed discussions I will refer only to volume and page number in the translation.

2. In fact, since Vicitravīrya dies childless, Dhṛtarāṣṭra and Pāṇḍu are fathered by their uncle Kṛṣṇa Dvaipāyana (known as Vyāsa), acting under the law of levirate. Since he is also credited with the composition of the *Mahābhārata*, Vyāsa emerges as both the author of the story and the ancestor of its principal characters.

3. In fact, since Pāṇḍu has incurred a curse prohibiting sexual intercourse, his wives avail themselves of a boon enabling them to conceive by the gods of their choice. None of the Pāṇḍavas, then, is actually Pāṇḍu's son. Karṇa, the son of Sūrya (the Sun-god), has been conceived in the same way and is no more a bastard than his younger brothers are.

4. For an older comparison of heroic poetry, Indian, Greek, Anglo-Saxon, and other, see Sidhanta 1929: 70–90 and passim; many of Sidhanta's observations pertain to what we would now call type scene. In the introduction to his translation of the first volume of the *Rāmāyana* Goldman provides an excellent discussion of the Indian epic style, which he contrasts with that of Homer (1984: 96–117). Although he speaks with the *Rāmāyana* in view, many of Goldman's observations hold for the *Mahābhārata* as well.

5. For a convenient introduction to dharma, see de Bary 1958: 206–30.

6. Dumézil's major treatment of the *Mahābhārata* is in the first volume of *Mythe et épopée* (1968). Hiltebeitel (1976) tries to incorporate Dumézilean and other perspectives into a treatment of myth and epic more sensitized to the peculiarities of the *Mahābhārata* and its tradition.

7. A common designation for Yudhiṣṭhira is *dharma-rāja*, which means "dharma-king"; the story makes him quite literally the son of the god Dharma, whom Kuntī (the mother of several of the Pāṇḍavas) invoked through her boon. According to Dumézil, Yudhiṣṭhira is representative of the first function (corresponding to the priestly or brahmanical class). For a brief statement of this view, see Dumézil 1973: 54–58.

8. The dicing match appears in *The Book of the Assembly Hall* (*Sabhāparvan*), *Mahābhārata* 2.43–72, van Buitenen 2: 106–69.

9. For example, van Buitenen (2: 3–30 and esp. 27–30) argues that the dicing match is integral to the *rājasūya* or royal consecration ceremony by which Yudhiṣṭhira in this book has formalized his universal sovereignty. This connection with Vedic religion is not explicable through general, cross-cultural principles of contesting.

10. Since the dicing occurs in a familial setting (see van Buitenen 2: 28), it is a contest of the ingroup variety and ought to follow an irenic pathway. For more on this point, see chapters 2 and 5 of this study.

11. This episode is narrated in *Mahābhārata* 1.124–27, van Buitenen 1: 274–82.

12. One of many names for Arjuna.

13. Van Buitenen's word for "kshatriyas."

14. I.e., descendant of Bharata, or Arjuna.

15. These eminent gods are also the fathers of Arjuna and Karṇa, respectively.

16. Since van Buitenen's translation ends with book 5, in these passages from the *Karṇaparvan* (book 8) I follow the translation of Pratap Chandra Roy (1889: 361–62).

17. Indeed, Krishna's reference to the dicing match, in which Śakuni (Roy's "Cakuni") took advantage of Yudhiṣṭhira's lack of skill and experience, implicitly reaffirms this very criterion of comparability and fair play in contests.

18. My citations are based on Valerie Krishna's edition (1976). On dating, dialect, and other matters, see Krishna's introduction (1–34).

19. The origins of the Alliterative Revival and its possible relationship to oral tradition has been the subject of long critical debate. On this and other topics relating to orality in the later medieval period, see the review of scholarship in Parks 1986c. The *Alliterative Morte Arthure* has been the poem most often studied by those interested in oral residue in Middle English literature.

20. Much of what follows is based on Parks 1990, which concentrates more on the level of small-scale flytings. Scholarship on the poem is considerable, particularly in recent years. For an annotated bibliography covering 1950–1975, see M. Foley 1979; Göller (1981b) surveys the criticism in his introduction to a recent collection of essays on the poem.

21. For a treatment of the "theme of battle" that takes cognizance of oral-formulaic approaches, see Ritzke-Rutherford 1981. As Ritzke-Rutherford construes the poem, its author takes a harsh view of war and those who sponsor it. For contrasting interpretations, see Eadie 1982 and Porter 1983.

22. For more, see Parks 1987b, 1987c, 1989, and forthcoming.

23. For a detailed study of the narrative organization of the first approximately seven hundred lines of the poem, see Keiser 1974.

24. The reader will understand, of course, here and throughout, that I am trying to articulate the program of assumptions underlying the flyting, not my own assessment of such conduct.

25. See, for example, Benson 1966: 77.

26. Compare Arthur's behavior with, for example, that of Achilles toward the body of Hektor. On this subject, see Segal 1971.

27. For a recent study of this pivotal episode, see Janssen 1981. Also relevant is Höltgen's treatment of the motif of the Nine Worthies (1957).

28. The view that the poet intends to undercut Arthur's character and martial ambitions finds its strongest support in the Dream and the altered mood of the action that follows. Any holistic interpretation of the poem has to deal, in fact, with this opposition between the earlier "heroic" and later "tragic" segments; the reading one prefers is liable to be a function of the

narrative movement that one chooses to emphasize. Not surprisingly, scholarly opinions diverge widely. A seminal ironic reading of the poem is Matthews 1960. For several important later articles touching on this subject from various viewpoints, see Benson 1966, Finlayson 1968, Lumiansky 1968, Keiser 1975, Markus 1981 (along with other contributions to Göller 1981a), and Eadie 1982.

29. In this section I have used Brault's edition (1978, vol. 2) as my source text for the epic, which, together with his commentary (1978, vol. 1) I will henceforth refer to as *Roland*; I have had frequent recourse also to the commentaries of Bédier (1927) and especially Cook (1987). Particularly pertinent to oral-formulaic perspectives is Rychner 1955, which gives attention to formulas and motifs in the *chanson de geste*, and Duggan 1973, with its detailed study of formulas and formulaic density in *Roland*. For brief, general treatments of the *chanson de geste* genre, see Brault 1978 and Duggan 1986, the latter sociological in outlook. Jones (1963), who stresses the martial and secular resonances particularly as these register in the poem's vocabulary, exposes the kind of mind-set in which flyting or contesting occurs; Cook (1987) provides an eloquent defense of Roland and the heroic ideal that he embodies. I would like to reiterate, in these inquiries into *Roland* and *Gawain* in particular, that I am concentrating on that particular stratum of ethical and artistic awareness that houses the flyting movements. Both of these poems give signs of allegorizing and other complex strategies relating to the artistic *use* of contesting that I will not be able here to explore in full.

30. As Brault points out in his discussion of the "meaning" of *Roland*, "The essential point made by Turoldus is that Christianity transcends all other faiths. It is so superior, in fact, as to be in a class by itself, other forms of belief being poor excuses for religion" (*Roland* 1978, 1: 40).

31. On the idea that right is measured by success and that combat is a *iudicium dei*, see Jones 1963: esp. 12–16.

32. This reading accords well with Brault's view that "Turoldus and his contemporaries considered Ganelon to be completely evil" (*Roland* 1978, 1: 100).

33. The French council is counterposed, in fact, to that of the Saracens earlier; it belongs to a larger program of mirrorings that interrelate and contrast the activities of these two forces. The dispute between Ganelon and Roland has, naturally, been the subject of much discussion; surveying pertinent issues, Brault (in *Roland* 1978, 1: 135–40) observes that the quarrel scene is "innately ambiguous" (135). As I will try to argue, much of this ambiguity is due to the quarrel's (designedly) uncertain relationship to heroic flyting. Cook (1987: 8–27) unravels the political and military realities underlying the interaction, arguing that Roland, unlike Ganelon, advises for the good of the army and not from personal animus.

34. Actually we cannot be certain precisely what Ganelon's intentions at this juncture are. Brault insists that Ganelon falls on account of greed; and by this view we could not construe his corruption as having taken place yet.

Nonetheless, Ganelon's behavior already and plainly signals a divergence between public profession and private aim.

35. As Brault observes (*Roland* 1978, 1: 165), the term that Ganelon uses, "fillastre" (743), echoes the terms by which Roland nominated his father-in-law earlier, *parastre* (277).

36. Bédier 1927: 150–52. For detailed commentary and justification of Roland's reactions, see Cook 1987: 43–53.

37. I am not taking up the problem of Roland's unwillingness to blow his horn and the resultant quarrel with Oliver, which has commonly been interpreted as the poet's indictment of Roland's undiscriminating heroism (for a revisionist reading, see Cook 1987: 62–76). Yet by the terms of sheer contesting, which is my exclusive focus here, no one could fault Roland.

38. As Brault points out (*Roland* 1978, 1: 309), this duel, thoroughly formulaic in character, is closely paralleled by the Pinabel-Thierry exchange (which we will be discussing shortly). Both are *adjudicative*—through them God renders his verdict.

39. The *iudicium dei*, judicial combat, and related practices, found in many parts of medieval Europe, have been the subject of considerable study. Much of this is cited and annotated in Alford and Seniff 1984.

40. The Green Knight characterizes his challenge and contest as a *gomen* from the very first speeches in which he proposes it (see 273 and 283). This and all subsequent citations from the poem—henceforth called *Gawain*—are based on the text of Tolkien and Gordon, revised by Norman Davis (1967). Criticism of this poem is, of course, voluminous; I have found particularly helpful Benson's classic study (1965). For an excellent guide to criticism through 1978, see Blanch 1983; Miller and Chance (1986) provide a more recent introduction to basic materials and approaches.

41. On the relationship between deception and the *Gawain* poet's quite writerly deployment of oral-formulaic structure, see Camargo 1987. The use of oral-formulaic techniques in *Gawain* is studied at length by Benson, especially in his chapter on style (1965: 110–66). Also pertinent is Renoir's discussion of the poet's literary use of the oral-formulaic "hero on the beach" theme (1986: esp. 132–35).

42. This motif is a common one; for parallels in French romance literature see the note to lines 90ff. in Tolkien and Gordon's edition (1967: 76).

43. Here again the *Gawain* poet shows his keen interest in the theme of play, an interest that suffuses the poem on all levels. As one would expect, the ludic dimensions of this romance have often been sounded in critical discussion, commonly with allusion to Huizinga 1955; see, for example, Leyerle 1975.

44. It is true, of course, that the beheading game makes its appearance in Irish and French literature, notably *Le Livre de Caradoc*; for reviews of sources and the *Gawain* poet's use of them, see Kittredge 1960: 9–76 and Benson 1965: 3–37. Nonetheless, the heroic contest pattern is, as I have argued in chapter 1, a type of intraspecific combat; and one of the normal characteristics of the human species is that, when members are decapitated, they die.

Thus normal human combat could hardly adopt conventions by which one contestant (barring the miraculous) always kills his adversary before the adversary has the chance for a return stroke. Kittredge points out (1960: 21–22, 218–23) that an alternation of blows was common practice in ancient dueling; on this matter Saxo Grammaticus observes that "in days of old when contests were arranged they did not try to exchange a rain of blows but hit at one another in a definite sequence with a gap between each turn" (1979, 1: 55). Nonetheless, the conditions of attack and defense in the duels recounted by Saxo and Kittredge were such as to prevent a mere, unimpeded slaughter (except in the *Gawain* analogues, of course). Quite obviously the decapitation motif represents the intrusion of the fabulous into *Gawain* and similar tales. Its forces lie precisely in its violation of normal contest procedures.

45. For a superb discussion of honor and shame in *Gawain*, a topic with major bearing on the heroic flyting exchange, see Burrow 1984: 117–31.

46. On Gawain as representative of the honor of Round Table, see again Burrow 1984.

47. The renewal of flyting between phases of a martial conflict is common enough fare in heroic literature; see, for example, the duel between Odysseus and Sokos in *Il.*11.427–55.

48. Prince Hal, for example, flyts (according to his fashion) before killing Hotspur in Shakespeare's *Henry IV, Part I* (5.4.58–74).

49. For a masterful, broad-ranging study of the agonistic theme in Western cultural history, see Ong 1981.

CHAPTER V

1. Most of the following discussion of sounding will be based on Labov 1972: 298–353. The literature on this verbal dueling genre is fairly extensive; see, for example, Dollard 1939; Abrahams 1962 and 1970: esp. 39–60; Ayoub and Barnett 1965; and assorted references in Foster 1974. For further citations, see Szwed, Abrahams, et al. 1978, especially under the entry "Verbal and Musical Dueling," 1: 803–4.

2. For an important introduction to verbal dueling with bibliography of scholarship treating the phenomenon in several cultures, see McDowell 1985. On an insult genre related to those studied by Dundes, Leach, and Özkök 1972, see Razvratnikov 1977.

3. For these poems, see the editions of Cranstoun (1887: 59–86) and Kinsley (1979: 76–95); Kinsley's notes (1979: esp. 282–86) provide a useful introduction to the topic. For further study of Scottish flyting and its historical backgrounds, see Bawcutt 1983. On other English flytings, see Gray 1984.

4. See, for example, Elliott's discussion of drumming duels among Greenland Eskimos and a south Italian insult game known as *la legge* or "the Law" (1960: 70–74); Eibl-Eibesfeldt quotes from a tavern song duel among Tyrolean Austrians (1979: 98–99); Huizinga cites many instances of related phenomena (1955: 65–71 and throughout). For a superb Nordic instance, see Lönnroth's (1979) discussion and citation from *Örvar-Odds saga*.

212 · Notes to Chapter V

5. For a fine inquiry into the rhetorical strategies and social and folkloristic backgrounds, see Lindahl 1987: esp. 71–155.

6. Although I will not base my analysis explicitly on speech act principles, nonetheless, speech act theory has relevance and will come into the discussion from time to time. The pioneering study in speech act theory is Austin 1975; more relevant to generic study is Pratt 1977. The field of pragmatics has much blossomed over the past decade; for a useful introduction, see Levinson 1983, who is somewhat critical of speech act theory and discourse analysis, preferring the more empirical conversational analysis. In the literary field, for a pragmatic study upholding the generic distinction between the *mannjafnaðr* and the *senna* in *Harbarðsljóð*, see Bax and Padmos 1983.

7. On the debate tradition as a background to *The Owl and the Nightingale*, see Hume 1975: 35–50.

8. On this subject, see Walther 1920; Raby (1957, 2: 282–308) provides an overview.

9. With the widespread interest in matters "ludic" over the past decade or two, I wish to stress the particular refinement I am giving to the use of this expression at this turn. As Huizinga (1955) has shown, "game" (*ludus*) suffuses human culture at all levels; and it plainly takes part in those flyting modes that I have called serious or nonludic. I do not mean to deny any of this; my distinction between the ludic and the nonludic here applies only to linguistic *reference*.

10. 1979: 62. For a fuller discussion of the rules governing assertions and other speech acts, see Searle 1969: 54–71.

11. The problem of fictionalization and nonfictionalization is distinct from the problem of figurative language, even though the two share the superficial characteristic of meaning in a nonliteral way. The "ludic" verbal contest, by the same token, should not be confused with some kind of "metaphorical" exchange or struggle. For a pragmatic analysis of these issues, see "Metaphor," in Searle 1979: 76–116. The belief in a "real world" outside of language and textuality has been much under fire in recent critical discourse; yet one need not subscribe to some naively intransigent world-mind dualism in order to affirm the existence of things outside one's own subjectivity, or even the subjectivity of language. On these problems, see especially Scholes 1985; I take world-denying textualism to task in Parks (forthcoming).

12. The connection between verbal dueling as I am studying it here and the courtroom is one that merits further study. While I am unfamiliar with scholarship exploring this association explicitly, Drew (1985) has provided a valuable introduction (with bibliography) to courtroom interaction viewed as discourse and dialogue.

13. I am conceiving of the "ritualization" of contests in terms of the channeling and circumscription of violence. For a far-ranging and provocative exploration into such questions, see Girard 1977. Although ultimately relevant to the present discussion, Girard takes scapegoating and sacrificial violence, not contesting, as his starting point.

14. See Clover 1980: 452–53.

15. On Scottish flyting, see, in addition to Bawcutt 1983, the editor's notes to "The Flyting of Dunbar and Kennedie" (Kinsley 1979: esp. 282–86).

16. Labov 1972: 336 and passim; see my discussion on this point in chapter 3.

17. The same is generally true in the animal world (see chapter 1).

18. See, for example, Valla 1948: 166: "*Ant.* 'Do you think I affirm something rather than raise the question for the sake of argument? Again you seem to seek excuses by your speech and, giving ground, decline to fight.' *Lor.* 'As if I fought for the sake of victory rather than truth!'"

CONCLUSION

1. For an eloquent discussion of Homer's treatment of heroism, see Schein 1984:esp. 67-88.

2. In what is nonetheless a superb review of animal and predatorial imagery in Homer, Vermeule in her chapter "The Happy Hero" (1979:83-117) fails, as I see it, to make this necessary distinction between the predatorial and the contestational. Polyphemos behaves like a predator; Achilles does not.

3. On this topic, see Ong 1981:119-48.

Bibliography

Editions and Translations

The Alliterative Morte Arthure: A Critical Edition. 1976. Edited by Valerie Krishna. New York: Burt Franklin.

The Anglo-Saxon Poetic Records: A Collective Edition. 1931–1953. Edited by George Philip Krapp and Elliott van Kirk Dobbie. 6 vols. New York: Columbia University Press.

Aristotle. 1934. *The Nicomachean Ethics*, rev. ed. Edited and translated by H. Rackham. Loeb Classical Library. Cambridge, Mass.: Harvard University Press.

The Battle of Maldon. 1981. Edited by D. G. Scragg. Manchester: Manchester University Press.

Beowulf and the Fight at Finnsburg, 3d ed. 1950. Edited by Friedrich Klaeber. Lexington, Mass.: D. C. Heath.

Chadwick, N. Kershaw, ed. and trans. 1927. *An Early Irish Reader.* Cambridge: Cambridge University Press.

Chaucer, Geoffrey. 1987. *The Riverside Chaucer*, 3d ed. General editor, Larry D. Benson. Boston: Houghton Mifflin.

Cranstoun, James, ed. 1887. "Polwart and Montgomerie Flyting." In *The Poems of Alexander Montgomerie*, 59–86. Scottish Text Society 9–11. Edinburgh: Blackwood.

Diodorus of Sicily. 1939. *The Library of History.* Edited and translated by C. H. Oldfather. Vol 3. Loeb Classical Library. Cambridge, Mass.: Harvard University Press.

Garmonsway, G. N., and Jacqueline Simpson, ed. and trans. 1980. *Beowulf and Its Analogues*, rev. ed. London: J. M. Dent.

Homeri Opera. 1917–1920. Vols. 1 and 2, *Iliadis Libros I–XII*, and *Iliadis Libros XIII–XXIV*, 3d ed. Edited by David B. Monro and Thomas W. Allen. Vols. 3 and 4, *Odysseae Libros I–XII*, and *Odysseae Libros XIII–XXIV*, 2d ed. Edited by Thomas W. Allen. Oxford: Clarendon.

Ihara, Saikaku. 1965. *This Scheming World.* Translated by Masanori Takatsuka and David C. Stubbs. Rutland, Vt.: Tuttle.

Kinsley, James, ed. 1979. "The Flyting of Dunbar and Kennedie." In *The Poems of William Dunbar*, 76–95, 282–98. Oxford: Clarendon Press.

Lattimore, Richmond, trans. 1951. *The Iliad of Homer.* Chicago: University of Chicago Press.

Narasimhan, Chakravarthi V. 1965. *The Mahābhārata: An English Version Based on Selected Verses.* New York: Columbia University Press.

Paul the Deacon. 1974. *History of the Lombards.* Translated by William Dudley Foulke, 1907. Reprint. Edited by Edward Peters. Philadelphia: University of Pennsylvania Press.

Roy, Pratap Chandra, trans. 1889. *The Mahābhārata, or Krishna Dwaipāyana Vyāsa. Karṇa Parva.* Calcutta: Bharata Press.
Saxo Grammaticus. 1979. *The History of the Danes.* Vol. 1, *English Text.* Vol. 2, *Commentary.* Edited and translated by Hilda Ellis Davidson and Peter Fish. Totowa, N.J.: Rowman and Littlefield.
Sir Gawain and the Green Knight. 1967. Edited by J.R.R. Tolkien and E. V. Gordon. 2d ed. Revised by Normand Davis. Oxford: Clarendon Press.
The Song of Roland: An Analytical Edition. 1978. Edited and translated by Gerald J. Brault. Vol. 1, *Introduction and Commentary.* Vol. 2, *Oxford Text and English Translation.* University Park: Pennsylvania State University Press.
Valla, Lorenzo. 1948. *Dialogue on Free Will.* Translated by Charles Edward Trinkaus. In *The Renaissance Philosophy of Man,* edited by Ernst Cassirer, Paul Oskar Kristeller, and John Herman Randall, 155–82. Chicago: University of Chicago Press.
van Buitenen, J.A.B., trans. 1973 and 1975. *The Mahābhārata.* Vol. 1, *The Book of the Beginning.* Vol. 2, *The Book of the Assembly Hall* and *The Book of the Forest.* Chicago: University of Chicago Press.
Waldere. 1979. Edited by Arne Zettersten. Manchester: Manchester University Press.
Wolfram von Eschenbach. 1980. *Parzival.* Translated by A. T. Hatto. Harmondsworth, Middlesex: Penguin.

SCHOLARLY STUDIES

Abrahams, Roger D. 1962. "Playing the Dozens." *Journal of American Folklore* 75: 209–18.
———. 1970. *Deep Down in the Jungle: Negro Narrative Folklore from the Streets of Philadelphia,* rev. ed. Chicago: Aldine.
Adler, Norman T. 1979. "On the Physiological Organization of Social Behavior: Sex and Aggression." In *Handbook of Behavioral Neurobiology,* vol. 3, *Social Behavior and Communication,* edited by Peter Marler and J. G. Vandenbergh, 29–71. New York: Plenum Press.
Alcock, John. 1984. *Animal Behavior: An Evolutionary Approach,* 3d ed. Sunderland, Mass.: Sinauer.
Alford, John A., and Dennis P. Seniff. 1984. *Literature and Law in the Middle Ages: A Bibliography of Scholarship.* New York: Garland.
Anderson, Earl R. 1970. "*Flyting* in *The Battle of Maldon.*" *Neuphilologische Mitteilungen* 71: 197–202.
Anderson, John R. 1985. *Cognitive Psychology and Its Implications,* 2d ed. New York: Freeman.
Andersson, Theodore M. 1976. *Early Epic Scenery: Homer, Virgil, and the Medieval Legacy.* Ithaca, N.Y.: Cornell University Press.
Arend, Walter. 1933. *Die typischen Scenen bei Homer.* Problemata 7. Berlin: Weidmann.
Arieti, James A. 1985. "Achilles' Guilt." *Classical Journal* 80: 193–203.
———. 1986. "Achilles' Alienation in *Iliad* 9." *Classical Journal* 82: 1–27.

Austin, J. L. 1975. *How to Do Things with Words*. 2d ed. Edited by J. O. Urmson and Marina Sbisà. Cambridge, Mass.: Harvard University Press.

Axelrod, Robert M. 1984. *The Evolution of Cooperation*. New York: Basic Books.

Ayoub, Millicent R., and Stephen A. Barnett. 1965. "Ritualized Verbal Insult in White High School Culture." *Journal of American Folklore* 78: 337–44.

Baird, Joseph. 1970. "Unferth the *þyle*." *Medium Ævum* 39: 1–12.

Bakhtin, M. M. 1981. *The Dialogic Imagination: Four Essays*. Edited by Michael Holquist, translated from the Russian by Caryl Emerson and Michael Holquist. Austin: University of Texas Press.

Barash, David P. 1982. *Sociobiology and Behavior*. New York: Elsevier.

Barney, Stephen A. 1985. *Wordhoard: An Introduction to Old English Vocabulary*, 2d ed. New Haven: Yale University Press.

Baron, Robert A. 1977. *Human Aggression*. New York: Plenum Press.

Baugh, Albert C. 1959. "Improvisation in the Middle English Romance." *Proceedings of the American Philosophical Association* 103: 418–54.

Bauman, Richard. 1986. "Performance and Honor in 13th-Century Iceland." *Journal of American Folklore* 99: 131–50.

Bawcutt, Priscilla. 1983. "The Art of Flyting." *Scottish Literary Journal* 10, no. 2: 5–24.

Bax, Marcel. 1981. "Rules for Ritual Challenges: A Speech Convention among Medieval Knights." *Journal of Pragmatics* 5: 423–44.

Bax, Marcel, and Tineke Padmos. 1983. "Two Types of Verbal Dueling in Old Icelandic: The Interactional Structure of the *senna* and the *mannjafnaðr* in *Hárbarðsljóð*." *Scandinavian Studies* 55: 149–74.

Bédier, Joseph. 1927. *La Chanson de Roland commentée*. Paris: H. Piazza.

Benson, Larry D. 1965. *Art and Tradition in Sir Gawain and the Green Knight*. New Brunswick, N.J.: Rutgers University Press.

———. 1966. "The Alliterative *Morte Arthure* and Medieval Tragedy." *Tennessee Studies in Literature* 11: 75–88.

Bessinger, J. B. 1962. "*Maldon* and *Óláfsdrápa*: An Historical Caveat." *Comparative Literature* 14: 23–35.

———, ed. 1978. *A Concordance to the Anglo-Saxon Poetic Records*. Programmed by Philip H. Smith, Jr., with an index of compounds compiled by Michael W. Twomey. Ithaca, N.Y.: Cornell University Press.

Beye, Charles Rowan. 1964. "Homeric Battle Narratives and Catalogues." *Harvard Studies in Classical Philology* 68: 345–73.

Blanch, Robert J. 1983. *Sir Gawain and the Green Knight: A Reference Guide*. Troy, N.Y.: Whitston Publishing.

Blanchard, D. Caroline, and Robert J. Blanchard. 1984. "Affect and Aggression: An Animal Model Applied to Human Behavior." In *Advances in the Study of Aggression*, edited by Robert. J. Blanchard and D. Caroline Blanchard, 1: 1–62. Orlando, Fla.: Academic Press.

Bloch, R. Howard. 1983. *Etymologies and Genealogies: A Literary Anthropology of the French Middle Ages*. Chicago: University of Chicago Press.

Bloomfield, Morton W. 1969. "Beowulf, Byrhtnoth, and the Judgment of God: Trial by Combat in Anglo-Saxon England." *Speculum* 44: 545–59.

Bø, Olav. 1969. "*Hólmganga* and *einvígi*: Scandinavian Forms of the Duel." *Mediaeval Scandinavia* 2: 132–48.

Bosworth, Joseph, and T. Northcote Toller. 1898. *An Anglo-Saxon Dictionary*. Oxford: Oxford University Press, 1898. *Supplement* by Toller. Oxford: Clarendon, 1921.

Bowra, C. M. 1952. *Heroic Poetry*. London: Macmillan.

Brandes, Stanley. 1980. *Metaphors of Masculinity: Sex and Status in Andalusian Folklore*. Philadelphia: University of Pennsylvania Press.

Brault, Gerald J. 1978. "The French Chansons de Geste." In Oinas 1978: 193–215.

Brennan, Malcolm M. 1985. "Hrothgar's Government." *Journal of English and German Philology* 84: 3–15.

Burrow, J. A. 1984. "Honour and Shame in *Sir Gawain and the Green Knight*." In *Essays on Medieval Literature*, 117–31. Oxford: Clarendon Press.

Butler, Kenneth Dean. 1969. "The *Heike Monogatari* and the Japanese Warrior Ethic." *Harvard Journal of Asiatic Studies* 29: 93–108.

Byock, Jesse L. 1982. *Feud in the Icelandic Saga*. Berkeley and Los Angeles: University of California Press.

Camargo, Martin. 1987. "Oral Traditional Structure in *Sir Gawain and the Green Knight*." In J. Foley 1987a: 121–37.

Carpenter, Rhys. 1946. *Folk Tale, Fiction, and Saga in the Homeric Epics*. Berkeley and Los Angeles: University of California Press.

Chadwick, H. Munro. 1912. *The Heroic Age*. Cambridge: Cambridge University Press.

Chadwick, H. Munro, and N. Kershaw Chadwick. 1932–1940. *The Growth of Literature*. 3 vols. Cambridge: Cambridge University Press.

Chance, Jane. 1986. *Woman as Hero in Old English Literature*. Syracuse, N.Y.: Syracuse University Press, 1986.

Chantraine, Pierre. 1968, 1970, 1974, 1977, and 1980. *Dictionnaire étymologique de la langue grecque*. Vols. 1–3; 4, no. 1; and 4, no. 2. Paris: Klincksieck.

Chatman, Seymour. 1978. *Story and Discourse: Narrative Structure in Fiction and Film*. Ithaca, N.Y.: Cornell University Press.

Clanchy, M. T. 1979. *From Memory to Written Record: England, 1066–1307*. Cambridge, Mass.: Harvard University Press.

Clark, Francelia. "Flyting in *Beowulf* and Rebuke in *The Song of Bagdad*: The Question of Theme." In J. Foley 1981a: 164–93.

Claus, David B. 1975. "*Aidôs* in the Language of Achilles." *Transactions of the American Philological Association* 105: 13–28.

Clover, Carol J. 1974. "Scene in Saga Composition." *Arkiv för nordisk filologi* 89: 57–83.

———. 1979. "*Hárbarðsljóð* as Generic Farce." *Scandinavian Studies* 51: 124–45.

———. 1980. "The Germanic Context of the Unferþ Episode." *Speculum* 55: 444–68.

Clutton-Brock, T. H., F. E. Guinness, and S. D. Albon. 1982. *Red Deer: Behavior and Ecology of Two Sexes*. Chicago: University of Chicago Press.

Conquergood, Dwight. 1981. "Boasting in Anglo-Saxon England: Performance and the Heroic Ethos." *Literature in Performance* 1, no. 2: 24–35.

Cook, Robert Francis. 1987. *The Sense of the Song of Roland*. Ithaca, N.Y.: Cornell University Press.

Coote, Mary P. 1981. "Lying in Passages." *Canadian-American Slavic Studies* 15: 5–23.

Crabtree, Michael, and Kenneth E. Moyer. 1977 and 1981. *Bibliography of Aggressive Behavior: A Reader's Guide to the Research Literature*. 2 vols. New York: Alan R. Liss.

Crowne, David K. 1960. "The Hero on the Beach: An Example of Composition by Theme in Anglo-Saxon Poetry." *Neuphilologische Mitteilungen* 61: 362–72.

Curtius, Ernst Robert. 1973. *European Literature and the Latin Middle Ages*. Translated from the 1948 German original by Willard R. Trask. Bollingen series 36. Princeton: Princeton University Press.

de Barry, William Theodore, gen. ed. 1958. *Sources of Indian Tradition*. Vol. 1. New York: Columbia University Press.

de Waal, Frans. 1982. *Chimpanzee Politics: Power and Sex among Apes*. New York: Harper and Row.

Dodds, E. R. 1951. *The Greeks and the Irrational*. Berkeley and Los Angeles: University of California Press.

Dollard, John. 1939. "The Dozens: The Dialect of Insult." *American Imago* 1: 3–24.

Drew, John. 1985. "Analyzing the Use of Language in Courtroom Interaction." In van Dijk 1985: 133–47.

Duggan, Joseph J. 1973. *The Song of Roland: Formulaic Style and Poetic Craft*. Publications of the Center for Medieval and Renaissance Studies, University of California, Los Angeles, 6. Berkeley and Los Angeles: University of California Press.

———. 1986. "Social Functions of the Medieval Epic in the Romance Literatures." *Oral Tradition* 1: 728–66.

Dumézil, Georges. 1943. *Servius et la fortune: Essai sur la fonction sociale de louange et de blâme et sur les éléments indo-européens du cens romain*. Paris: Librairie Gaillaird.

———. 1968. *Mythe et épopée*, vol. 1, *L'idéologie des trois fonctions dans les épopées des peuples indo-européens*. Paris: Editions Gallimard.

———. 1973. *Gods of the Ancient Northmen*. Translated from the 1959 French original by John Lindow, Alan Toth, Francis Charat, and George Gopen. Berkeley and Los Angeles: University of California Press.

Dundes, Alan, Jerry W. Leach, and Bora Özkök. 1972. "The Strategy of Turkish Boys' Verbal Dueling Rhymes." In *Directions in Sociolinguistics: The*

Ethnography of Communication, edited by John J. Gumperz and Dell Hymes, 130–60. New York: Holt, Rinehart and Winston.

Eadie, J. 1982. "The Alliterative *Morte Arthure*: Structure and Meaning." *English Studies* 63: 1–12.

Earl, James W. 1983. "The Role of the Men's Hall in the Development of the Anglo-Saxon Superego." *Psychiatry* 46: 139–60.

Edwards, Mark W. 1970. "Homeric Speech Introductions." *Harvard Studies in Classical Philology* 74: 1–36.

———. 1975. "Type–Scenes and Homeric Hospitality." *Transactions of the American Philological Association* 105: 51–72.

———. 1980. "Convention and Individuality in *Iliad* 1." *Harvard Studies in Classical Philology* 84: 1–28.

———. 1986. "Homer and Oral Tradition: The Formula, Part I." *Oral Tradition* 1: 171–230.

———. 1988. "Homer and Oral Tradition: The Formula, Part II." *Oral Tradition* 3: 11–60.

Eibl-Eibesfeldt, Irenäus. 1979. *The Biology of Peace and War: Men, Animals, and Aggression*. Translated from the German by Eric Mosbacher. New York: Viking.

Einarsson, Stefán. 1934. "Old English *Beot* and Old Icelandic *Heitstrenging*." *PMLA* 49: 975–93.

Eliason, Norman E. 1963. "The Þyle and Scop in *Beowulf*." *Speculum* 38: 267–84.

Elliott, Robert C. 1960. *The Power of Satire: Magic, Ritual, Art*. Princeton: Princeton University Press.

Feldman, Thalia Phillies. 1979. "The Taunter in Ancient Epic: The *Iliad*, *Odyssey*, *Aeneid*, and *Beowulf*." *Papers on Language and Literature* 15: 3–16.

Fenik, Bernard C. 1968. *Typical Battle Scenes in the Iliad: Studies in the Narrative Techniques of Homeric Battle Description*. Wiesbaden: Steiner.

———, ed. 1978a. *Homer: Tradition and Invention*. Cincinnati Classical Studies, new series 2. Leiden: E. J. Brill.

———. 1978b. "Stylization and Variety: Four Monologues in the *Iliad*." In Fenik 1978a: 68–90.

———. 1986. *Homer and the Nibelungenlied: Comparative Studies in Epic Style*. Cambridge, Mass.: Harvard University Press.

Finley, M. I. 1978. *The World of Odysseus*, rev. ed. New York: Viking.

Finkelberg, Margalit. 1986. "Is ΚΛΕΟΣ ΑΦΘΙΤΟΝ a Homeric Formula?" *Classical Quarterly* 36: 1–5.

Finlayson, John. 1968. "The Concept of the Hero in 'Morte Arthure.'" In *Chaucer und seine Zeit: Symposion für Walter F. Schirmer*, edited by Arno Esch, Buchreihe der *Anglia*, Zeitschrift für englische Philologie, 14, 249–74. Tübingen: Max Niemeyer.

Foley, John Miles. 1978a. "The Oral Singer in Context: Halil Bajgorić, *Guslar*." *Canadian-American Slavic Studies* 12: 230–46.

———. 1978b. "The Traditional Structure of Ibro Bašić's 'Alagić Alija and Velagić Selim.'" *Slavic and East European Journal* 22: 1–14.

———. 1980. "Beowulf and Traditional Narrative Song: The Potential and Limits of Comparison." In *Old English Literature in Context: Ten Essays*, edited by John D. Niles, 117–36 and 173–78. Totowa, N.J.: Rowman and Littlefield.

———, ed. 1981a. *Oral Traditional Literature: A Festschrift for Albert Bates Lord.* Columbus, Ohio: Slavica.

———. 1981b. "Introduction: The Oral Theory in Context." In J. Foley 1981a: 27–122.

———. 1983. "Literary Art and Oral Tradition in Old English and Serbian Poetry." *Anglo-Saxon England* 12: 183–214.

———. 1985. *Oral-Formulaic Theory and Research: An Introduction and Annotated Bibliography.* New York: Garland.

———, ed. 1986a. *Oral Tradition in Literature: Interpretation in Context.* Columbia: University of Missouri Press.

———. 1986b. "Introduction." In J. Foley 1986a: 1–18.

———. 1986c. "Tradition and the Collective Talent: Oral Epic, Textual Meaning, and Receptionalist Theory." *Cultural Anthropology* 1: 203–22.

———, ed. 1987a. *Comparative Research on Oral Traditions: A Memorial for Milman Parry.* Columbus, Ohio: Slavica.

———. 1987b. "Reading the Oral Traditional Text: Aesthetics of Creation and Response." In J. Foley 1987a: 185–212.

———. 1988. *The Theory of Oral Composition: History and Methodology.* Bloomington: Indiana University Press.

Foley, Michael. 1979. "The Alliterative *Morte Arthure*: An Annotated Bibliography, 1950–75." *Chaucer Review* 14: 166–87.

Foster, Herbert L. 1974. *Ribbin', Jivin', and Playin' the Dozens: The Unrecognized Dilemma of Inner City Schools.* Cambridge, Mass.: Ballinger.

Frame, Douglas. 1978. *The Myth of Return in Early Greek Epic.* New Haven: Yale University Press.

Friedrich, Paul. 1973. "Defilement and Honor in the *Iliad*." *Journal of Indo-European Studies* 1: 119–26.

Fry, Donald K. 1968. "Old English Formulaic Themes and Type-Scenes." *Neophilologus* 52: 48–54.

———. 1969. *Beowulf and the Fight at Finnsburh: A Bibliography.* Charlottesville: University Press of Virginia.

———. 1974. *Finnsburh: Fragment and Episode.* London: Methuen.

Gaier, Claude. 1985 and 1986. "Technique des combats singuliers d'après les auteurs 'bourguignons' du XVᵉ siècle." *Le moyen âge* 4th ser., 40: 415–57, and 41: 5–40.

Gaisser, Julia H. 1969. "Adaption of Traditional Material in the Glaucus-Diomedes Episode." *Transactions of the American Philological Association* 100: 165–76.

Gardiner, E. Norman. 1970. *Greek Athletic Sports and Festivals.* London: Macmillan. Reprint of 1910 edition.

Genette, Gérard. 1980. *Narrative Discourse: An Essay in Method.* Translated by Jane E. Lewin. Ithaca, N.Y.: Cornell University Press.

Girard, René. 1977. *Violence and the Sacred.* Translated from the 1972 French original by Patrick Gregory. Baltimore: John Hopkins University Press.

Goldman, Robert P. 1984. "Introduction." In *The Rāmāyana of Vālmiki: An Epic of Ancient India,* vol. 1, *Bālakāṇḍa,* 3–117. Translated by Robert P. Goldman. Princeton: Princeton University Press.

Göller, Karl Heinz, ed. 1981a. *The "Alliterative Morte Arthure": A Reassessment of the Poem.* Cambridge: D. S. Brewer.

———. 1981b. "A Summary of Research." In Göller 1981a: 7–14, 153–57.

Goodall, Jane. 1986. *The Chimpanzees of Gombe: Patterns of Behavior.* Cambridge, Mass.: Belknap Press of Harvard University Press.

Gossen, Gary H. 1974. *Charmulas in the World of the Sun: Time and Space in a Maya Oral Tradition.* Cambridge, Mass.: Harvard University Press.

Gouldner, Alvin W. 1965. *Enter Plato: Classical Greece and the Origins of Social Theory.* New York: Basic Books.

Gray, Douglas. 1984. "Rough Music: Some Early Invectives and Flytings." In *The Yearbook of English Studies,* no. 14, *Satire Special Number: Essays in Memory of Robert C. Elliott, 1914–1981,* 21–43. London: Modern Humanities Research Association.

Greenfield, Stanley B. 1955. "The Formulaic Expression of the Theme of 'Exile' in Anglo-Saxon Poetry." *Speculum* 30: 200–206.

Greenfield, Stanley B., and Daniel G. Calder. 1986. *A New Critical History of Old English Literature.* New York: New York University Press.

Grice, H. P. 1975. "Logic and Conversation." In *Syntax and Semantics,* vol. 3, *Speech Acts,* edited by Peter Cole and Jerry L. Morgan, 41–58. New York: Academic Press.

Griffin, Jasper. 1980. *Homer on Life and Death.* Oxford: Clarendon.

Hamilton, W. D. 1964. "The Genetical Evolution of Social Behavior." *Journal of Theoretical Biology* 7: 1–52.

Hansen, William F. 1972. *The Conference Sequence: Patterned Narration and Narrative Inconsistency in the Odyssey.* University of California Classical Studies, vol. 8. Berkeley and Los Angeles: University of California Press.

Harris, H. A. 1966. *Greek Athletes and Athletics.* Bloomington: Indiana University Press.

Harris, Joseph. 1979. "The *Senna*: From Description to Literary Theory." *Michigan Germanic Studies* 5: 65–74.

Havelock, Eric A. 1963. *Preface to Plato.* Cambridge, Mass.: Belknap Press of Harvard University Press.

———. 1978. *The Greek Concept of Justice: From Its Shadow in Homer to Its Substance in Plato.* Cambridge, Mass.: Harvard University Press.

Heusler, Andreas. 1943. *Die altgermanische Dichtung.* Potsdam: Athenaion.

Hermann, John P. 1982. "The Recurrent Motifs of Spiritual Warfare in Old English Poetry." *Annuale Mediaevale* 22: 7–35.

Hiltebeitel, Alf. 1976. *The Ritual of Battle: Krishna in the Mahābhārata.* Ithaca, N.Y.: Cornell University Press.

Hollowell, Ida Masters. 1976. "Unferð the þyle in Beowulf." *Studies in Philology* 73: 239–65.

Höltgen, Karl Josef. 1957. "König Arthur und Fortuna." *Anglia* 75: 35–54.

Holthausen, Ferdinand. 1963. *Altenglisches etymologisches Wörterbuch*, 2d ed. Heidelberg: C. Winter.

Holtsmark, Anne. 1966 and 1970. "Mannjevning" and "Senna." In *Kulturhistorisk leksikon for nordisk middelalder fra vikingetid til reformationstid*. Vol. 11, Copenhagen: Rosenkilde and Bagger, 325–26, and vol. 15, Oslo: Gyldendal, 149–52.

Huizinga, Johan. 1955. *Homo Ludens: A Study of the Play-Element in Culture*. Translated from the 1944 German edition. Boston: Beacon Press.

Hume, Kathryn. 1975. *The Owl and the Nightingale: The Poem and Its Critics*. Toronto: University of Toronto Press.

Irving, Edward B. 1968. *A Reading of Beowulf*. New Haven: Yale University Press.

Jakobson, Roman. 1960. "Closing Statement: Linguistics and Poetics." In *Style in Language*, edited by Thomas A. Sebeok, 350–77. Cambridge, Mass.: MIT Press.

———. 1973. "Two Aspects of Language: Metaphor and Metonymy." In *European Literary Theory and Practice: From Existential Phenomenology to Structuralism*, edited by Vernon W. Gras, 119–29. New York: Delta.

Janssen, Anke. 1981. "The Dream of the Wheel of Fortune." In Göller 1981a: 140–52, 179–81.

Jeanroy, Alfred. 1925. *Les Origins de la poésie lyrique en France au moyen âge*, 3d ed. Paris: Champion.

Jones, George Fenwick. 1963. *The Ethos of the Song of Roland*. Baltimore: John Hopkins Press.

Kahrl, Stanley J. 1972. "Feuds in *Beowulf*: A Tragic Necessity?" *Modern Philology* 69: 189–98.

Keiser, George Robert. 1974. "Narrative Structure in the Alliterative *Morte Arthure*, 26–720." *Chaucer Review* 9: 130–44.

———. 1975. "The Theme of Justice in the Alliterative *Morte Arthure*." *Annuale Mediaevale* 16: 94–109.

Keitel, Elizabeth. 1987. "Homeric Antecedents to the *Cohortatio* in the Ancient Historians." *Classical World* 80: 153–72.

Ker, W. P. 1897. *Epic and Romance: Essays on Medieval Literature*. London: Macmillan.

King, Katherine Callen. 1987. *Achilles: Paradigms of the War Hero from Homer to the Middle Ages*. Berkeley and Los Angeles: University of California Press.

Kirk, G. S. 1978. "The Formal Duels in Books 3 and 7 of the *Iliad*." In Fenik 1978a: 18–40.

Kittredge, George Lyman. 1960. *A Study of Sir Gawain and the Green Knight*. Gloucester, Mass.: Peter Smith. Reprint of the 1916 edition.

Klopfer, Peter H. 1985. "On Central Controls for Aggression." In *Perspectives in Ethology*, vol. 6, *Mechanisms*, edited by P.P.G. Bateson and Peter H. Klopfer, 33–44. New York and London: Plenum Press.

Knobloch, Heinrich. 1886. *Die Streitgedichte im Provenzalichen und Altfranzösischen*. Breslau: Korn.

Kroll, Norma. 1986. "Beowulf: The Hero as Keeper of Human Polity." *Modern Philology* 84: 117–29.

Labov, William. 1972. *Language in the Inner City: Studies in the Black English Vernacular.* Philadelphia: University of Pennsylvania Press.

Levinson, Stephen C. 1983. *Pragmatics.* Cambridge: Cambridge University Press.

Leyerle, John. 1965. "Beowulf the Hero and King." *Medium Ævum* 34: 89–102.

———. 1975. "The Game and Play of Hero." In *Concepts of the Hero in the Middle Ages and the Renaissance,* edited by Norman T. Burns and Christopher J. Reagan, 49–82. Albany: State University of New York Press.

Leyhausen, Paul. 1979. *Cat Behavior: The Predatory and Social Behavior of Domestic and Wild Cats,* rev. ed. Translated from the German by Barbara A. Tonkin. New York: Garland.

Liddell, Henry George, and Robert Scott. 1925–1940. *A Greek-English Lexicon,* 9th ed. Revised by Henry Stuart Jones. Oxford: Clarendon.

Lindahl, Carl. 1987. *Earnest Games: Folkloric Patterns in the "Canterbury Tales."* Bloomington: Indiana University Press.

Lindow, John. 1976. *Comitatus, Individual, and Honor: Studies in North Germanic Institutional Vocabulary.* University of California Publications in Linguistics, 83. Berkeley and Los Angeles: University of California Press.

Lönnroth, Lars. 1979. "The Double Scene of Arrow-Odd's Drinking Contest." In *Medieval Narrative: A Symposium,* edited by Hans Bekker-Nielsen, Peter Foot, Andreas Haarder, and Preben Mealengracht Sorensen, 94–114. Odense: Odense University Press.

Lord, Albert B. 1938. "Homer and Huso II: Narrative Inconsistencies in Homer and Oral Poetry." *Transactions of the American Philological Association* 69: 439–45.

———. 1965a. "Beowulf and Odysseus." *Franciplegius: Medieval and Linguistic Studies in Honor of Francis Peabody Magoun,* edited by Jess B. Bessinger and Robert P. Creed, 86–91. New York: New York University Press.

———. 1965b. *The Singer of Tales.* New York: Atheneum.

———. 1969. "The Theme of the Withdrawn Hero in Serbo-Croatian Oral Epic." *Prilozi za književnost, jezik, istoriju i folklor* 35: 18–30.

———. 1986. "The Merging of Two Worlds: Oral and Written Poetry as Carriers of Ancient Values." In J. Foley 1986a: 19–64.

Lorenz, Konrad. 1966. *On Aggression.* Translated from the 1963 German edition, *Das Sogenannte Böse,* by Marjorie Kerr Wilson. New York: Harcourt, Brace and World.

Luce, J. V. 1975. *Homer and the Heroic Age.* London: Thames and Hudson.

Lumiansky, Robert M. 1952. "The Dramatic Audience in *Beowulf.*" *Journal of English and German Philology* 51: 545–50.

———. 1968. "The Alliterative *Morte Arthure,* the Concept of Medieval Tragedy, and the Cardinal Virtue Fortitude." In *Medieval and Renaissance Studies: Proceedings of the Southeastern Institute of Medieval and Renaissance Studies,*

Summer, 1967, edited by J. M. Headley, 95–118. Chapel Hill: University of North Carolina Press.

Markus, Manfred. 1981. "The Language and Style: The Paradox of Heroic Poetry." In Göller 1981a: 57–69, 164–67.

Martindale, Colin. 1981. *Cognition and Consciousness*. Homewood, Ill.: Dorsey.

Matthews, William. 1960. *The Tragedy of Arthur: A Study of the Alliterative Morte Arthure*. Berkeley and Los Angeles: University of California Press.

Maynard Smith, John. 1979. "Games Theory and the Evolution of Behavior." *Proceedings of the Royal Society of London* ser. B, 205: 475–88.

———. 1982. *Evolution and the Theory of Games*. Cambridge: Cambridge University Press.

McDowell, John H. 1985. "Verbal Dueling." In van Dijk 1985: 203–11.

Miller, Mirian Youngerman, and Jane Chance, ed. 1986. *Approaches to Teaching Sir Gawain and the Green Knight*. New York: Modern Language Association of America.

Morgan, Gerald. 1972. "The Treachery of Hrothulf." *English Studies* 53: 23–39.

Morton, Eugene S. 1977. "The Occurrence and Significance of Motivation-Structure Rules in Some Bird and Mammal Sounds." *American Naturalist* 111: 84–92.

Moyer, Kenneth E. 1976. *The Psychobiology of Aggression*. New York: Harper and Row.

Mueller, Martin. 1984. *The Iliad*. London: Allen and Unwin.

Murnaghan, Sheila. 1987. *Disguise and Recognition in the Odysseay*. Princeton: Princeton University Press.

Murphy, Michael. 1985. "Vows, Boasts and Taunts, and the Role of Women in Some Medieval Literature." *English Studies* 66: 105–12.

Nagler, Michael N. 1974. *Spontaneity and Tradition: A Study in the Oral Art of Homer*. Berkeley and Los Angeles: University of California Press.

Nagy, Gregory. 1979. *The Best of the Achaeans: Concepts of the Hero in Archaic Greek Poetry*. Baltimore: John Hopkins University Press.

———. 1986. "Ancient Greek Epic and Praise Poetry: Some Typological Considerations." In J. Foley 1986a: 89–102.

Neumann, Erich. 1954. *The Origins and History of Consciousness*. Translated from the German by R.F.C. Hull. Princeton: Princeton University Press.

Niles, John D. 1983. *Beowulf: The Poem and Its Tradition*. Cambridge, Mass.: Harvard University Press.

Nimis, Steve. 1986. "The Language of Achilles: Construction vs. Representation." *Classical World* 79: 217–25.

Nolan, Barbara, and Morton W. Bloomfield. 1980. "*Beotword*, *Gilpcwidas*, and the *Gilphlæden* Scop of *Beowulf*." *Journal of English and Germanic Philology* 79: 499–516.

Notopoulos, James A. 1952. "The Warrior as an Oral Poet: A Case History." *Classical Weekly* 46, no. 2: 17–19.

Ogilvy, J.D.A. 1964. "Unferth: Foil to Beowulf?" *PMLA* 79: 370–75.

Oinas, Felix J., ed. 1978. *Heroic Epic and Saga: An Introduction to the World's Great Folk Epics.* Bloomington: Indiana University Press.

Olivová, Věra. 1985. *Sports and Games in the Ancient World.* New York: St. Martin's Press.

Olrik, Alex. 1965. "Epic Laws of Folk Narrative." In *The Study of Folklore,* edited by Alan Dundes, 129–41. Englewood Cliffs, N.J.: Prentice-Hall. Originally published as "Epische Gesetze der Volksdichtung," 1909.

Olsen, Alexandra Hennessey. 1986. "Oral-Formulaic Research in Old English Studies: I." *Oral Tradition* 1: 548–606.

———. 1988. "Oral-Formulaic Research in Old English Studies: II." *Oral Tradition* 3: 138–90.

Ong, Walter J. 1981. *Fighting for Life: Contest, Sexuality, and Consciousness.* Ithaca, N.Y.: Cornell University Press.

———. 1982. *Orality and Literacy: The Technologizing of the Word.* London: Methuen.

Opland, Jeff. 1980. *Anglo-Saxon Oral Poetry: A Study of the Traditions.* New Haven: Yale University Press.

Panzer, Friedrich. 1910. *Studien zur germanischen Sagengeschichte,* vol. 1, "*Beowulf.*" Munich: Beck.

Parks, Ward. 1981. "Generic Identity and the Guest-Host Exchange: A Study of Return Songs in the Homeric and Serbo-Croatian Traditions." *Canadian-American Slavic Studies* 15: 24–41.

———. 1983. "The Return Song and a Middle English Romance: *Sir Orfeo,* 'Četić Osmanbey,' 'Đulic Ibrahim,' and the *Odyssey.*" *Southeastern Europe* 10: 222–41.

———. 1986a. "Flyting and Fighting: Pathways in the Realization of the Epic Contest." *Neophilologus* 70: 292–306.

———. 1986b. "Flyting, Sounding, Debate: Three Verbal Contest Genres." *Poetics Today* 7: 439–58.

———. 1986c. "The Oral–Formulaic Theory in Middle English Studies." *Oral Tradition* 1: 636–94.

———. 1987a. "The Flyting Speech in Traditional Heroic Narrative." *Neophilologus* 71: 285–95.

———. 1987b. "The Traditional Narrator and the 'I Heard' Formulas in Old English Poetry." *Anglo-Saxon England* 16: 45–66.

———. 1987c. "Orality and Poetics: Synchrony, Diachrony, and the Axes of Narrative Transmission." In Foley 1987a: 511–32.

———. 1988. "Ring Structure and Narrative Embedding in Homer and *Beowulf.*" *Neuphilologische Mitteilungen* 89: 127–51.

———. 1989. "Interperformativity in *Beowulf.*" *Narodna umjetnost* 26:25–35.

———. 1990. "The Flyting Contract and Adversarial Patterning in the Alliterative *Morte Arthure.*" In *New Views on Old Masterpieces: Essays on British Literature of the Middle Ages and Renaissance,* edited by David G. Allen and Robert A. White, 59–74. Newark: University of Delaware Press.

———. Forthcoming. "The Textualization of Orality in Literary Criticism." In *Con-Texts: Orality and Textuality and the Middle Ages,* edited by Carol Braun Pasternack and A. N. Doane. Madison: University of Wisconsin Press.

Parry, Adam. 1956. "The Language of Achilles." *Transactions of the American Philological Association* 87: 1–7.

Parry, Milman. 1971. *The Making of Homeric Verse: The Collected Papers of Milman Parry*. Edited by Adam Parry. Oxford: Clarendon Press.

Peabody, Berkley. 1975. *The Winged Word: A Study in the Technique of Ancient Greek Oral Composition as Seen Principally through Hesiod's "Works and Days."* Albany: State University of New York Press.

Peristiany, J. G., ed. 1966. *Honour and Shame: The Values of Mediterranean Society*. Chicago: University of Chicago Press.

Phillpotts, Bertha S. 1920. *The Eldar Edda and Ancient Scandinavian Drama*. Cambridge: Cambridge University Press.

Pizarro, Joaquín Martínez. 1976. "Studies on the Function and Context of the *Senna* in Early Germanic Narrative." Ph.D. dissertation, Harvard University.

Porter, Elizabeth. 1983. "Chaucer's Knight, the Alliterative *Morte Arthure*, and Medieval Laws of War: A Reconsideration." *Nottingham Medieval Studies* 27: 56–78.

Powell, Barry B. 1977. *Composition by Theme in the Odyssey*. Beiträge zur klassischen Philologie, 81. Meisenheim am Glan: Hain.

Pratt, Mary Louise. 1977. *Toward a Speech Act Theory of Literary Discourse*. Bloomington: Indiana University Press.

Prince, Gerald. 1982. *Narratology: The Form and Functioning of Narrative*. Amsterdam: Mouton.

Pritchett, W. Kendrick. 1985. *The Greek State at War: Part IV*. Berkeley and Los Angeles: University of California Press.

Propp, V. 1968. *Morphology of the Folktale*, 2d ed. Translated from the Russian by Laurence Scott. Austin: University of Texas Press.

Raby, F.J.E. 1957. *A History of Secular Latin Poetry in the Middle Ages*, 2 vols., 2d ed. Oxford: Clarendon Press.

Razvratnikov, Boris Sukritch. 1977. "Latent Accusative Tendencies in the Skopje Dialect *or* Where to Go and What to Do with It in North-Central Macedonia." *Maledicta* 1: 69–73.

Reinhard, John R. 1932. "Some Illustrations of the Mediaeval *Gab*." In *Essays and Studies in English and Comparative Literature*, University of Michigan Publications, Language and Literature, 8: 27–57. Ann Arbor: University of Michigan.

Renoir, Alain. 1963. "The Heroic Oath in *Beowulf*, the *Chanson de Roland*, and the *Nibelungenlied*." In *Studies in Old English Literature in Honor of Arthur C. Brodeur*, edited by Stanley B. Greenfield, 237–66. Eugene: University of Oregon Press.

———. 1986. "Oral-Formulaic Rhetoric and the Interpretation of Written Texts." In J. Foley 1986a: 103–35.

Richardson, John. 1987. "The Critic on the Beach." *Neophilologus* 71: 114–19.

Ritzke-Rutherford, Jean. 1981. "Formulaic Macrostructure: The Theme of Battle." In Göller 1981a: 83–95, 169–71.

Rose, Peter W. 1988. "Thersites and the Plural Voices of Homer." *Arethusa* 21: 5–25.

Rosenberg, Bruce. 1969. "The Necessity of Unferth." *Journal of the Folklore Institute* 6: 50–60.

———. 1975. "Folktale Morphology and the Structure of *Beowulf*: A Counterproposal." *The Journal of the Folklore Institute* 11: 199–209.

Rosier, James L. 1962. "Design for Treachery: The Unferth Intrigue." *PMLA* 77: 1–7.

Rychner, Jean. 1955. *La Chanson de geste: Essai sur l'art épique des jongleurs.* Geneva: Droz.

Sacks, Harvey, Emanuel A. Schegloff, and Gail Jefferson. 1978. "A Simplest Systematics for the Organization of Turn Taking for Conversation." In *Studies in the Organization of Conversational Interaction*, edited by Jim Schenkein, 7–55. New York: Academic Press.

Schein, Seth L. 1984. *The Mortal Hero: An Introduction to Homer's "Iliad."* Berkeley and Los Angeles: University of California Press.

Schofield, Malcolm. 1986. "*Eubolia* in the *Iliad*." *Classical Quarterly* 36: 6–31.

Scholes, Robert. 1985. *Textual Power: Literary Theory and the Teaching of English.* New Haven: Yale University Press.

Schriffin, Deborah. "Everyday Argument: The Organization of Diversity in Talk." In van Dijk 1985: 35–46.

Scully, Stephen. 1984. "The Language of Achilles: The ΟΧΘΗΣΑΣ Formulas." *Transactions of the American Philological Association* 114: 11–27.

Searle, John R. 1969. *Speech Acts: An Essay in the Philosophy of Language.* Cambridge: Cambridge University Press.

———. 1979. *Expression and Meaning: Studies in the Theory of Speech Acts.* Cambridge: Cambridge University Press.

Sebeok, Thomas A., ed. 1977. *How Animals Communicate.* Bloomington: Indiana University Press.

Segal, Charles P. 1971. *The Theme of the Mutilation of the Corpse in the Iliad.* Leiden: E. J. Brill.

Selbach, Ludwig. 1886. *Das Streitgedicht in der altprovenzalischen Lyrik und sein Verhältniss zu ähnlichen Dichtungen anderer Litteraturen.* Marburg: Elwert.

Sidhanta, N. K. 1929. *The Heroic Age of India: A Comparative Study.* London: Kegan Paul, Trench, Trubner.

Smithers, G. V. 1970. "Destiny and the Heroic Warrior in *Beowulf*." In *Philological Essays: Studies in Old and Middle English Language and Literature in Honour of Herbert Dean Meritt*, edited by James L. Rosier, 65–81. The Hague: Mouton.

Swanton, Michael. 1977. "Heroes, Heroism, and Heroic Literature." *Essays and Studies* 30: 1–21.

Szwed, John F., Roger D. Abrahams, et al. 1978. *Afro-American Folk Culture: An Annotated Bibliography of Materials from North, Central, and South American and the West Indies*, 2 vols. Philadelphia: Institute for the Study of Human Issues.

Tinbergen, Niko. 1961. *The Herring Gull's World: A Study of the Social Behavior of Birds*, rev. ed. New York: Basic Books.

Tolkien, J.R.R. 1953. "The Homecoming of Beorhtnoth, Beorhthelm's Son." *Essays and Studies* new ser., 6: 1–18.

———. 1982. *Finn and Hengest: The Fragment and the Episode*. Edited by Alan Bliss. London: Allen and Unwin.

Torrini-Roblin, Gloria. 1984. "*Gomen* and *Gab*: Two Models for Play in Medieval Literature." *Romance Philology* 38: 32–40.

Trivers, Robert. 1985. *Social Evolution*. Menlo Park, Calif.: Benjamin/Cummings.

van Buitenen, J.A.B., and Edward C. Dimock. 1974. "The Indian Epic." In *The Literatures of India: An Introduction*, by Edward C. Dimock, Edwin Gerow, C. M. Naim, A. K. Ramanujan, Gordon Roadarmel, and J.A.B. van Buitenen, 47–80. Chicago: University of Chicago Press.

van Dijk, Teun A. 1985. *Handbook of Discourse Analysis*, vol. 3, *Discourse and Dialogue*. New York: Academic Press.

van Nooten, Barend A. 1971. *The Mahābhārata*. New York: Twayne.

———. 1978. "The Sanskrit Epics." In Oinas 1978: 49–75.

van Wees, Hans. 1988. "Kings in Combat: Battles and Heroes in the *Iliad*." *Classical Quarterly* 38: 1–24.

Vermeule, Emily. 1979. *Aspects of Death in Early Greek Art and Poetry*. Berkeley and Los Angeles: University of California Press.

Wagner, F. 1936. "L'Organisation du combat singulier au moyen âge dans les états scandinaves et dans l'ancienne république islandaise." *Revue de Synthèse* 11: 41–60.

Walther, Hans. 1920. *Das Streitgedichte in der lateinischen Literatur des Mittelalters*. Munich: Beck.

Ward, Donald. 1973. "On the Poets and Poetry of the Indo-Europeans." *Journal of Indo-European Studies* 1: 127–44.

Warnke, Frank J. 1986. "Amorous Agon, Erotic Flyting: Some Play-Motifs in the Literature of Love." In *Auctor Ludens: Essays on Play in Literature*, edited by Gerald Guinness and Andrew Hurley, 99–111. Philadelphia: John Benjamins.

Whitman, Cedric H. 1965. *Homer and the Heroic Tradition*. New York: Norton. Reprint of the 1958 edition.

Whitman, Cedric H., and Ruth Scodel. 1981. "Sequence and Simultaneity in *Iliad* N, Ξ, and O." *Harvard Studies in Classical Philology* 85: 1–15.

Wilson, Edward O. 1975. *Sociobiology: The New Synthesis*. Cambridge, Mass.: Belknap Press of Harvard University Press.

———. 1978. *On Human Nature*. Cambridge, Mass.: Harvard University Press.

Wynne-Edwards, V. C. 1986. *Evolution through Group Selection*. Oxford: Blackwell.

Zhirmunsky, Victor. 1966. "The Epic of 'Alpamysh' and the Return of Odysseus." *Proceedings of the British Academy* 52: 267–86.

Index

Achilles: vs. Agamemnon, esp. 91–95, also 20, 25–26, 27, 45, 85, 89, 107, 109, 127, 148, 191n.17; vs. Agenor, 56–57, 62; vs. Aineias, esp. 117–26, 162–63, 172–74, also 34, 36, 44–45, 47, 58, 101, 107, 108; vs. Asteropaios, esp. 50–51, also 36, 60, 108, 205n.18; and Briseis, 26; contrasting views of, 192n.27; vs. Hektor, esp. 64, 102, also 3, 34, 35, 36, 37, 49, 56, 62, 66, 91, 106, 110, 112, 113, 195n.59, 199n.38; and honor, 26–27, 94; vs. Iphition, 60; vs. Lykäon, esp. 59, also 35, 60, 101–2, 106, 107, 110, 113; as peacemaker, 90, 202n.67; vs. Tros, 198n.27; vs. Xanthos, 67
ad hominem argumentation, 6, 12, 26–27, 105, 167. *See also* verbal dueling, subject matter, contestant- or other-oriented
Adrestos, 59, 101
Aeschylus, 4, 191n.14
Agamemnon: vs. Achilles, esp. 91–95, also 20, 25–26, 27, 45, 85, 89, 109, 127, 148, 191n.17; and Menelaos, 22; vs. Odysseus, 89; vs. Peisandros and Hippolochos, 59, 101
Agenor, 56, 62, 197n.18
aggression: interspecific and intraspecific, 21–22; scholarship on, 189n.1; taxonomies of, 19. *See also* agonistic mindset
agonistic mindset: and the academy, 178, 181–82; and conceptions of the self, 8–9, 23–26, 180–81; the contemporary rejection of, 182–84; and culture, 14–15; and ritual contests, 16–18, 32; and verbal dueling, 161–62; virtues and vices of, 180–82
Aias: vs. Antenor, 61; vs. Hektor, esp. 65, 79, also 34, 46, 63, 66, 110, 199n.34
Aias (son of Oïleus), 90
Aineias: vs. Achilles, esp. 117–26, 162–

63, 172–74, also 34, 36, 44–45, 47, 58, 101, 107, 108; vs. Diomedes, 67; divine rescue, 62, 67, 197n.18; vs. Meriones, 61, 63, 105, 110
Akamas, 61, 65–66, 109
Alboin, 11, 41, 81
Alexander the Great, 39, 180
Alexandros. *See* Paris
Alkathoös, 61, 65
Alkinoös, 39, 73–75, 77, 81, 91, 92–93
Alliterative Morte Arthure, The, 52–53, 79, 129, 136–45, 151, 159, 194n.41, 208–9nn.18–20 and 28. *See also* Arthur: in *The Alliterative Morte Arthure*
Alliterative Revival, 208n.19
Anderson, J., 203n.5
Andersson, T., 204n.8
Andreas, 7, 88, 187n.8
Andreas Capellanus, 12, 188–89n.22
animal behavior: baboons, 33, 202n.67; cats, 17; dolphins, 22; herring gulls, 8, 18–19; *Macaca fuscatas*, 22; mantis shrimp, 21; rats, 17, 34; red deer, 8, 16–18, 20, 24, 34; sparrows, 32; squirrels, 22; tropical cleaner fish, 22; vampire bats, 22; whales, 22
Antenor, 61
Antilochos, 90
Antinoös, 3, 85–87
Aphrodite, 64–65, 67, 124, 200n.49
Apollo, 49, 58, 62, 66, 67
Arend, W., 43, 96
Ares, 60, 67
Aretos, 66
Aristophanes, 4
Aristotle, 27
Arjuna, 3, 107, 129–36
armor stripping, 56, 63, 68, 198n.22. *See also* contest pattern, elements in: Resolution
Artemis, 58, 67
Arthur
    in *The Alliterative Morte Arthure*: and Gawain, 3; vs. Giant of St. Michael's